W9-BXW-025

MANIFEST DESTINY

CHRIS DINGESS — WRITER

MATTHEW ROBERTS — PENCILLER & INKER

OWEN GIENI — COLORIST

PAT BROSSEAU — LETTERER

SEAN MACKIEWICZ — EDITOR

MATTHEW ROBERTS & OWEN GIENI
COVER ART

IMAGE COMICS, INC.
Robert Kirkman – Chief Operating Officer
Erik Larsen – Chief Financial Officer
Todd McFarlane – President
Marc Silvestri – Chief Executive Officer
Jim Valentino – Vice-President

Eric Stephenson – Publisher
Ron Richards – Director of Business Development
Jennifer de Guzman – Director of Trade Book Sales
Kat Salazar – Director of PR & Marketing
Corey Murphy – Director of Retail Sales
Jeremy Sullivan – Director of Digital Sales
Emilio Bautista – Sales Assistant
Branwyn Bigglestone – Senior Accounts Manager
Emily Miller – Accounts Manager
Jessica Ambriz – Administrative Assistant
Tyler Shainline – Events Coordinator
David Brothers – Content Manager
Jonathan Chan – Production Manager
Drew Gill – Art Director
Meredith Wallace – Print Manager
Monica Garcia – Senior Production Artist
Addison Duke – Production Artist
Tricia Ramos – Production Assistant
IMAGECOMICS.COM

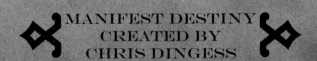

MANIFEST DESTINY
CREATED BY
CHRIS DINGESS

SKYBOUND
FOR SKYBOUND ENTERTAINMENT
Robert Kirkman – CEO
Sean Mackiewicz – Editorial Director
Shawn Kirkham – Director of Business Development
Brian Huntington – Online Editorial Director
June Alian – Publicity Director
Rachel Skidmore – Director of Media Development
Helen Leigh – Assistant Editor
Dan Petersen – Operations Manager
Sarah Effinger – Office Manager
Nick Palmer – Operations Coordinator
Lizzy Iverson – Administrative Assistant
Stephan Murillo – Administrative Assistant
International inquiries: ag@sequentialrights.com
Licensing inquiries: contact@skybound.com
www.skybound.com

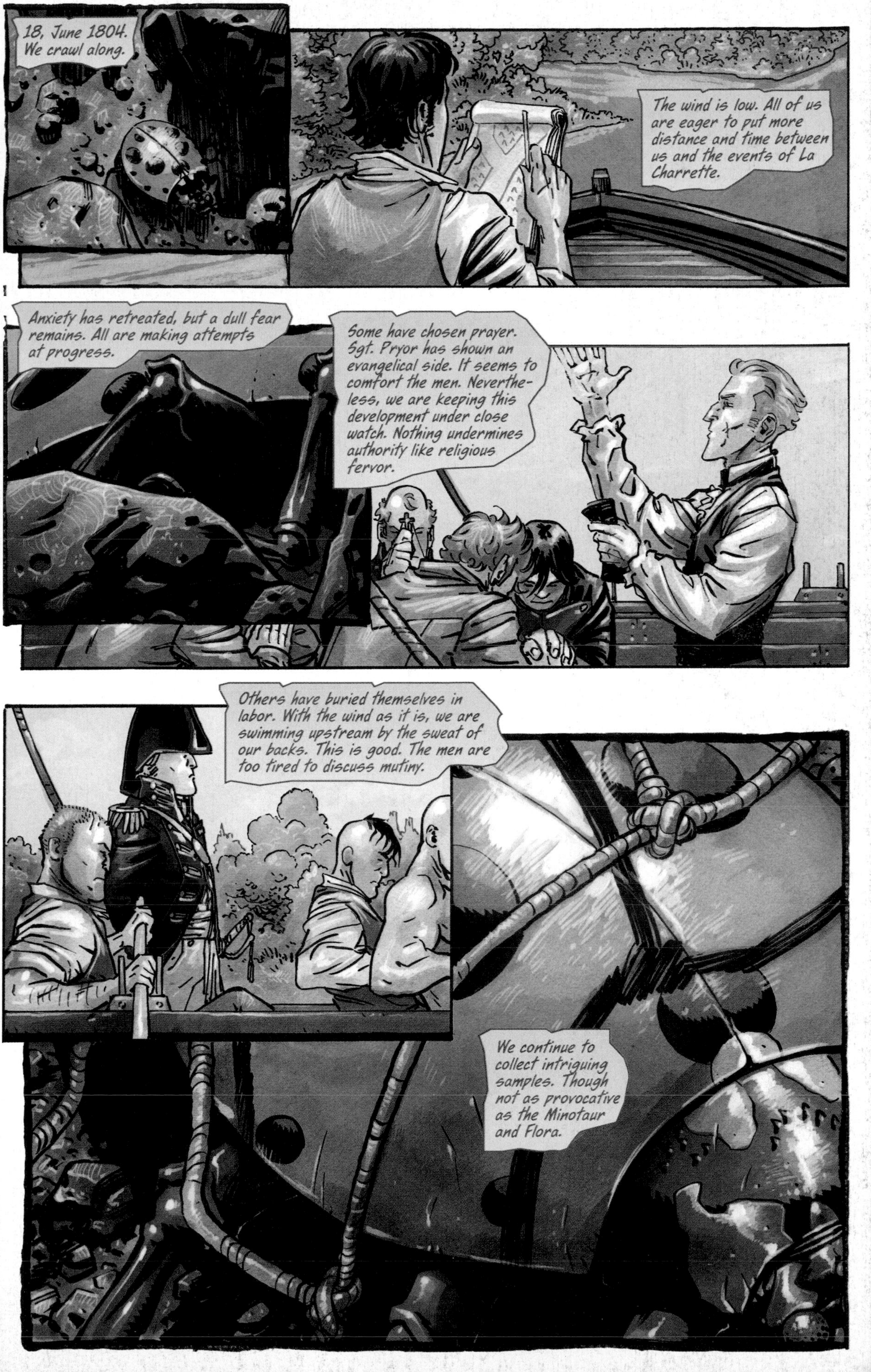
18, June 1804. We crawl along.
The wind is low. All of us are eager to put more distance and time between us and the events of La Charrette.
Anxiety has retreated, but a dull fear remains. All are making attempts at progress.
Some have chosen prayer. Sgt. Pryor has shown an evangelical side. It seems to comfort the men. Neverthe-less, we are keeping this development under close watch. Nothing undermines authority like religious fervor.
Others have buried themselves in labor. With the wind as it is, we are swimming upstream by the sweat of our backs. This is good. The men are too tired to discuss mutiny.
We continue to collect intriguing samples. Though not as provocative as the Minotaur and Flora.

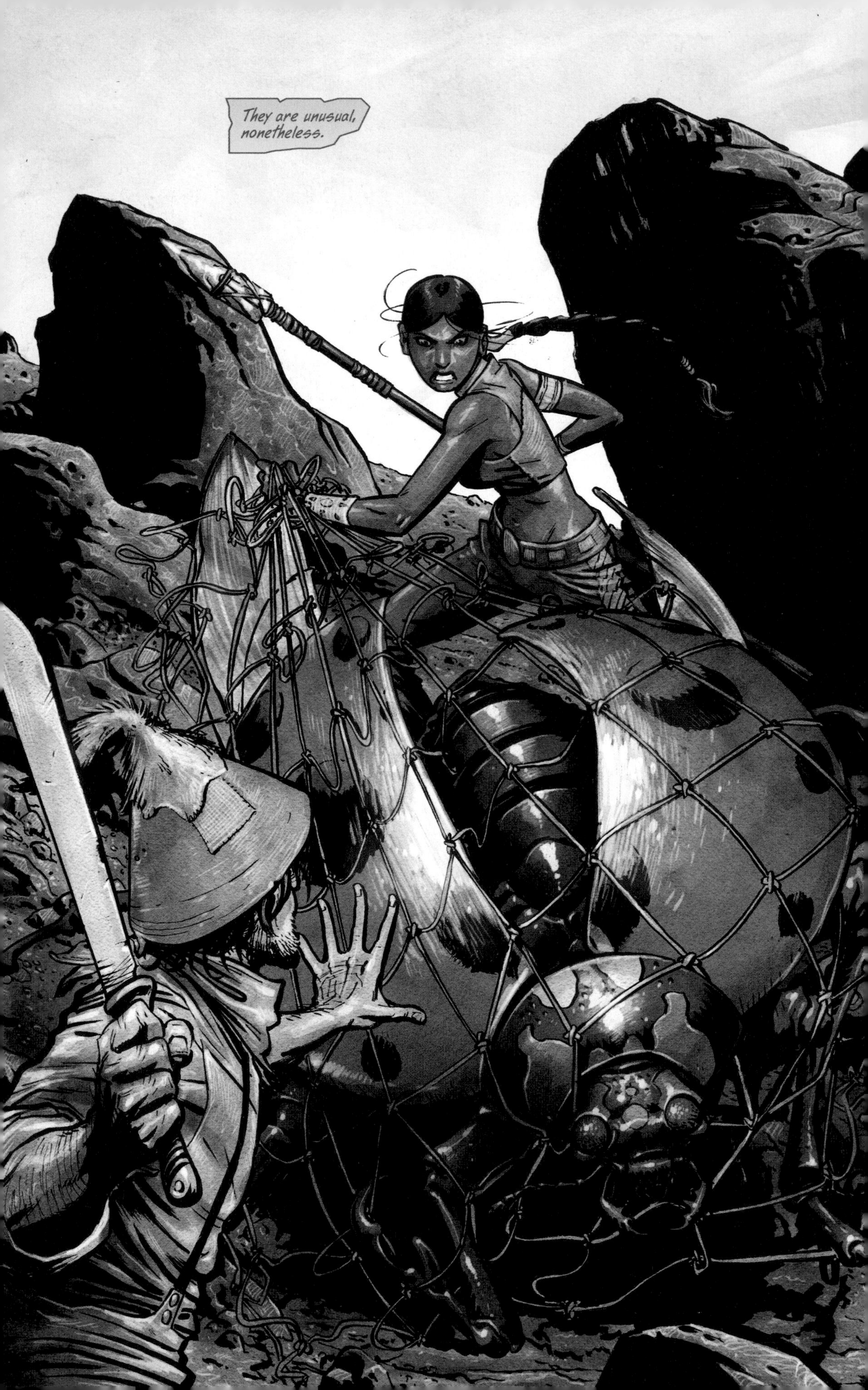
They are unusual, nonetheless.

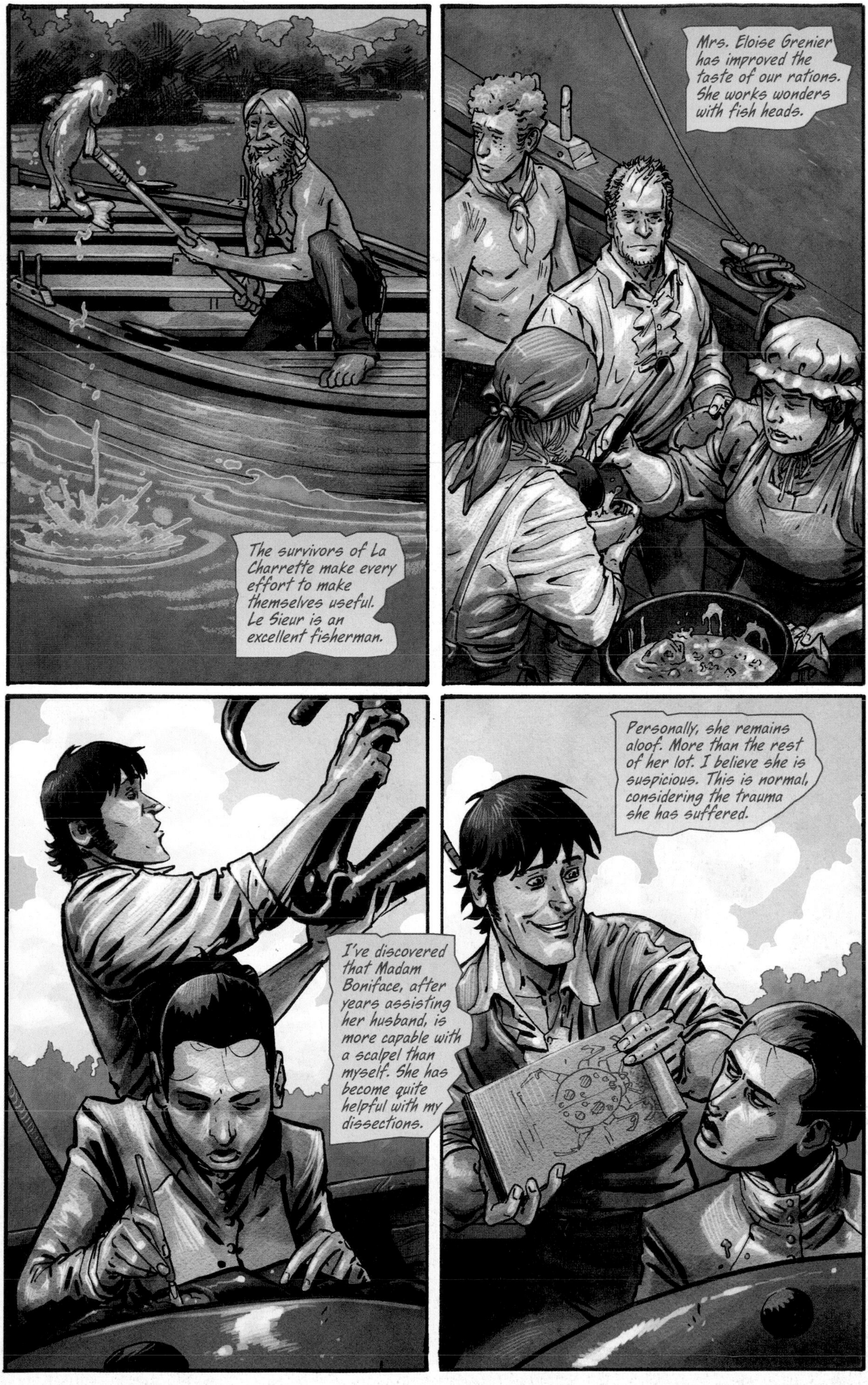
The survivors of La Charrette make every effort to make themselves useful. Le Sieur is an excellent fisherman.
Mrs. Eloise Grenier has improved the taste of our rations. She works wonders with fish heads.
I've discovered that Madam Boniface, after years assisting her husband, is more capable with a scalpel than myself. She has become quite helpful with my dissections.
Personally, she remains aloof. More than the rest of her lot. I believe she is suspicious. This is normal, considering the trauma she has suffered.

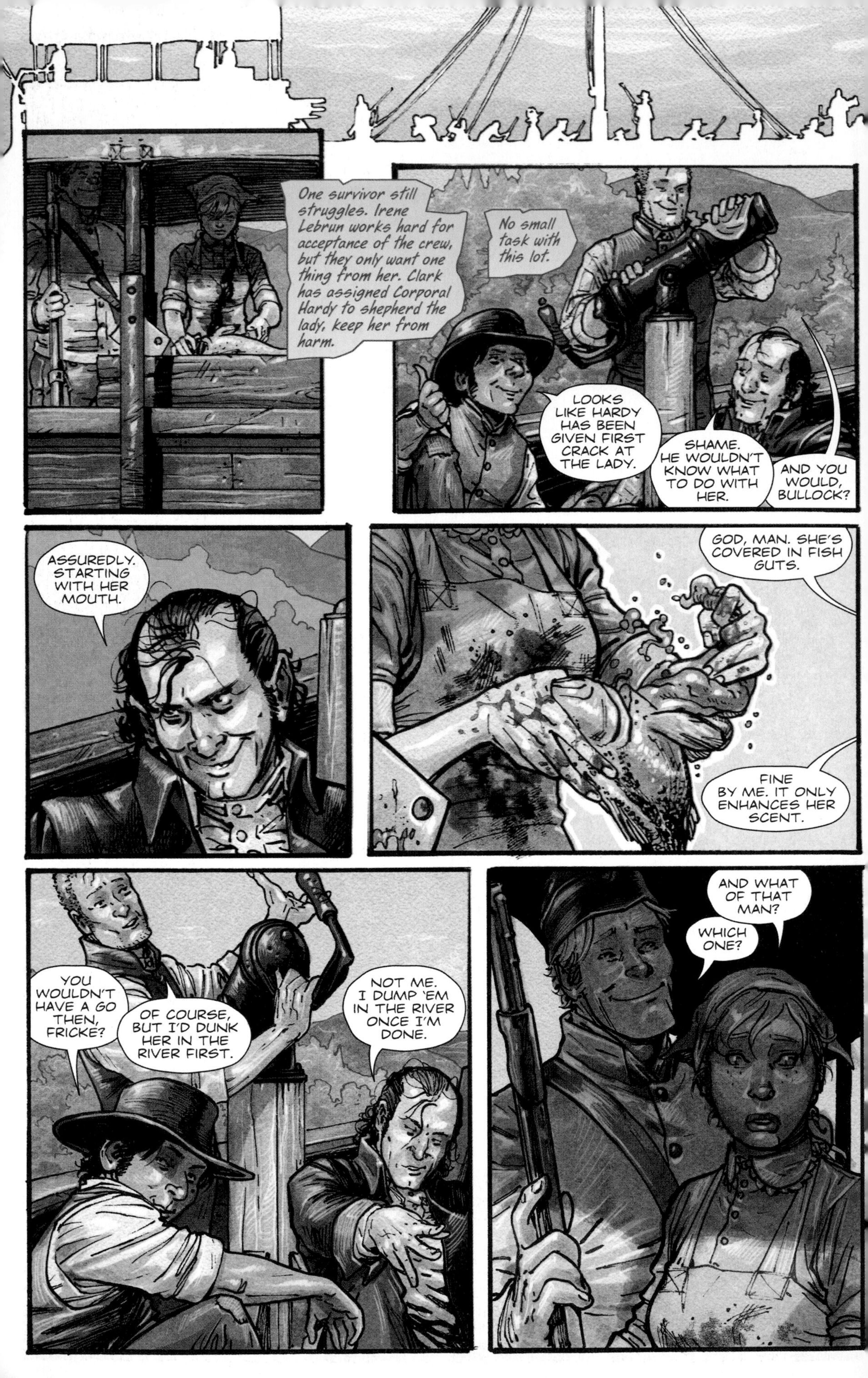
One survivor still struggles. Irene Lebrun works hard for acceptance of the crew, but they only want one thing from her. Clark has assigned Corporal Hardy to shepherd the lady, keep her from harm.
No small task with this lot.
LOOKS LIKE HARDY HAS BEEN GIVEN FIRST CRACK AT THE LADY.
SHAME. HE WOULDN'T KNOW WHAT TO DO WITH HER.
AND YOU WOULD, BULLOCK?
ASSUREDLY. STARTING WITH HER MOUTH.
GOD, MAN. SHE'S COVERED IN FISH GUTS.
FINE BY ME. IT ONLY ENHANCES HER SCENT.
YOU WOULDN'T HAVE A GO THEN, FRICKE?
OF COURSE, BUT I'D DUNK HER IN THE RIVER FIRST.
NOT ME. I DUMP 'EM IN THE RIVER ONCE I'M DONE.
AND WHAT OF THAT MAN?
WHICH ONE?

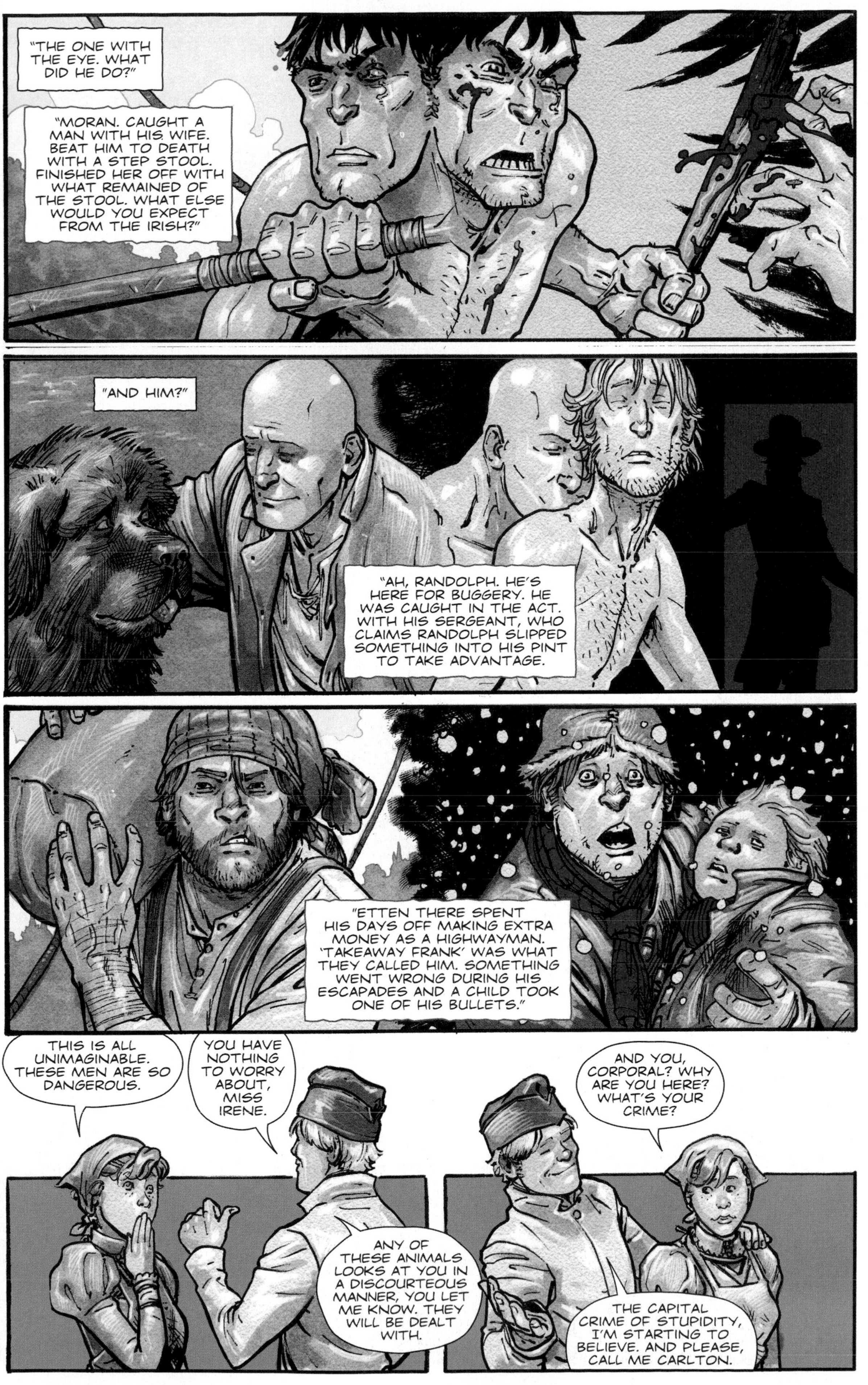

"THE ONE WITH THE EYE. WHAT DID HE DO?"
"MORAN. CAUGHT A MAN WITH HIS WIFE. BEAT HIM TO DEATH WITH A STEP STOOL. FINISHED HER OFF WITH WHAT REMAINED OF THE STOOL. WHAT ELSE WOULD YOU EXPECT FROM THE IRISH?"
"AND HIM?"
"AH, RANDOLPH. HE'S HERE FOR BUGGERY. HE WAS CAUGHT IN THE ACT. WITH HIS SERGEANT, WHO CLAIMS RANDOLPH SLIPPED SOMETHING INTO HIS PINT TO TAKE ADVANTAGE.
"ETTEN THERE SPENT HIS DAYS OFF MAKING EXTRA MONEY AS A HIGHWAYMAN. 'TAKEAWAY FRANK' WAS WHAT THEY CALLED HIM. SOMETHING WENT WRONG DURING HIS ESCAPADES AND A CHILD TOOK ONE OF HIS BULLETS."
THIS IS ALL UNIMAGINABLE. THESE MEN ARE SO DANGEROUS.
YOU HAVE NOTHING TO WORRY ABOUT, MISS IRENE.
ANY OF THESE ANIMALS LOOKS AT YOU IN A DISCOURTEOUS MANNER, YOU LET ME KNOW. THEY WILL BE DEALT WITH.
AND YOU, CORPORAL? WHY ARE YOU HERE? WHAT'S YOUR CRIME?
THE CAPITAL CRIME OF STUPIDITY, I'M STARTING TO BELIEVE. AND PLEASE, CALL ME CARLTON.

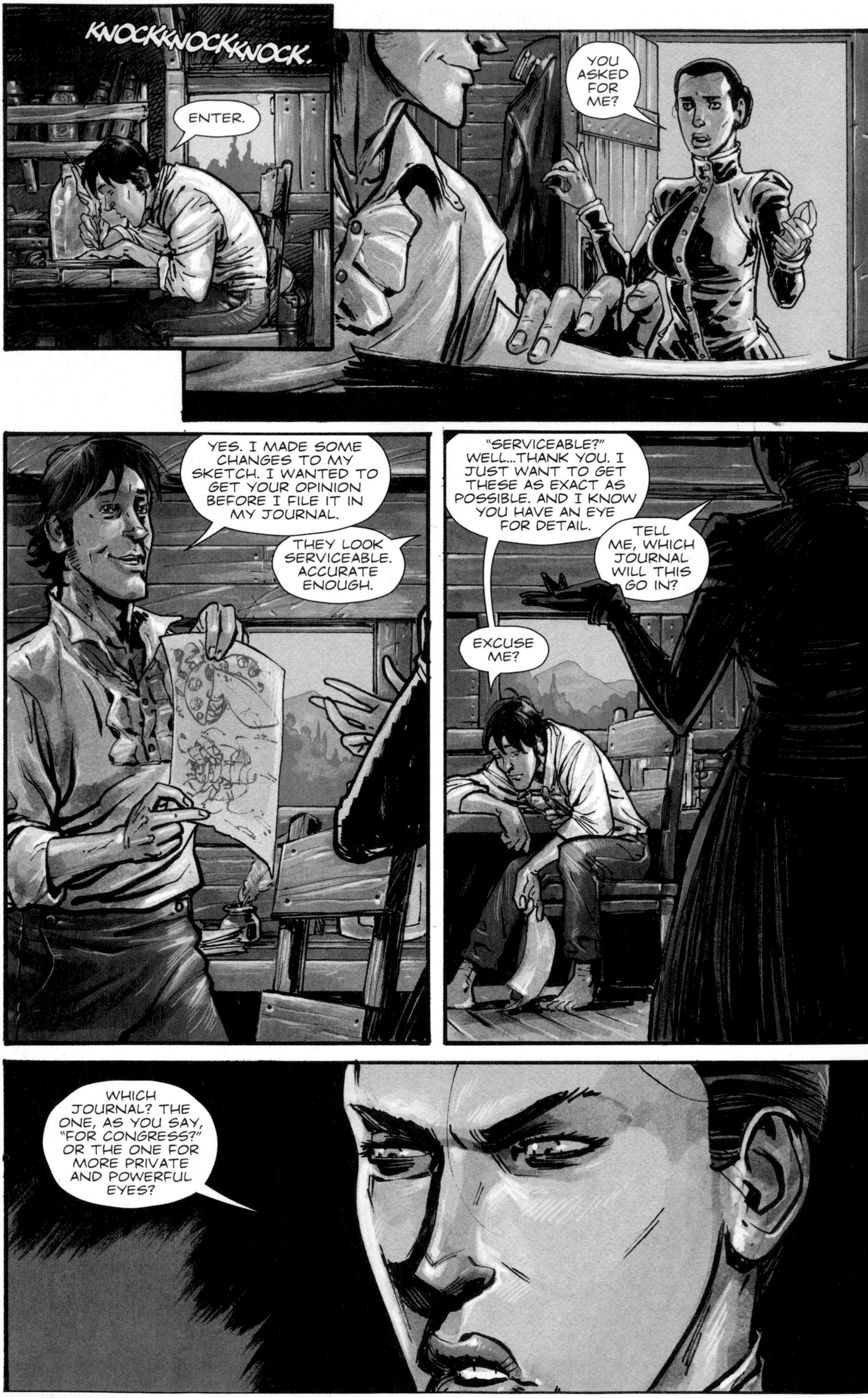
KNOCKKNOCKKNOCK.
ENTER.
YOU ASKED FOR ME?
YES. I MADE SOME CHANGES TO MY SKETCH. I WANTED TO GET YOUR OPINION BEFORE I FILE IT IN MY JOURNAL.
THEY LOOK SERVICEABLE. ACCURATE ENOUGH.
"SERVICEABLE?" WELL...THANK YOU. I JUST WANT TO GET THESE AS EXACT AS POSSIBLE. AND I KNOW YOU HAVE AN EYE FOR DETAIL.
TELL ME, WHICH JOURNAL WILL THIS GO IN?
EXCUSE ME?
WHICH JOURNAL? THE ONE, AS YOU SAY, "FOR CONGRESS?" OR THE ONE FOR MORE PRIVATE AND POWERFUL EYES?

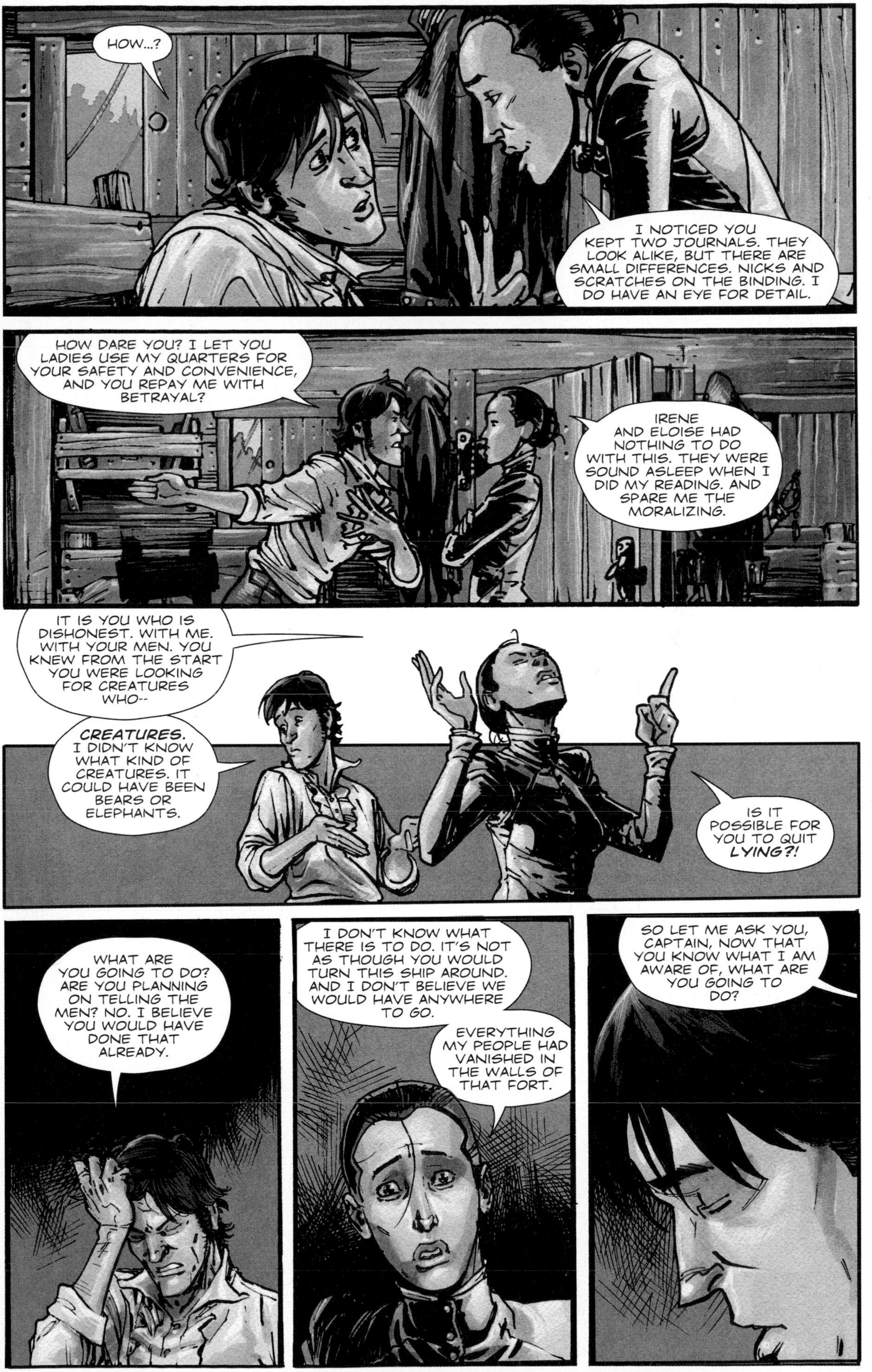
HOW...?
I NOTICED YOU KEPT TWO JOURNALS. THEY LOOK ALIKE, BUT THERE ARE SMALL DIFFERENCES. NICKS AND SCRATCHES ON THE BINDING. I DO HAVE AN EYE FOR DETAIL.
HOW DARE YOU? I LET YOU LADIES USE MY QUARTERS FOR YOUR SAFETY AND CONVENIENCE, AND YOU REPAY ME WITH BETRAYAL?
IRENE AND ELOISE HAD NOTHING TO DO WITH THIS. THEY WERE SOUND ASLEEP WHEN I DID MY READING. AND SPARE ME THE MORALIZING.
IT IS YOU WHO IS DISHONEST. WITH ME. WITH YOUR MEN. YOU KNEW FROM THE START YOU WERE LOOKING FOR CREATURES WHO--
CREATURES. I DIDN'T KNOW WHAT KIND OF CREATURES. IT COULD HAVE BEEN BEARS OR ELEPHANTS.
IS IT POSSIBLE FOR YOU TO QUIT LYING?!
WHAT ARE YOU GOING TO DO? ARE YOU PLANNING ON TELLING THE MEN? NO. I BELIEVE YOU WOULD HAVE DONE THAT ALREADY.
I DON'T KNOW WHAT THERE IS TO DO. IT'S NOT AS THOUGH YOU WOULD TURN THIS SHIP AROUND. AND I DON'T BELIEVE WE WOULD HAVE ANYWHERE TO GO.
EVERYTHING MY PEOPLE HAD VANISHED IN THE WALLS OF THAT FORT.
SO LET ME ASK YOU, CAPTAIN, NOW THAT YOU KNOW WHAT I AM AWARE OF, WHAT ARE YOU GOING TO DO?

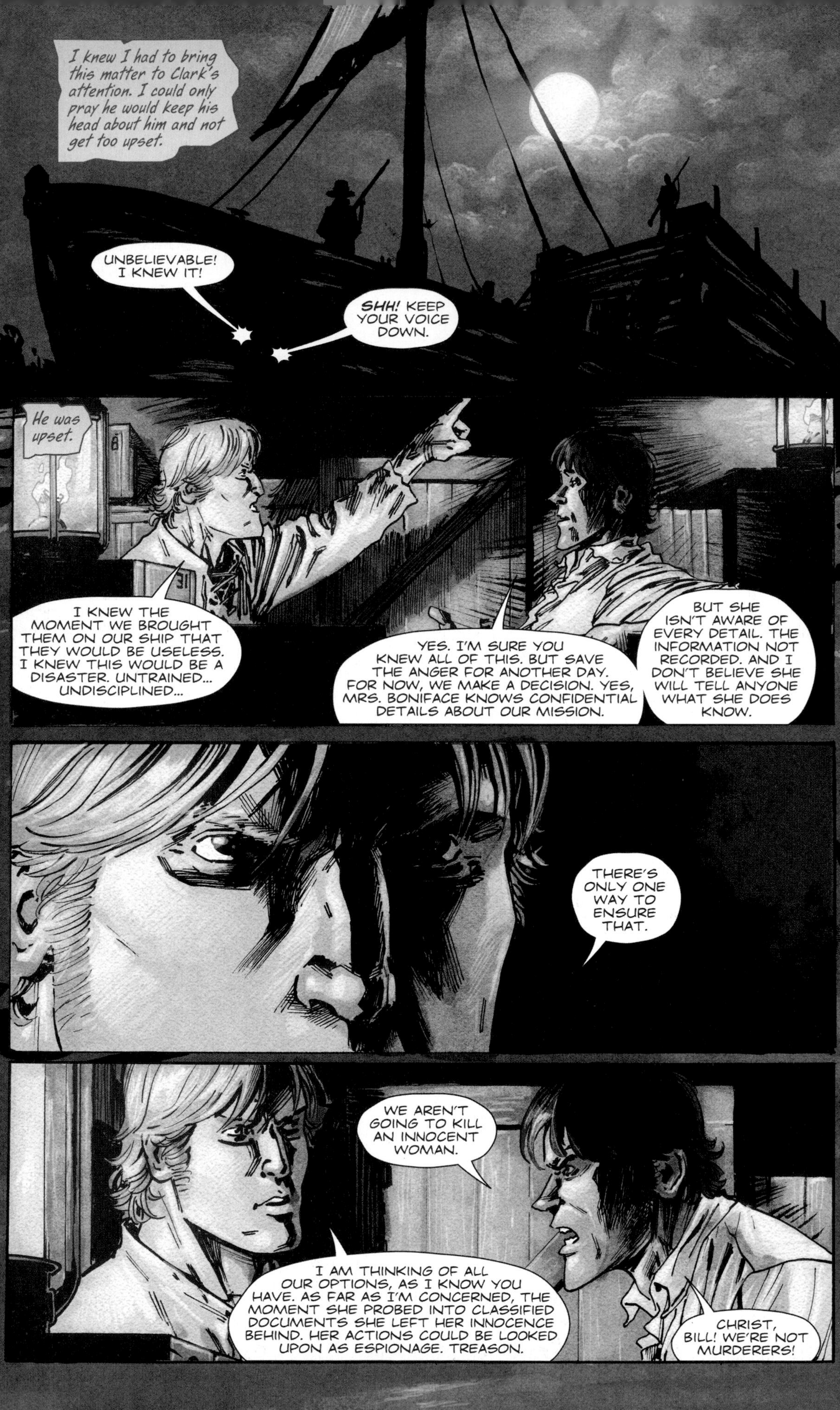
I knew I had to bring this matter to Clark's attention. I could only pray he would keep his head about him and not get too upset.
UNBELIEVABLE! I KNEW IT!
SHH! KEEP YOUR VOICE DOWN.
He was upset.
I KNEW THE MOMENT WE BROUGHT THEM ON OUR SHIP THAT THEY WOULD BE USELESS. I KNEW THIS WOULD BE A DISASTER. UNTRAINED... UNDISCIPLINED...
YES. I'M SURE YOU KNEW ALL OF THIS. BUT SAVE THE ANGER FOR ANOTHER DAY. FOR NOW, WE MAKE A DECISION. YES, MRS. BONIFACE KNOWS CONFIDENTIAL DETAILS ABOUT OUR MISSION.
BUT SHE ISN'T AWARE OF EVERY DETAIL. THE INFORMATION NOT RECORDED. AND I DON'T BELIEVE SHE WILL TELL ANYONE WHAT SHE DOES KNOW.
THERE'S ONLY ONE WAY TO ENSURE THAT.
WE AREN'T GOING TO KILL AN INNOCENT WOMAN.
I AM THINKING OF ALL OUR OPTIONS, AS I KNOW YOU HAVE. AS FAR AS I'M CONCERNED, THE MOMENT SHE PROBED INTO CLASSIFIED DOCUMENTS SHE LEFT HER INNOCENCE BEHIND. HER ACTIONS COULD BE LOOKED UPON AS ESPIONAGE. TREASON.
CHRIST, BILL! WE'RE NOT MURDERERS!

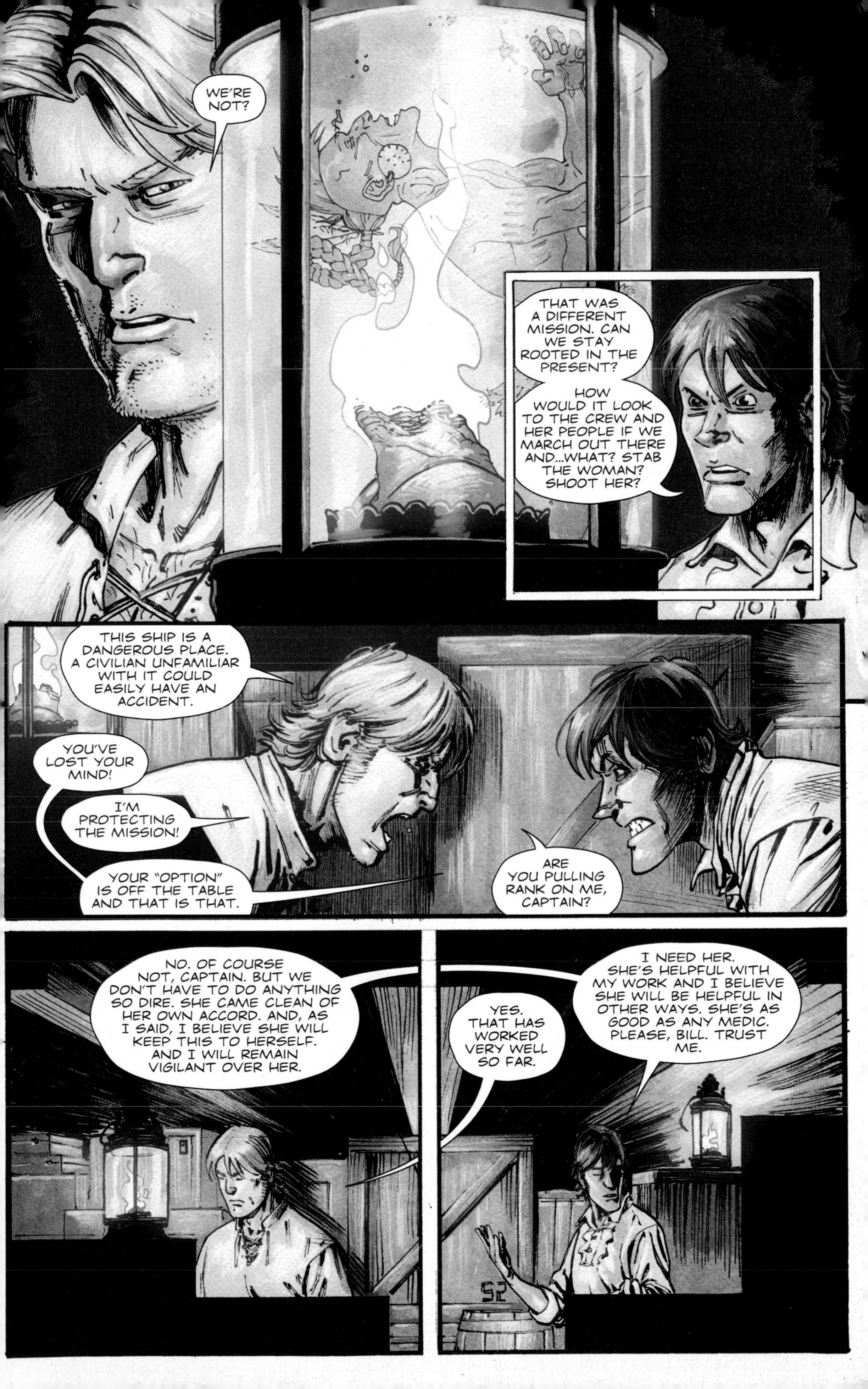
WE'RE NOT?
THAT WAS A DIFFERENT MISSION. CAN WE STAY ROOTED IN THE PRESENT?
HOW WOULD IT LOOK TO THE CREW AND HER PEOPLE IF WE MARCH OUT THERE AND...WHAT? STAB THE WOMAN? SHOOT HER?
THIS SHIP IS A DANGEROUS PLACE. A CIVILIAN UNFAMILIAR WITH IT COULD EASILY HAVE AN ACCIDENT.
YOU'VE LOST YOUR MIND!
I'M PROTECTING THE MISSION!
YOUR "OPTION" IS OFF THE TABLE AND THAT IS THAT.
ARE YOU PULLING RANK ON ME, CAPTAIN?
NO. OF COURSE NOT, CAPTAIN. BUT WE DON'T HAVE TO DO ANYTHING SO DIRE. SHE CAME CLEAN OF HER OWN ACCORD. AND, AS I SAID, I BELIEVE SHE WILL KEEP THIS TO HERSELF. AND I WILL REMAIN VIGILANT OVER HER.
YES. THAT HAS WORKED VERY WELL SO FAR.
I NEED HER. SHE'S HELPFUL WITH MY WORK AND I BELIEVE SHE WILL BE HELPFUL IN OTHER WAYS. SHE'S AS GOOD AS ANY MEDIC. PLEASE, BILL. TRUST ME.

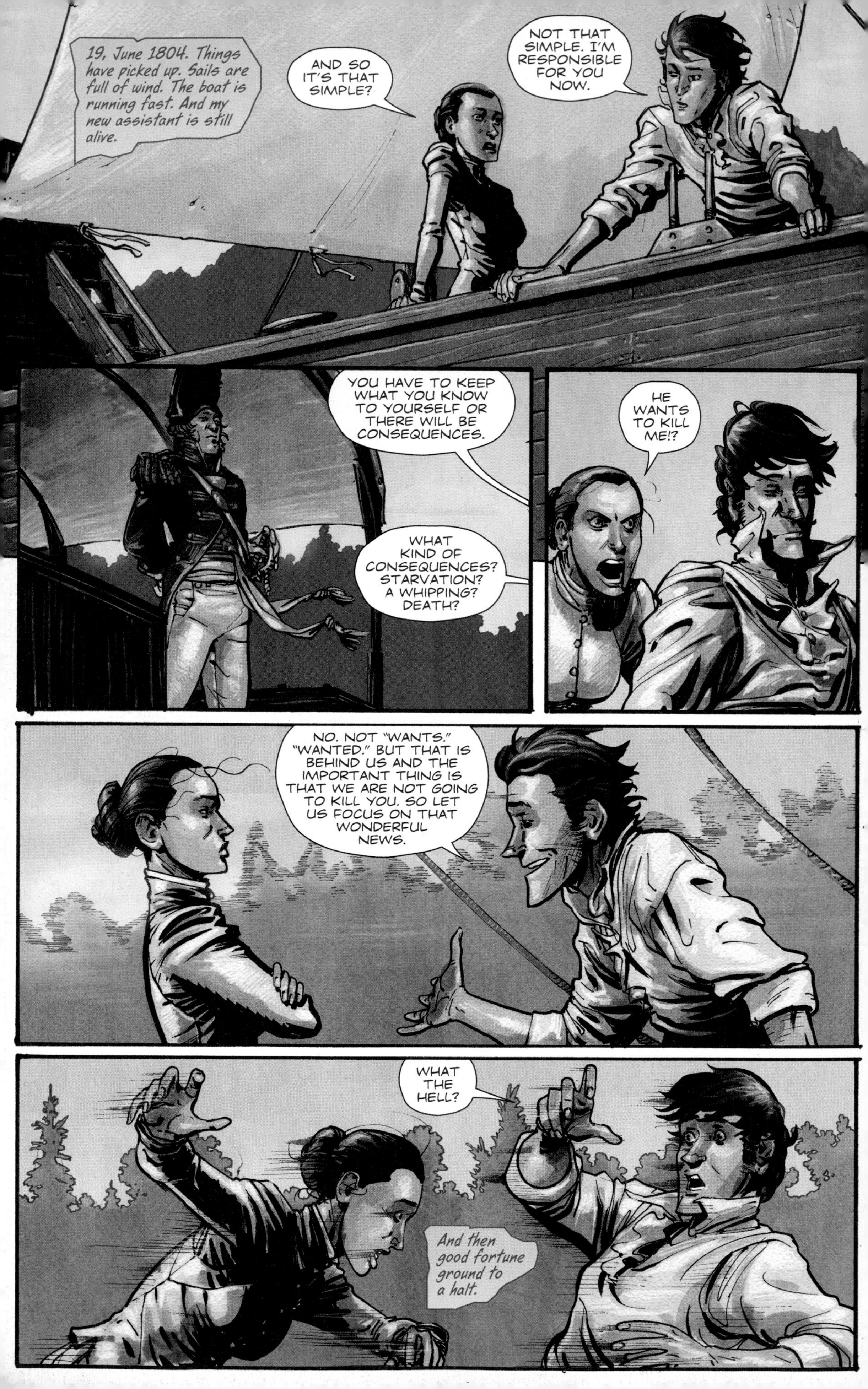
19, June 1804. Things have picked up. Sails are full of wind. The boat is running fast. And my new assistant is still alive.
AND SO IT'S THAT SIMPLE?
NOT THAT SIMPLE. I'M RESPONSIBLE FOR YOU NOW.
YOU HAVE TO KEEP WHAT YOU KNOW TO YOURSELF OR THERE WILL BE CONSEQUENCES.
WHAT KIND OF CONSEQUENCES? STARVATION? A WHIPPING? DEATH?
HE WANTS TO KILL ME!?
NO. NOT "WANTS." "WANTED." BUT THAT IS BEHIND US AND THE IMPORTANT THING IS THAT WE ARE NOT GOING TO KILL YOU. SO LET US FOCUS ON THAT WONDERFUL NEWS.
WHAT THE HELL?
And then good fortune ground to a halt.

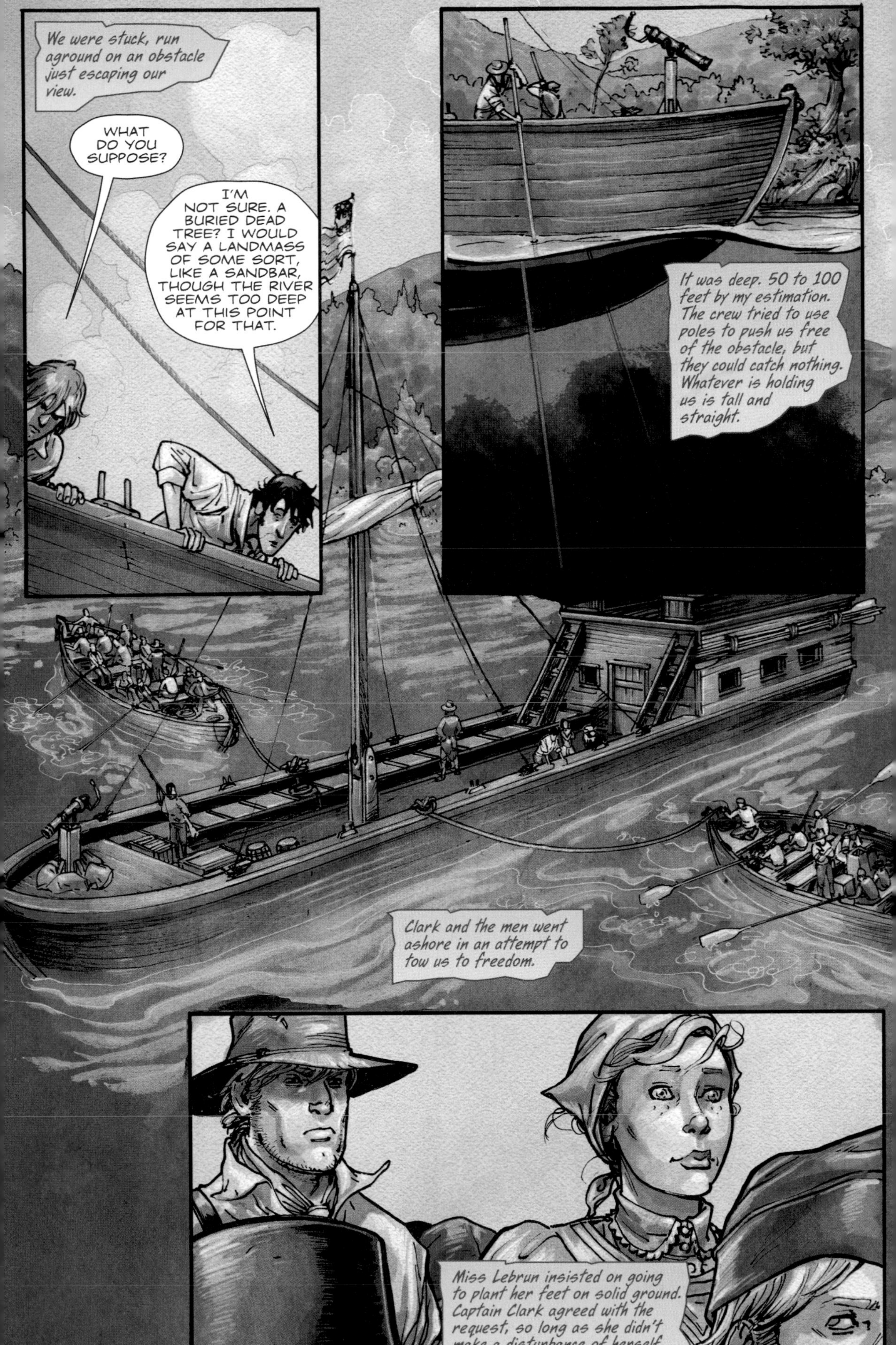
We were stuck, run aground on an obstacle just escaping our view.
WHAT DO YOU SUPPOSE?
I'M NOT SURE. A BURIED DEAD TREE? I WOULD SAY A LANDMASS OF SOME SORT, LIKE A SANDBAR, THOUGH THE RIVER SEEMS TOO DEEP AT THIS POINT FOR THAT.
It was deep. 50 to 100 feet by my estimation. The crew tried to use poles to push us free of the obstacle, but they could catch nothing. Whatever is holding us is tall and straight.
Clark and the men went ashore in an attempt to tow us to freedom.
Miss Lebrun insisted on going to plant her feet on solid ground. Captain Clark agreed with the request, so long as she didn't make a disturbance of herself.

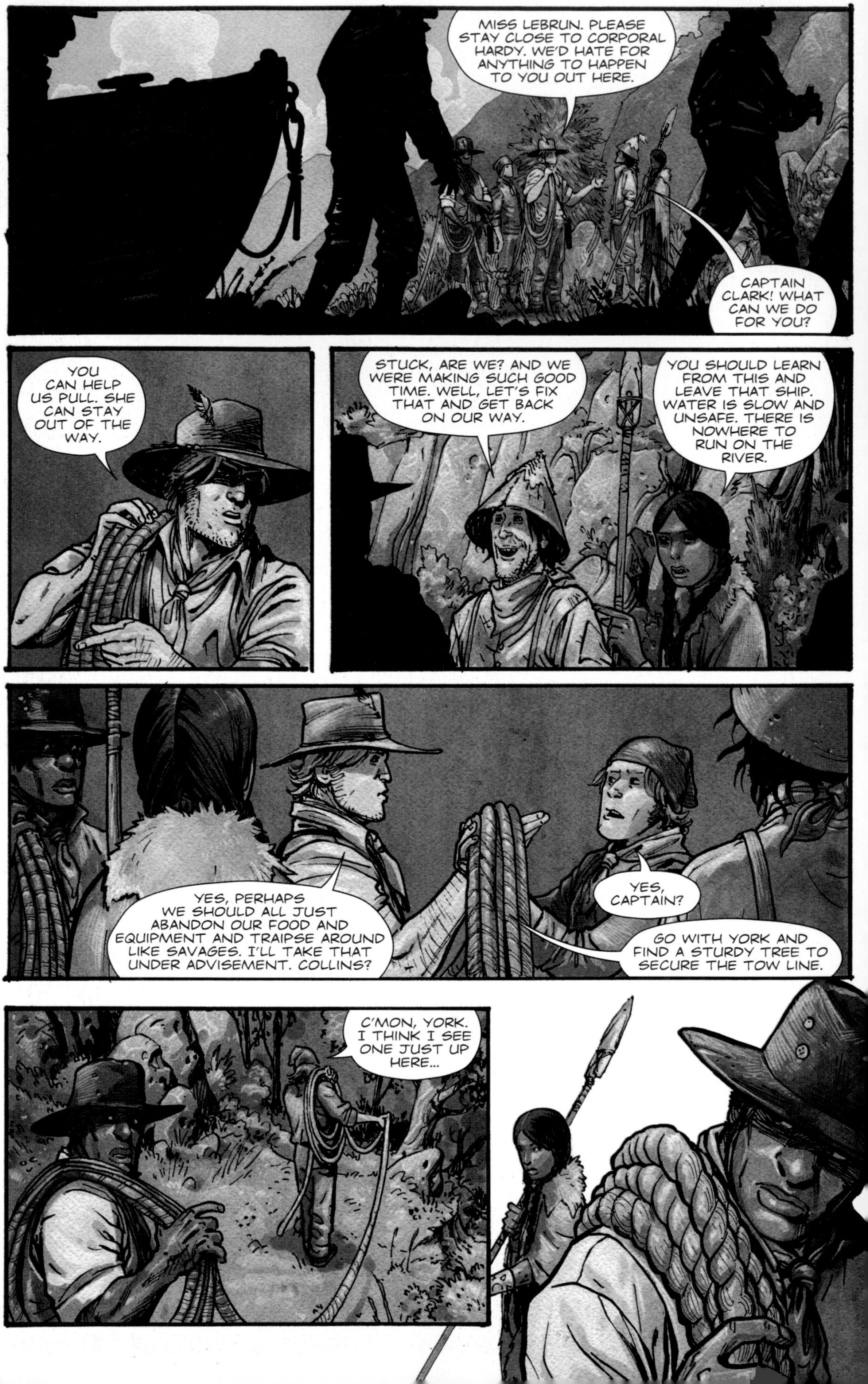
MISS LEBRUN. PLEASE STAY CLOSE TO CORPORAL HARDY. WE'D HATE FOR ANYTHING TO HAPPEN TO YOU OUT HERE.
CAPTAIN CLARK! WHAT CAN WE DO FOR YOU?
YOU CAN HELP US PULL. SHE CAN STAY OUT OF THE WAY.
STUCK, ARE WE? AND WE WERE MAKING SUCH GOOD TIME. WELL, LET'S FIX THAT AND GET BACK ON OUR WAY.
YOU SHOULD LEARN FROM THIS AND LEAVE THAT SHIP. WATER IS SLOW AND UNSAFE. THERE IS NOWHERE TO RUN ON THE RIVER.
YES, PERHAPS WE SHOULD ALL JUST ABANDON OUR FOOD AND EQUIPMENT AND TRAIPSE AROUND LIKE SAVAGES. I'LL TAKE THAT UNDER ADVISEMENT. COLLINS?
YES, CAPTAIN?
GO WITH YORK AND FIND A STURDY TREE TO SECURE THE TOW LINE.
C'MON, YORK. I THINK I SEE ONE JUST UP HERE...

I stayed behind to conduct my own business.

BE CAREFUL, SIR.

IT'LL BE FINE. YOU JUST STAY PREPARED. IF I GET IN TROUBLE, I WILL RING THIS BELL. UNDERSTOOD?

I THINK THIS IS FOOLISH.

I THINK IT'S VERY FOOLISH. AND YET, I MUST SEE WHAT'S GOT AHOLD OF THIS BOAT.

WHY?

BECAUSE I HAVE A FEELING. A FEELING THAT I GET WHEN I'M ABOUT TO SEE SOMETHING FOR THE FIRST TIME.

CAPTAIN LEWIS!

WHAT IS IT, TUTTLE?

THERE IS A LADY PRESENT!

MRS. BONIFACE IS A WOMAN OF SCIENCE AND ABOVE THE CONFINES OF MODESTY. ISN'T THAT RIGHT?

I'M MORE OFFENDED BY YOUR EYEWEAR.

THOSE RIDICULOUS THINGS WILL HELP YOU SEE UNDER-WATER?

FOR A MOMENT OR TWO, UNTIL THE WATER COMES IN. THEY ARE REMARKABLE THINGS. YOU'RE WELCOME TO COME IN AND TRY THEM WITH ME.

THAT'S QUITE ALRIGHT.

And so, I went in alone.

SHPLOOSH!

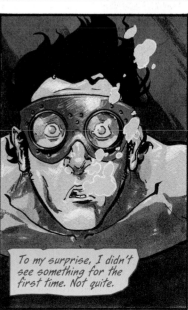

To my surprise, I didn't see something for the first time. Not quite.

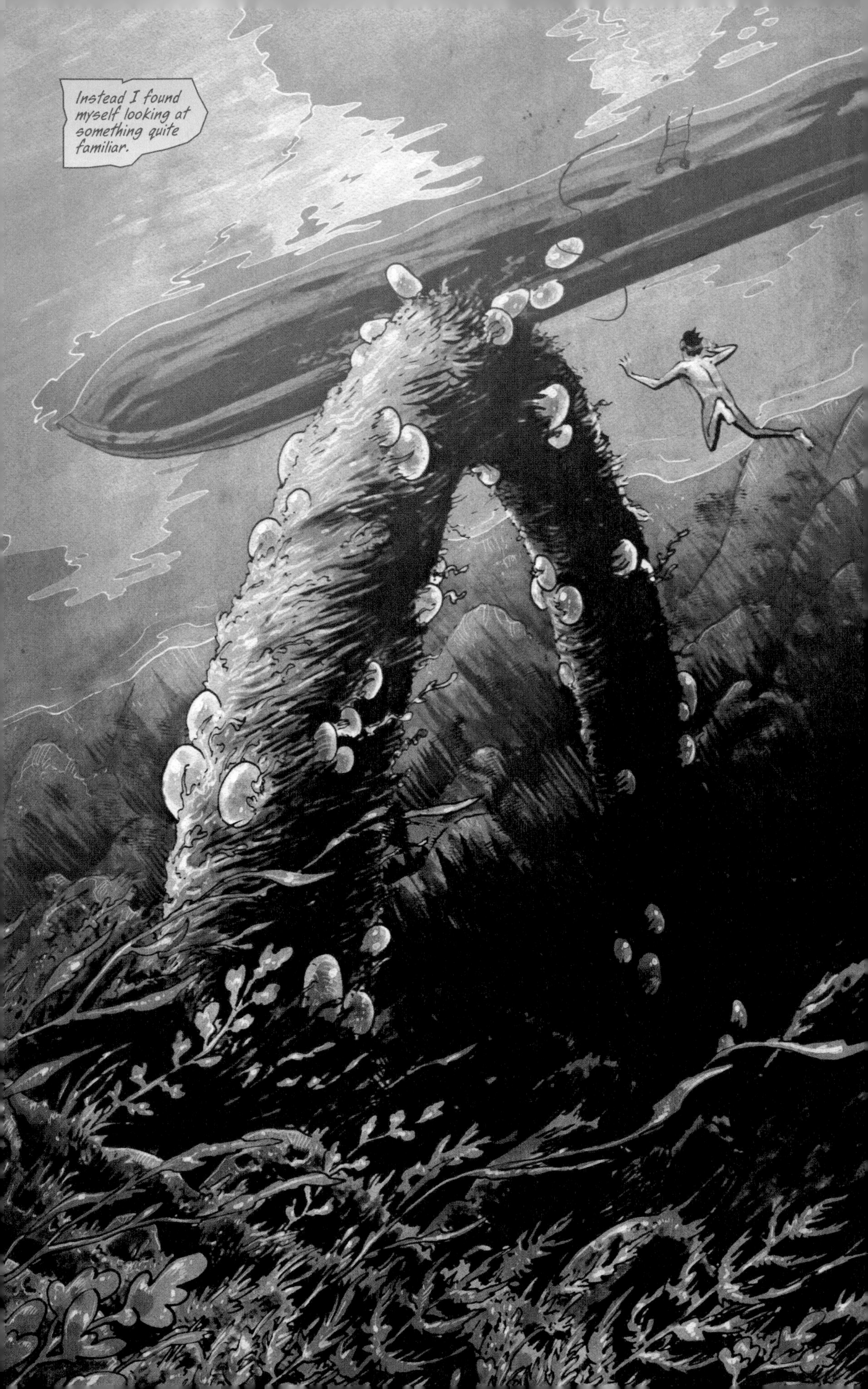
Instead I found myself looking at something quite familiar.

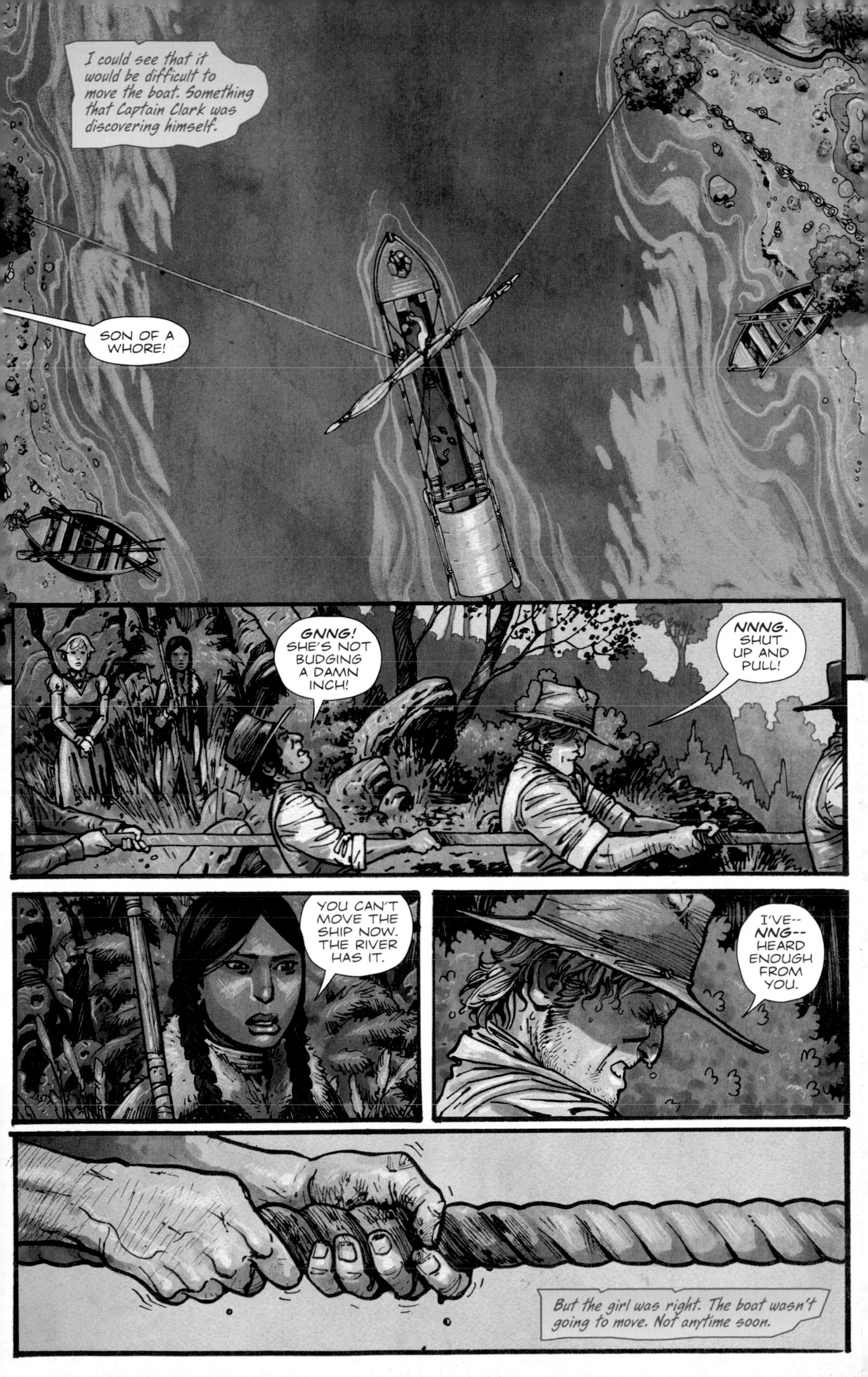
I could see that it would be difficult to move the boat. Something that Captain Clark was discovering himself.
SON OF A WHORE!
GNNG! SHE'S NOT BUDGING A DAMN INCH!
NNNG. SHUT UP AND PULL!
YOU CAN'T MOVE THE SHIP NOW. THE RIVER HAS IT.
I'VE-- NNG-- HEARD ENOUGH FROM YOU.
But the girl was right. The boat wasn't going to move. Not anytime soon.

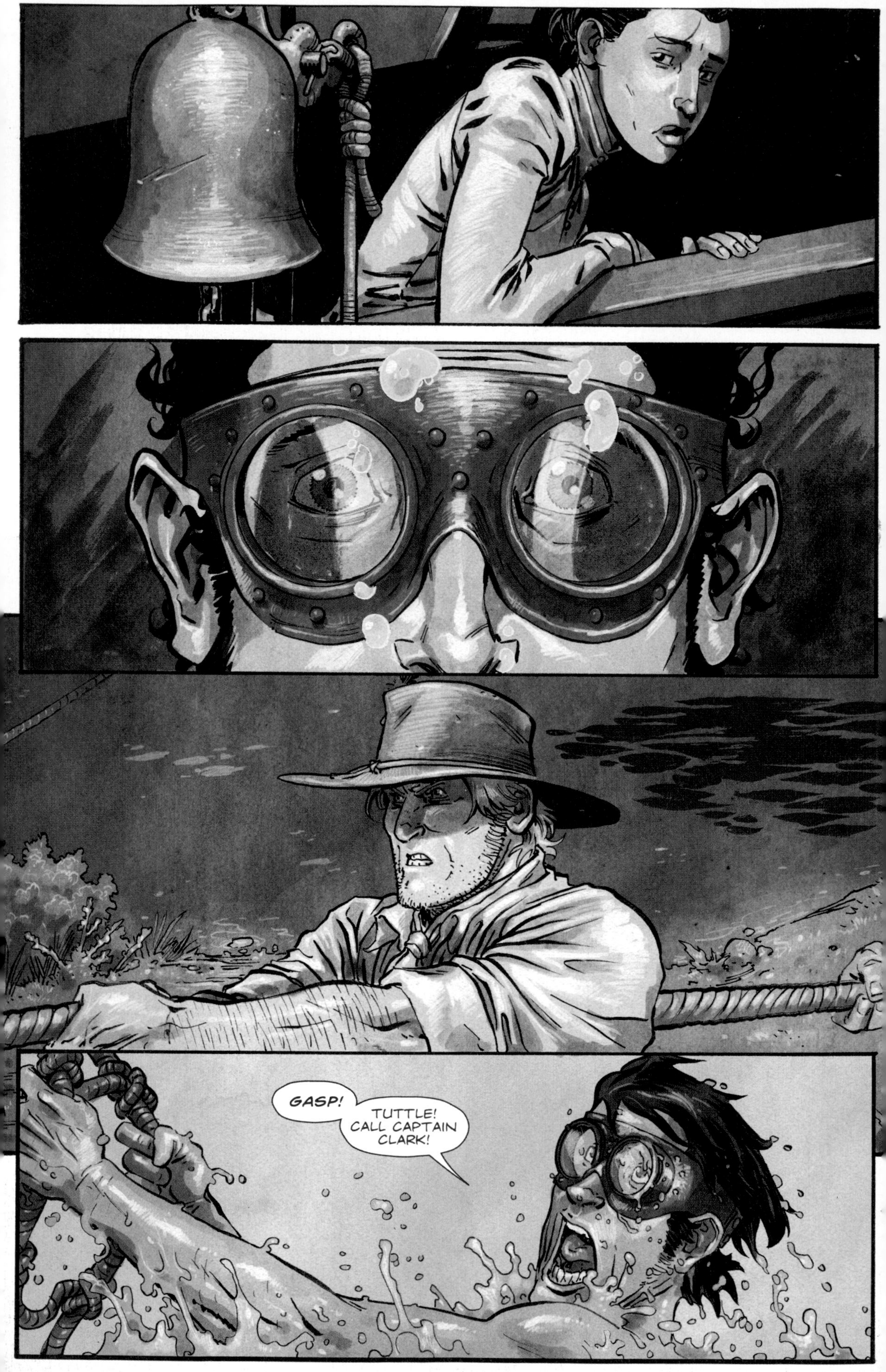
GASP!
TUTTLE! CALL CAPTAIN CLARK!

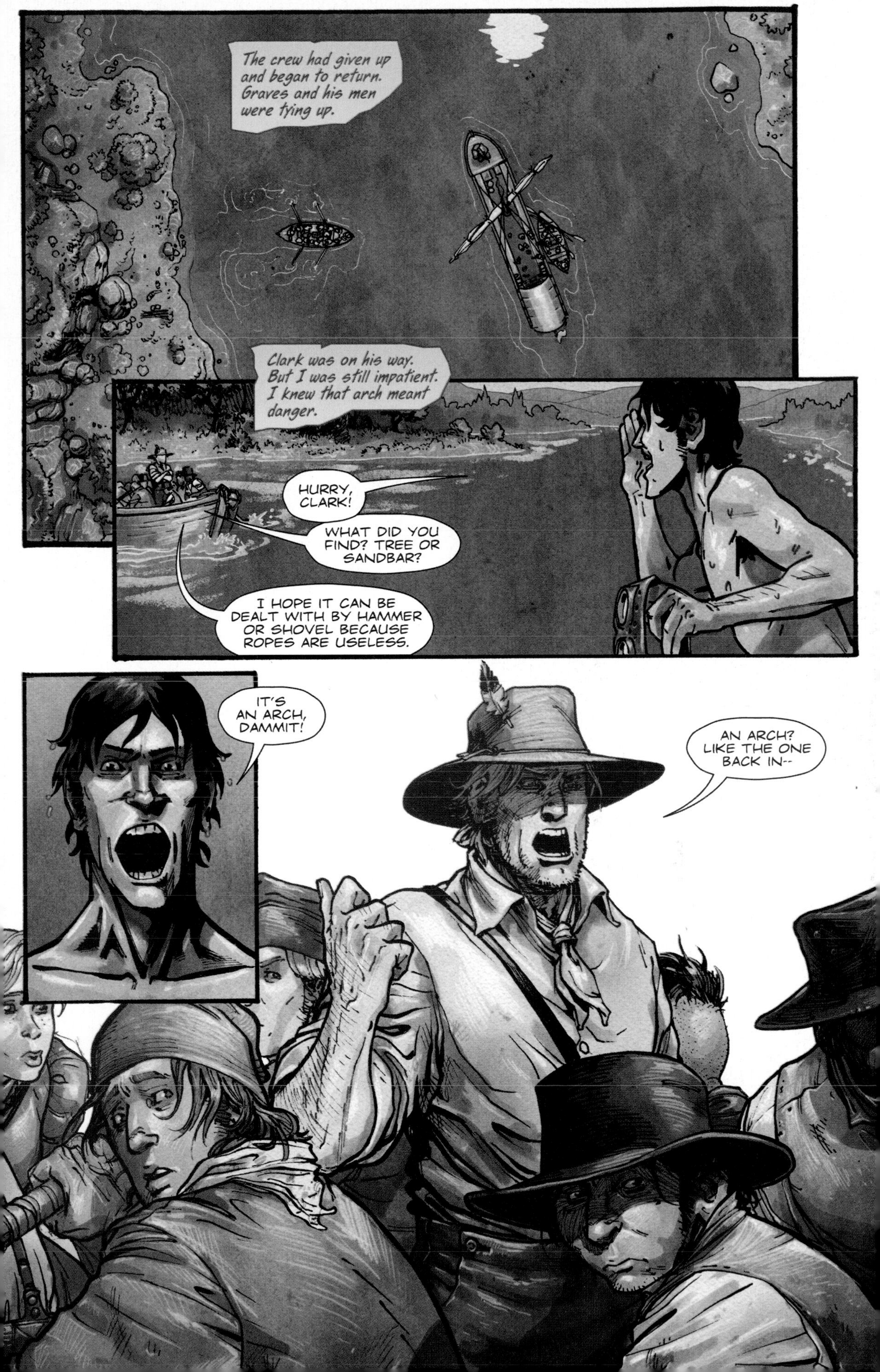
The crew had given up and began to return. Graves and his men were tying up.
Clark was on his way. But I was still impatient. I knew that arch meant danger.
HURRY, CLARK!
WHAT DID YOU FIND? TREE OR SANDBAR?
I HOPE IT CAN BE DEALT WITH BY HAMMER OR SHOVEL BECAUSE ROPES ARE USELESS.
IT'S AN ARCH, DAMMIT!
AN ARCH? LIKE THE ONE BACK IN--

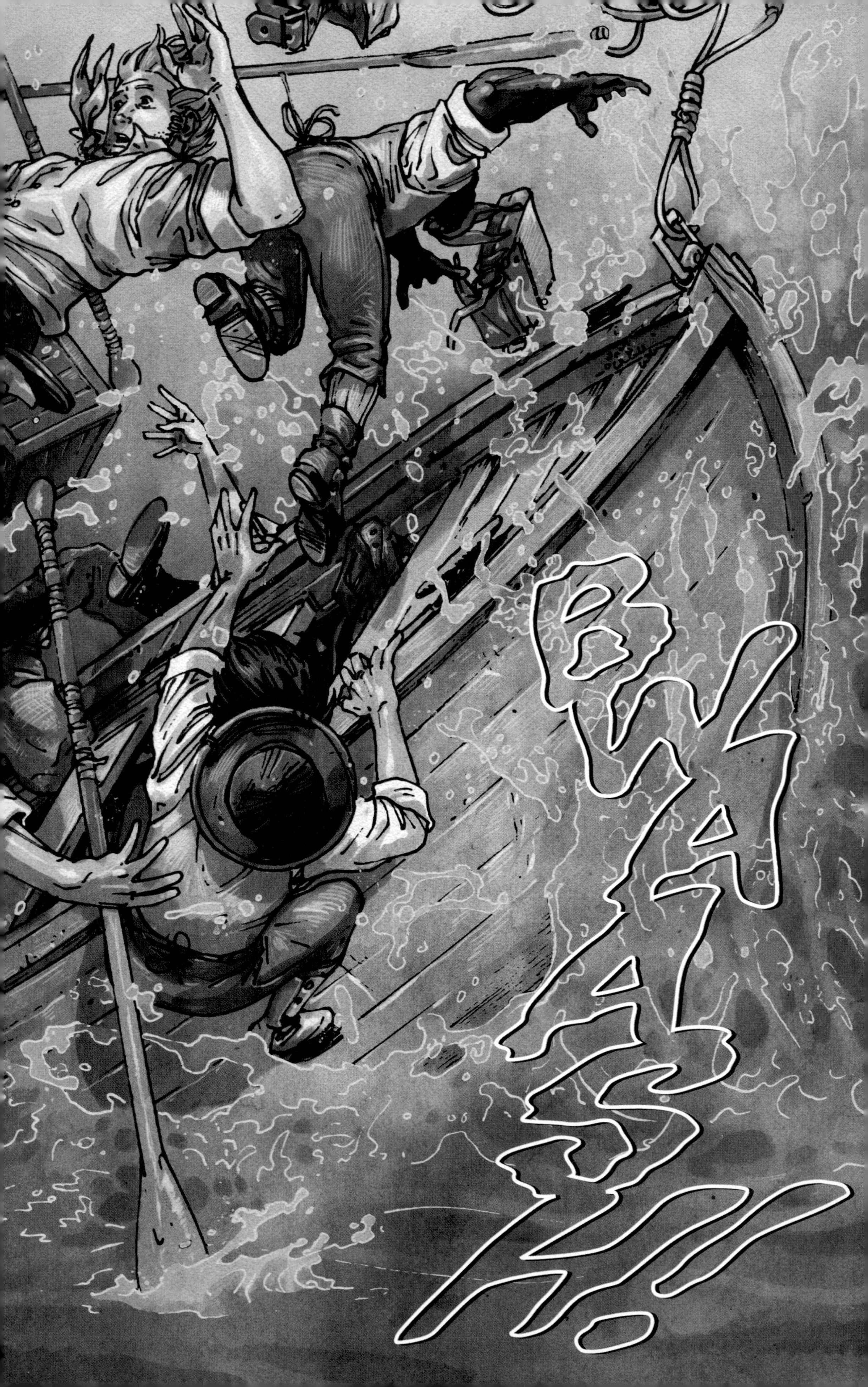
BWAASH!!

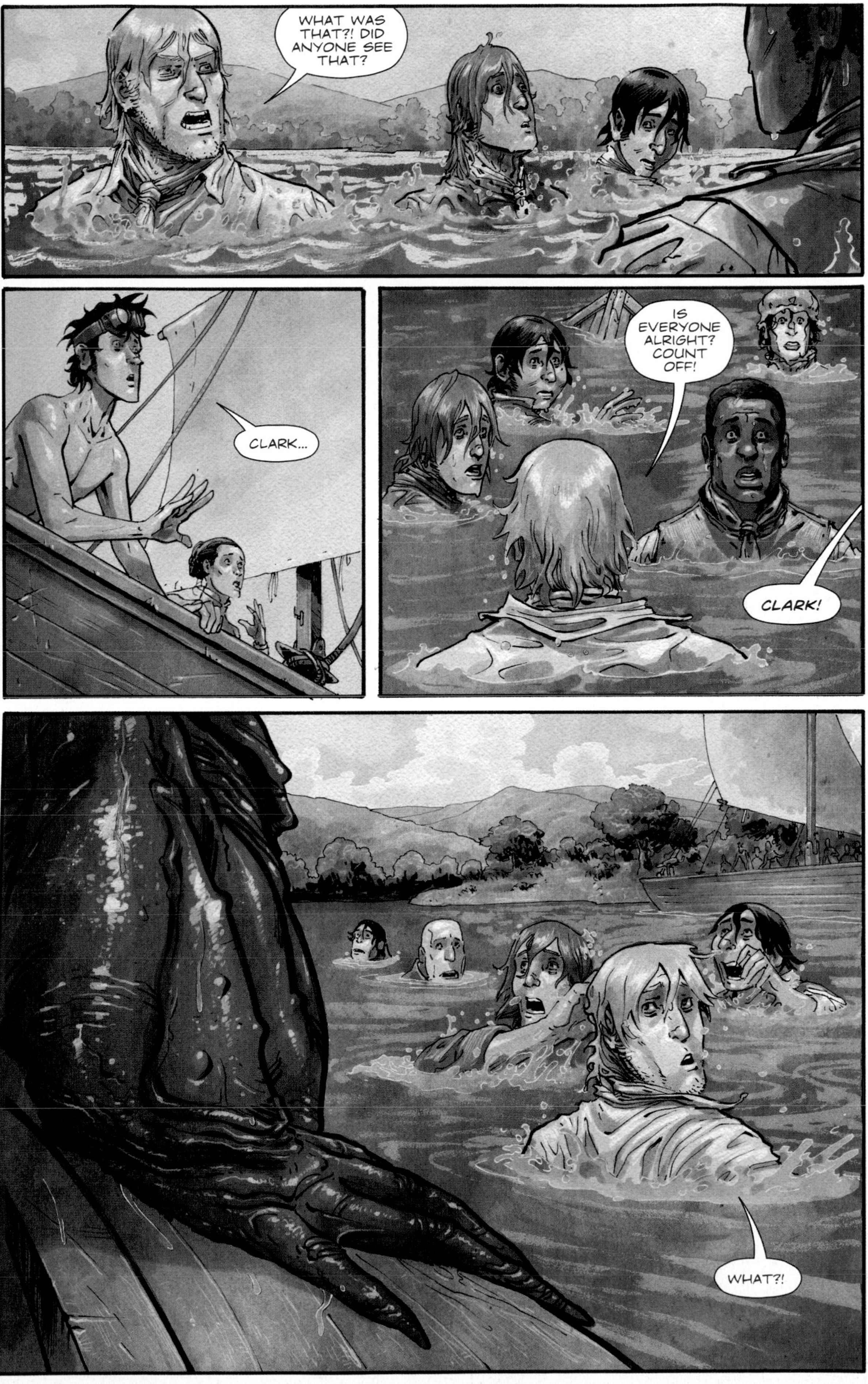
WHAT WAS THAT?! DID ANYONE SEE THAT?
CLARK...
IS EVERYONE ALRIGHT? COUNT OFF!
CLARK!
WHAT?!

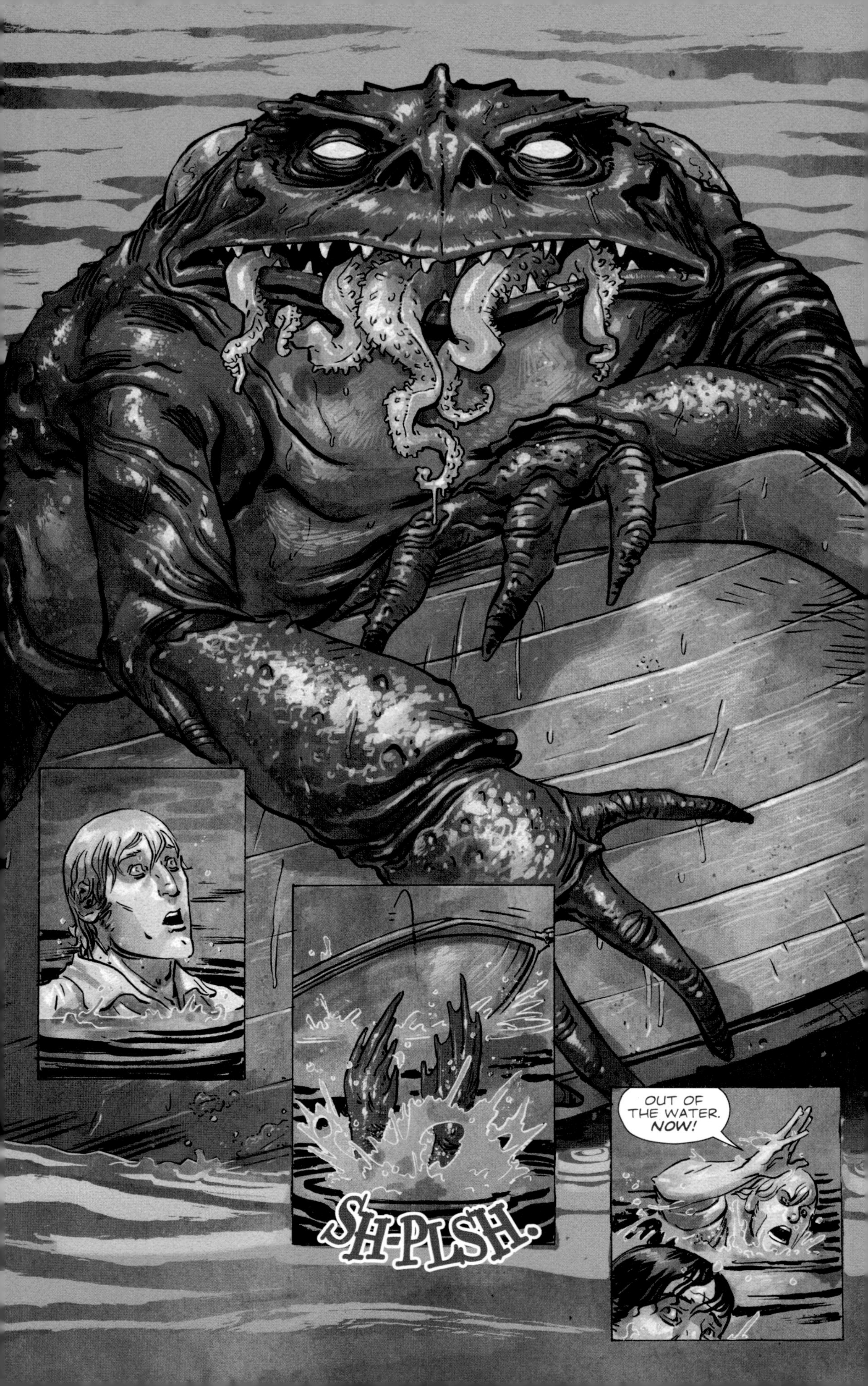
SH-PLSH.
OUT OF THE WATER. NOW!

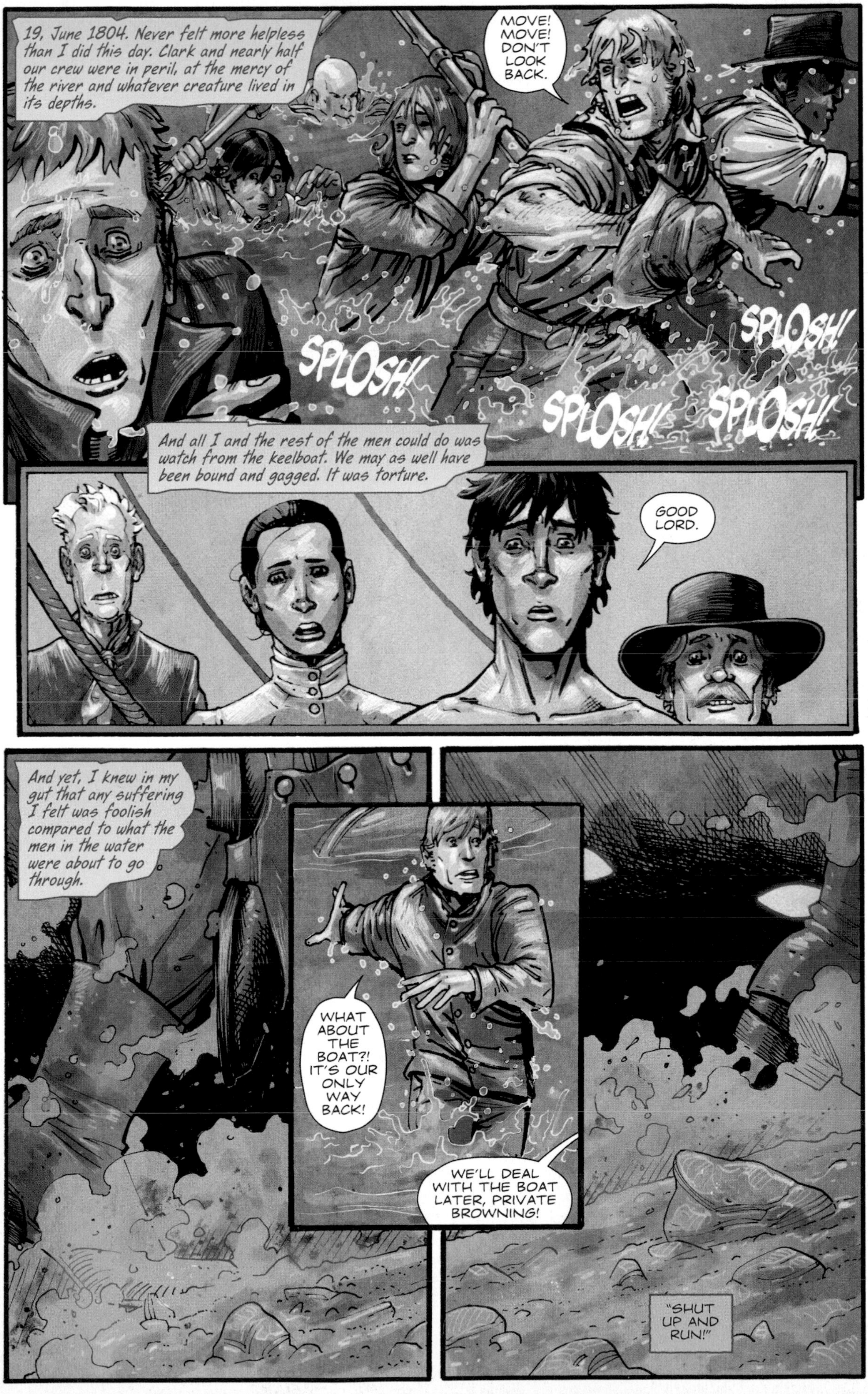
19, June 1804. Never felt more helpless than I did this day. Clark and nearly half our crew were in peril, at the mercy of the river and whatever creature lived in its depths.
MOVE! MOVE! DON'T LOOK BACK.
SPLOSH!
SPLOSH!
SPLOSH!
SPLOSH!
And all I and the rest of the men could do was watch from the keelboat. We may as well have been bound and gagged. It was torture.
GOOD LORD.
And yet, I knew in my gut that any suffering I felt was foolish compared to what the men in the water were about to go through.
WHAT ABOUT THE BOAT?! IT'S OUR ONLY WAY BACK!
WE'LL DEAL WITH THE BOAT LATER, PRIVATE BROWNING!
"SHUT UP AND RUN!"

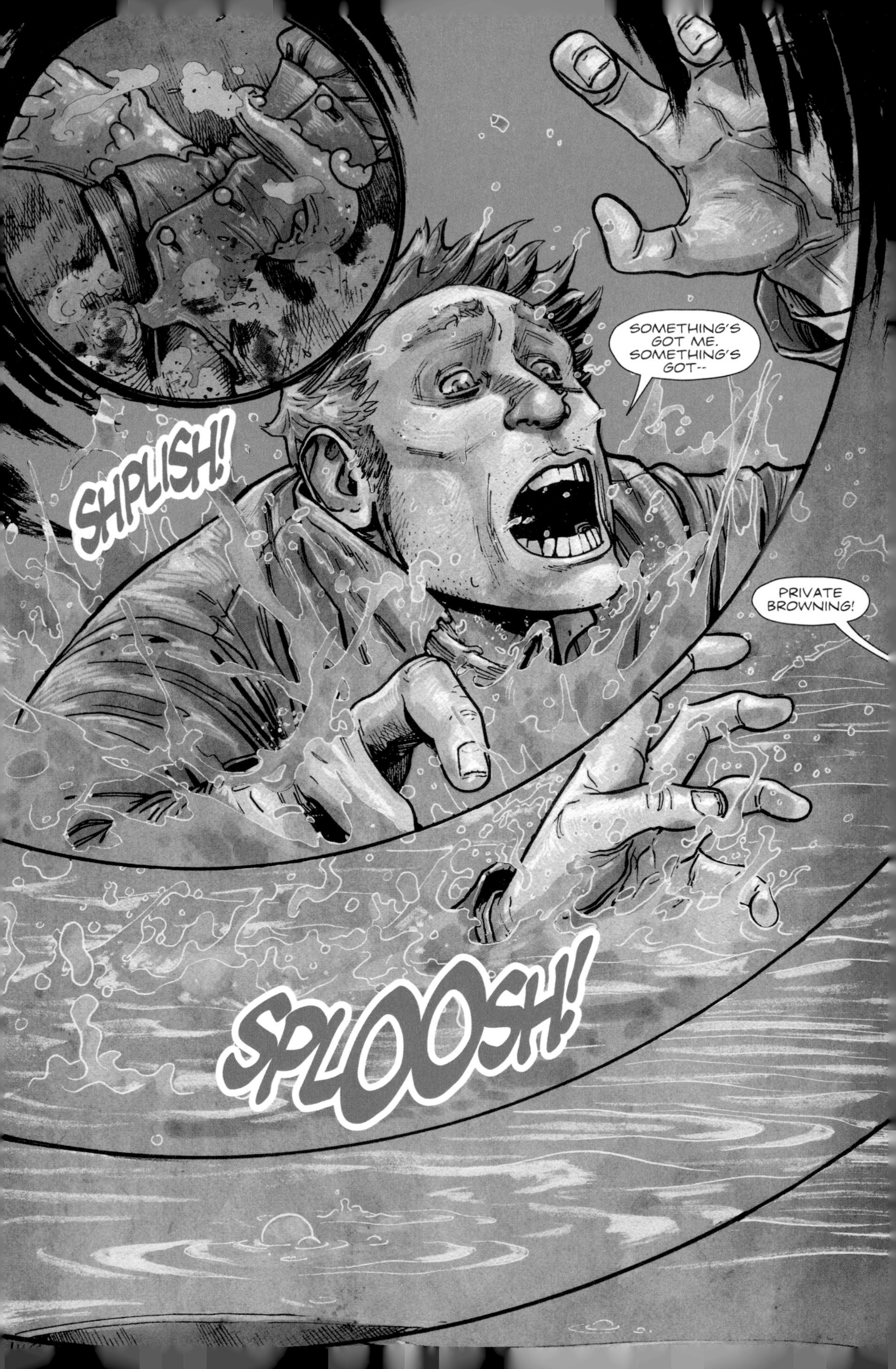
SOMETHING'S GOT ME. SOMETHING'S GOT--
SHPLISH!
PRIVATE BROWNING!
SPLOOSH!

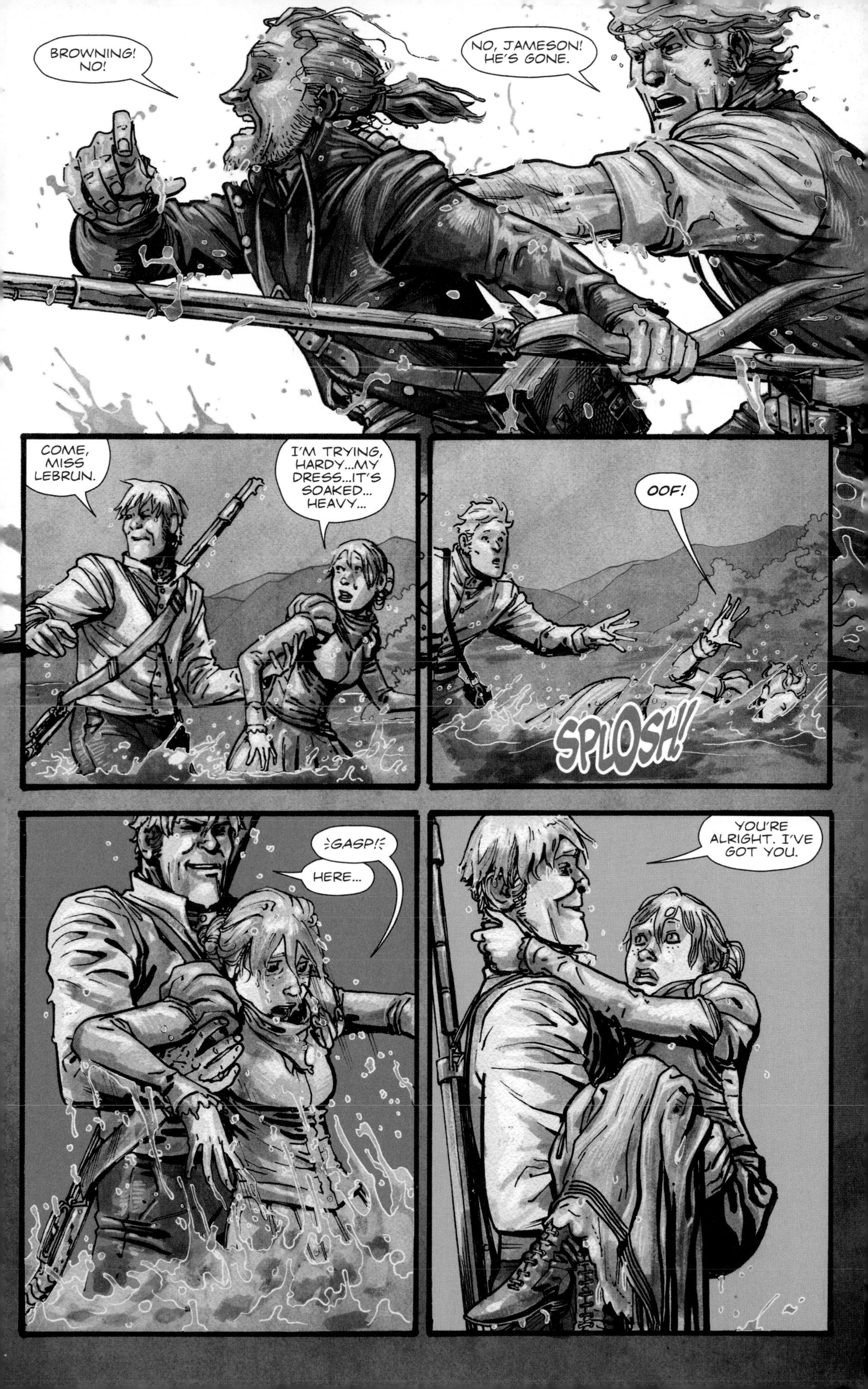
BROWNING! NO!
NO, JAMESON! HE'S GONE.
COME, MISS LEBRUN.
I'M TRYING, HARDY...MY DRESS...IT'S SOAKED... HEAVY...
OOF!
SPLOSH!
GASP!
HERE...
YOU'RE ALRIGHT. I'VE GOT YOU.

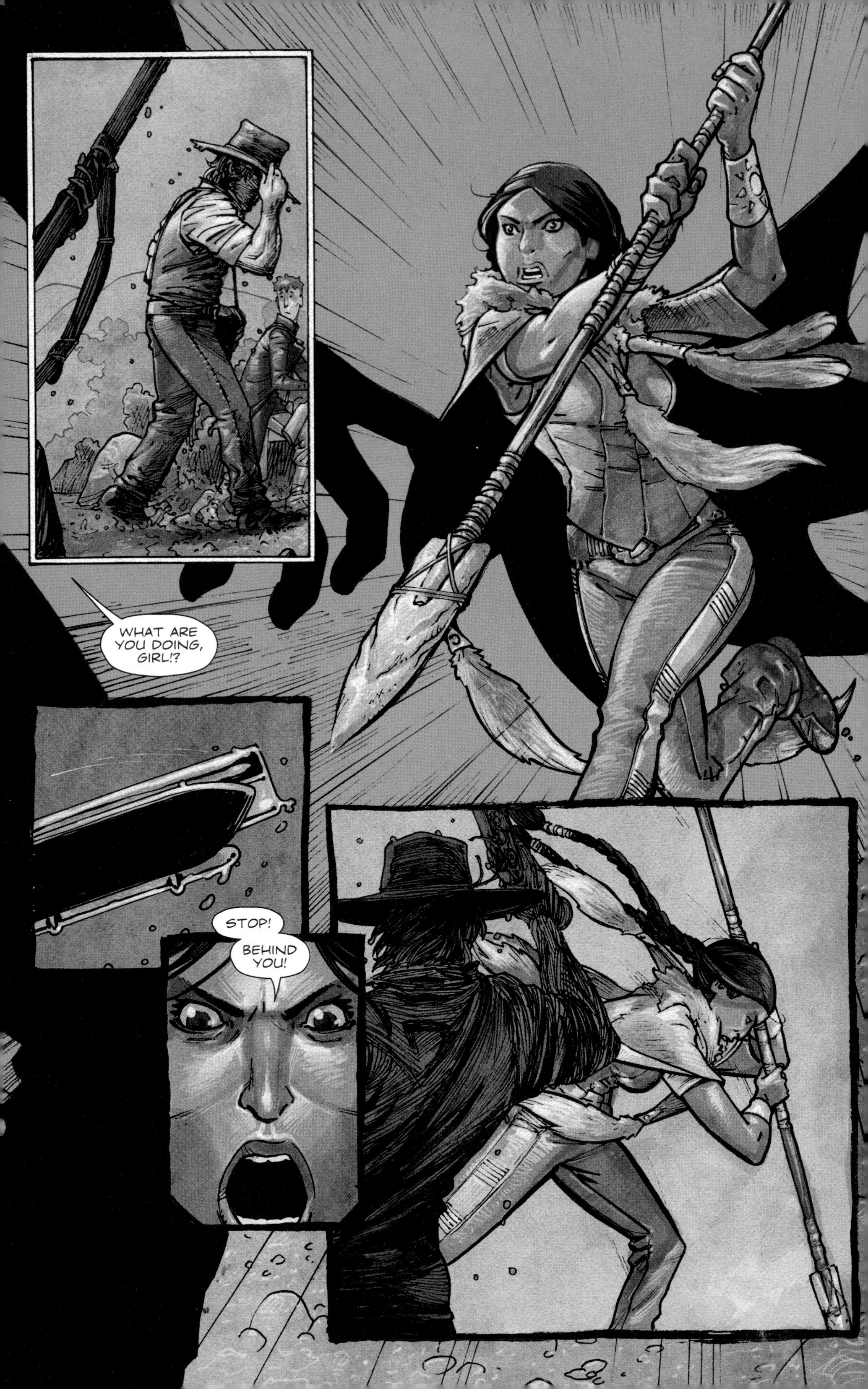
WHAT ARE YOU DOING, GIRL!?
STOP!
BEHIND YOU!

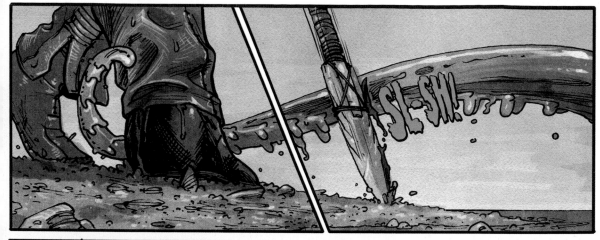

TWO TIMES. TWO TIMES I HAVE SAVED YOU.

SOMEONE PICK UP THAT PIECE OF TONGUE.

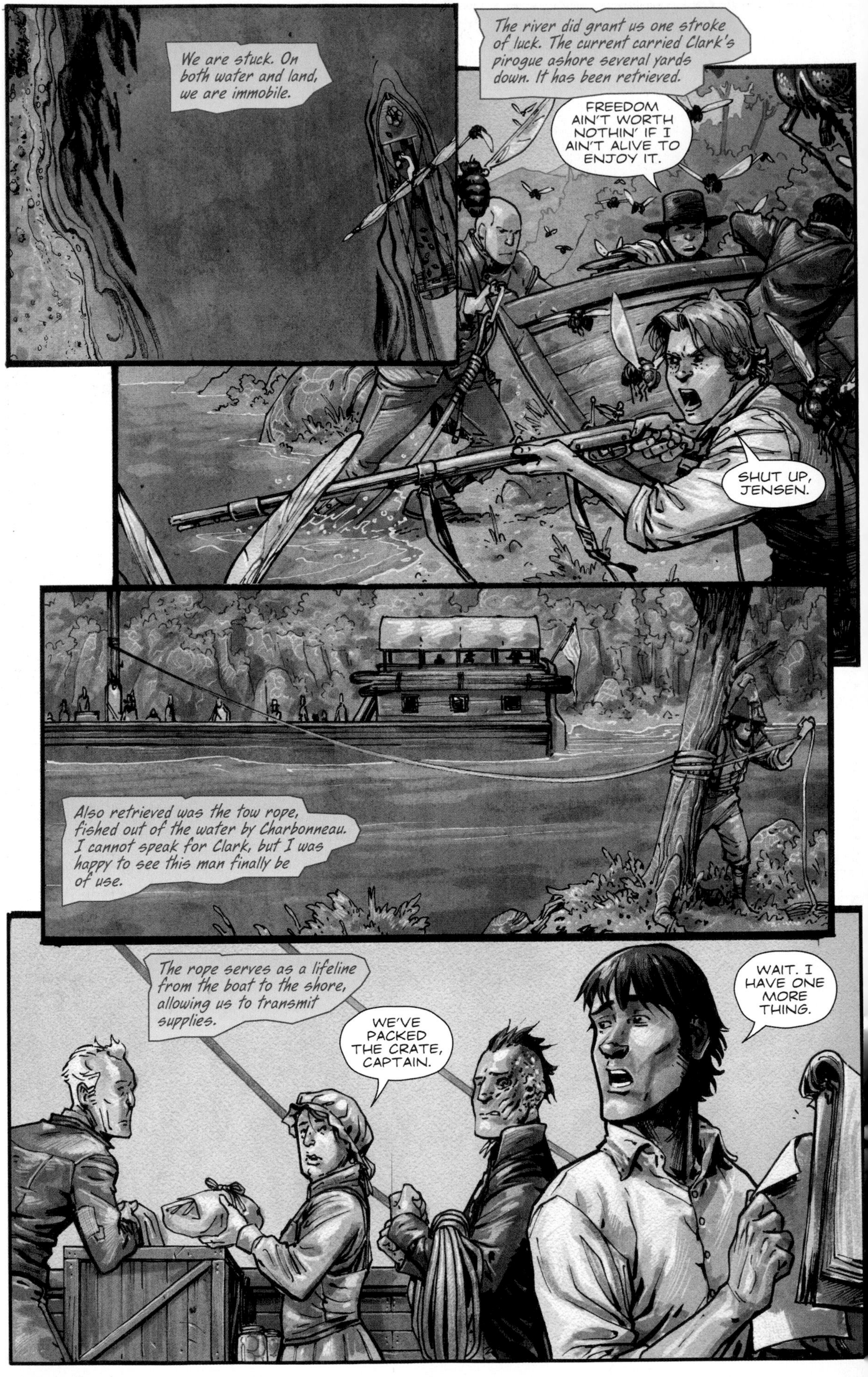
We are stuck. On both water and land, we are immobile.
The river did grant us one stroke of luck. The current carried Clark's pirogue ashore several yards down. It has been retrieved.
FREEDOM AIN'T WORTH NOTHIN' IF I AIN'T ALIVE TO ENJOY IT.
SHUT UP, JENSEN.
Also retrieved was the tow rope, fished out of the water by Charbonneau. I cannot speak for Clark, but I was happy to see this man finally be of use.
The rope serves as a lifeline from the boat to the shore, allowing us to transmit supplies.
WE'VE PACKED THE CRATE, CAPTAIN.
WAIT. I HAVE ONE MORE THING.

It also delivered details of just how dire our situation is.

CHRIST ON HIS THRONE...

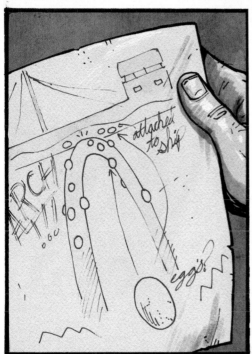

attached to ship

RCH

eggs?

WE'LL MOVE TWENTY YARDS INTO THE TREELINE. WE CAN SCOUT OUT A SITE AND CAMP FOR THE NIGHT.

NO.

WHAT ARE YOU DOING?

HERE IS BETTER. HERE YOU KNOW WHAT DEVILS THERE ARE. NOT IN THE WOODS.

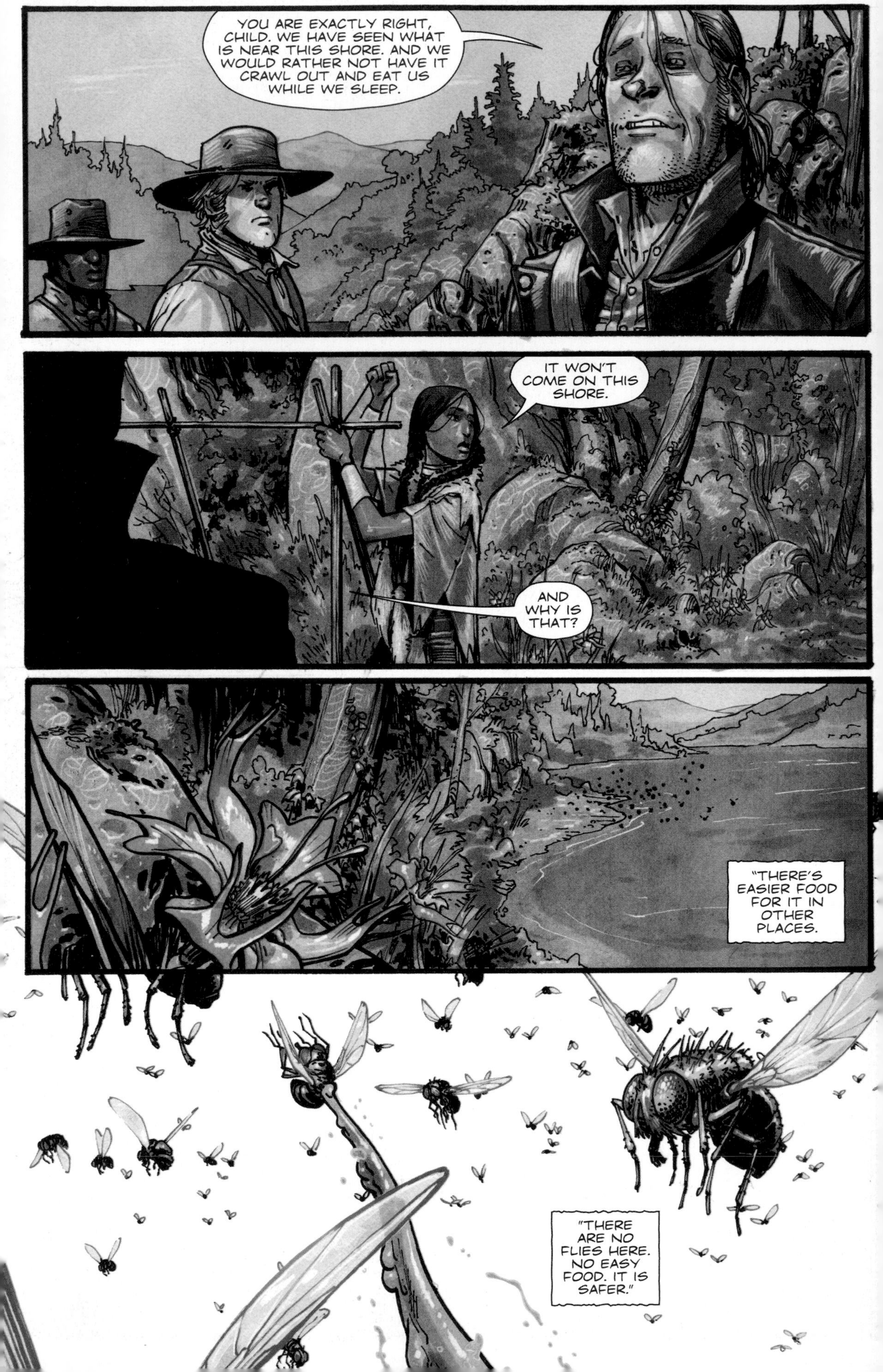
YOU ARE EXACTLY RIGHT, CHILD. WE HAVE SEEN WHAT IS NEAR THIS SHORE. AND WE WOULD RATHER NOT HAVE IT CRAWL OUT AND EAT US WHILE WE SLEEP.
IT WON'T COME ON THIS SHORE.
AND WHY IS THAT?
"THERE'S EASIER FOOD FOR IT IN OTHER PLACES.
"THERE ARE NO FLIES HERE. NO EASY FOOD. IT IS SAFER."

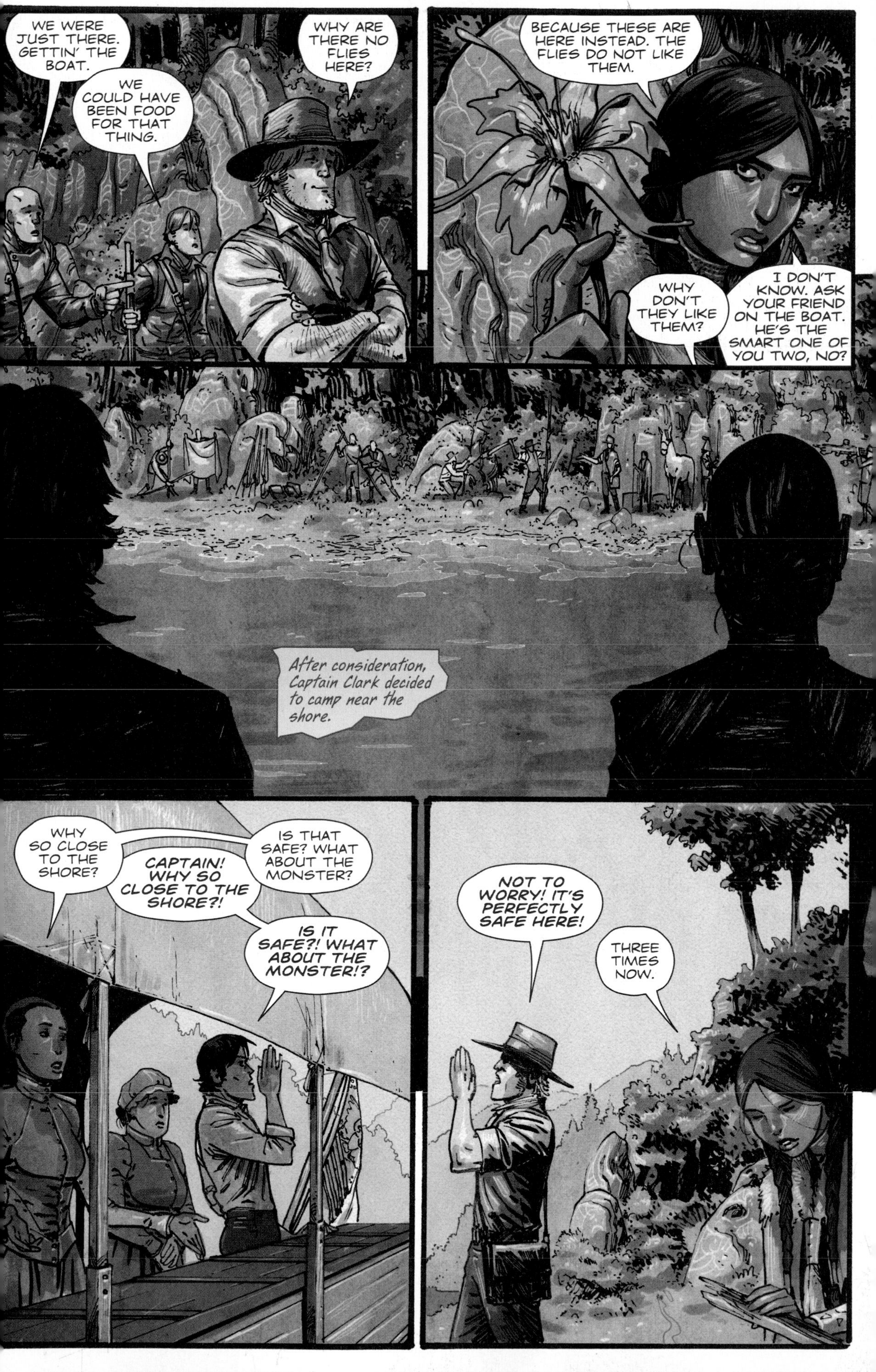
WE WERE JUST THERE. GETTIN' THE BOAT.
WE COULD HAVE BEEN FOOD FOR THAT THING.
WHY ARE THERE NO FLIES HERE?
BECAUSE THESE ARE HERE INSTEAD. THE FLIES DO NOT LIKE THEM.
WHY DON'T THEY LIKE THEM?
I DON'T KNOW. ASK YOUR FRIEND ON THE BOAT. HE'S THE SMART ONE OF YOU TWO, NO?
After consideration, Captain Clark decided to camp near the shore.
WHY SO CLOSE TO THE SHORE?
IS THAT SAFE? WHAT ABOUT THE MONSTER?
CAPTAIN! WHY SO CLOSE TO THE SHORE?!
IS IT SAFE?! WHAT ABOUT THE MONSTER!?
NOT TO WORRY! IT'S PERFECTLY SAFE HERE!
THREE TIMES NOW.

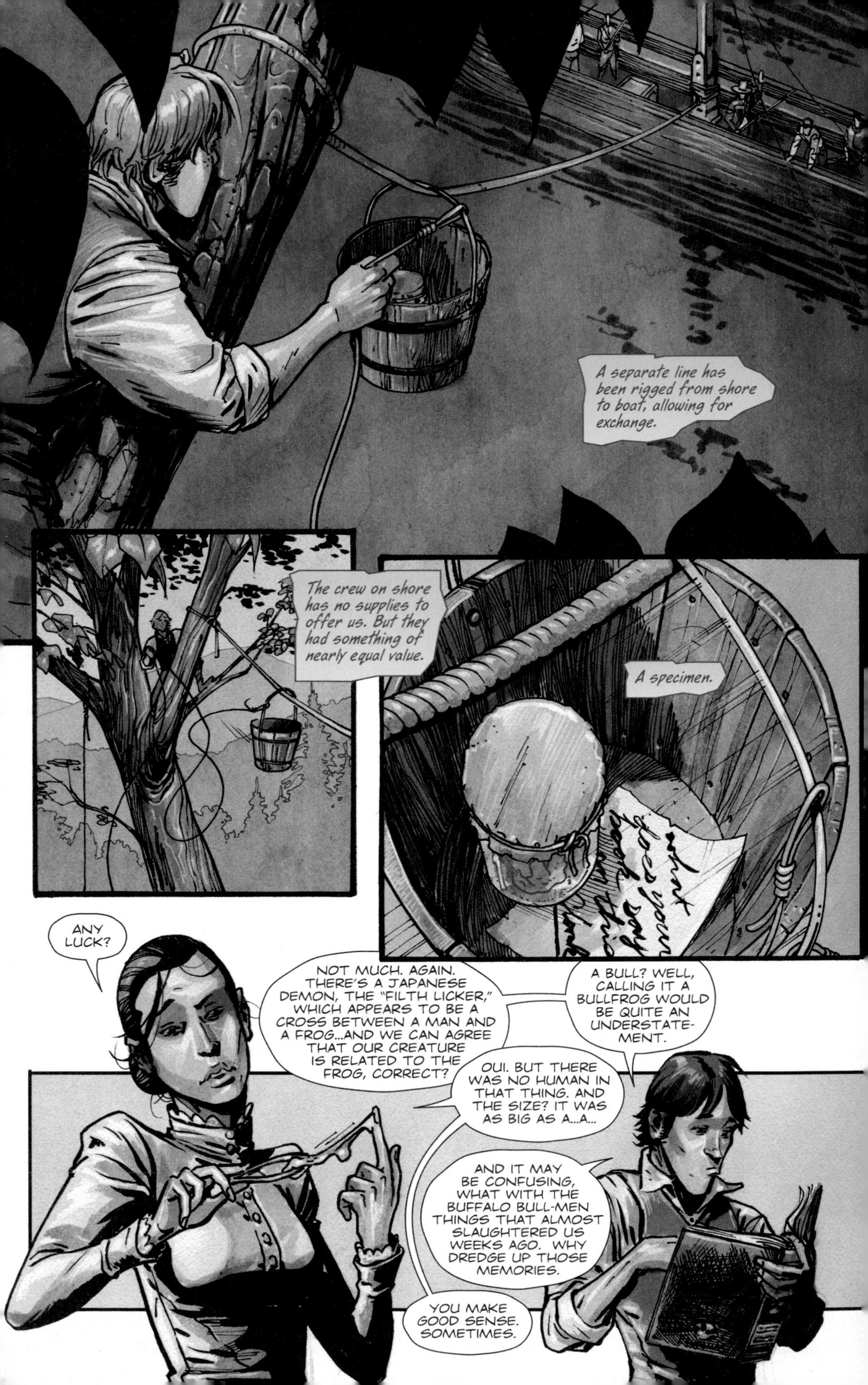
A separate line has been rigged from shore to boat, allowing for exchange.
The crew on shore has no supplies to offer us. But they had something of nearly equal value.
A specimen.
ANY LUCK?
NOT MUCH. AGAIN. THERE'S A JAPANESE DEMON, THE "FILTH LICKER," WHICH APPEARS TO BE A CROSS BETWEEN A MAN AND A FROG...AND WE CAN AGREE THAT OUR CREATURE IS RELATED TO THE FROG, CORRECT?
OUI. BUT THERE WAS NO HUMAN IN THAT THING. AND THE SIZE? IT WAS AS BIG AS A...A...
A BULL? WELL, CALLING IT A BULLFROG WOULD BE QUITE AN UNDERSTATEMENT.
AND IT MAY BE CONFUSING, WHAT WITH THE BUFFALO BULL-MEN THINGS THAT ALMOST SLAUGHTERED US WEEKS AGO. WHY DREDGE UP THOSE MEMORIES.
YOU MAKE GOOD SENSE. SOMETIMES.

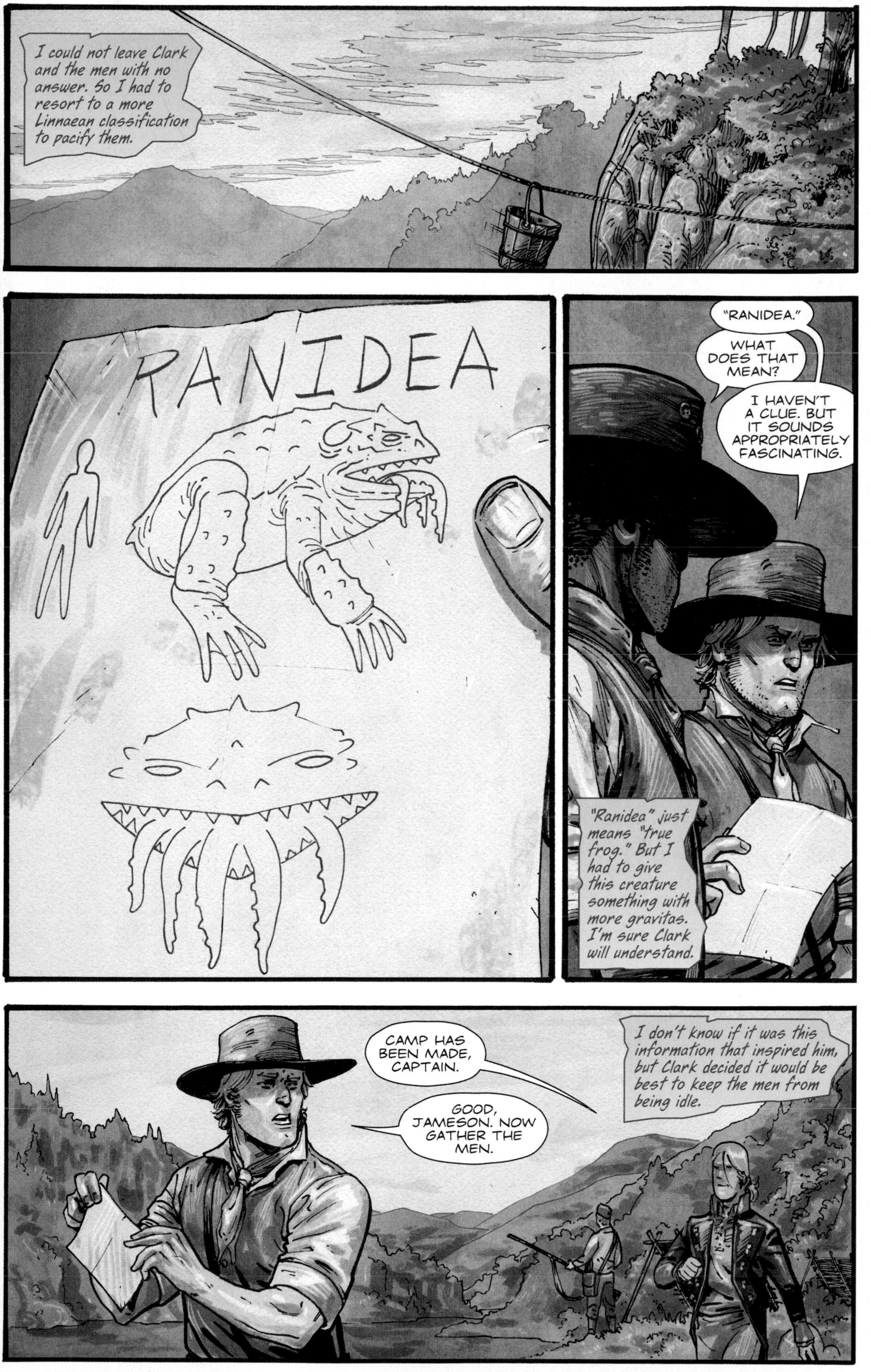
I could not leave Clark and the men with no answer. So I had to resort to a more Linnaean classification to pacify them.
RANIDEA
"RANIDEA."
WHAT DOES THAT MEAN?
I HAVEN'T A CLUE. BUT IT SOUNDS APPROPRIATELY FASCINATING.
"Ranidea" just means "true frog." But I had to give this creature something with more gravitas. I'm sure Clark will understand.
CAMP HAS BEEN MADE, CAPTAIN.
GOOD, JAMESON. NOW GATHER THE MEN.
I don't know if it was this information that inspired him, but Clark decided it would be best to keep the men from being idle.

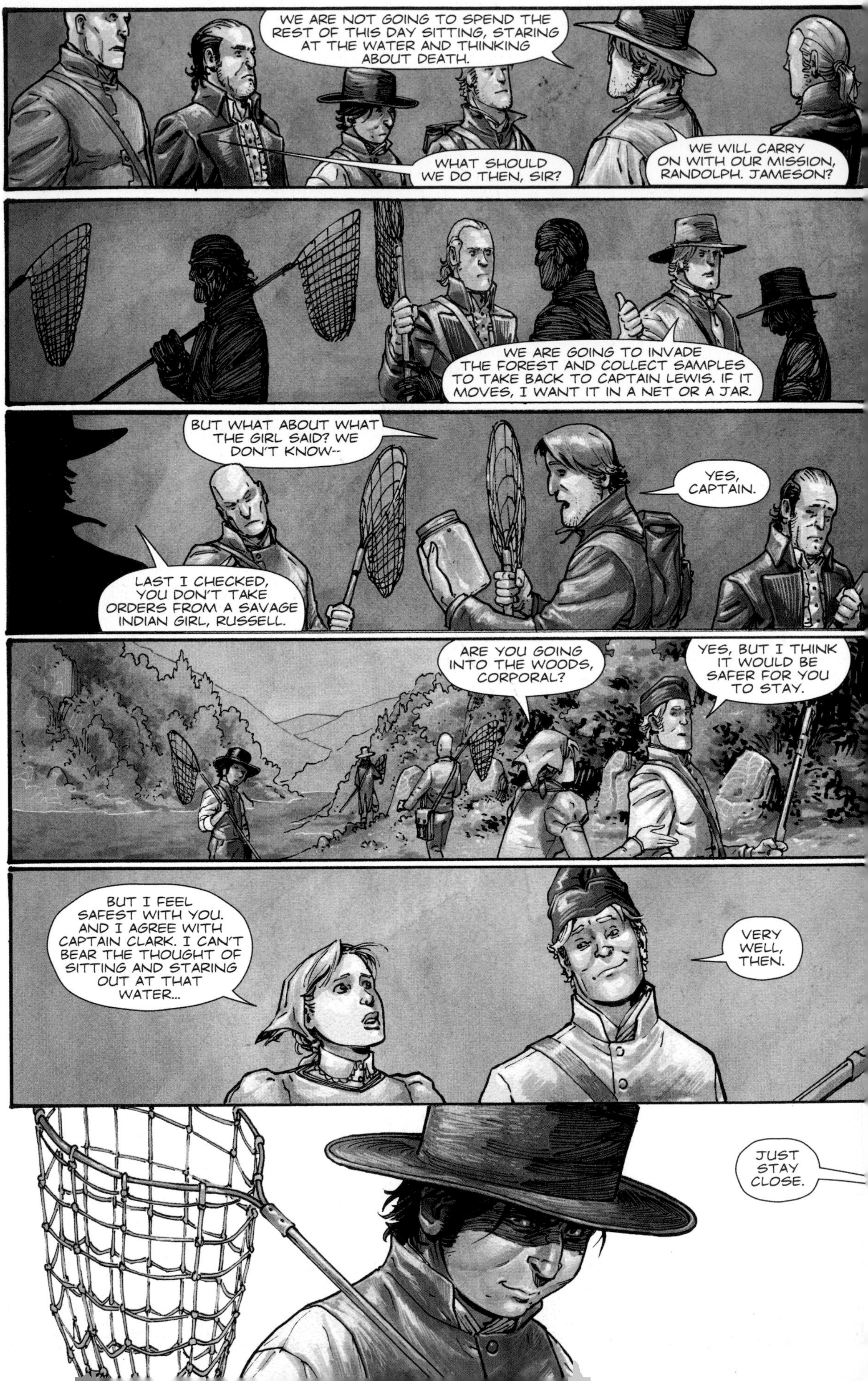
WE ARE NOT GOING TO SPEND THE REST OF THIS DAY SITTING, STARING AT THE WATER AND THINKING ABOUT DEATH.
WHAT SHOULD WE DO THEN, SIR?
WE WILL CARRY ON WITH OUR MISSION, RANDOLPH. JAMESON?
WE ARE GOING TO INVADE THE FOREST AND COLLECT SAMPLES TO TAKE BACK TO CAPTAIN LEWIS. IF IT MOVES, I WANT IT IN A NET OR A JAR.
BUT WHAT ABOUT WHAT THE GIRL SAID? WE DON'T KNOW--
LAST I CHECKED, YOU DON'T TAKE ORDERS FROM A SAVAGE INDIAN GIRL, RUSSELL.
YES, CAPTAIN.
ARE YOU GOING INTO THE WOODS, CORPORAL?
YES, BUT I THINK IT WOULD BE SAFER FOR YOU TO STAY.
BUT I FEEL SAFEST WITH YOU. AND I AGREE WITH CAPTAIN CLARK. I CAN'T BEAR THE THOUGHT OF SITTING AND STARING OUT AT THAT WATER...
VERY WELL, THEN.
JUST STAY CLOSE.

MY MEN DON'T NEED YOUR HELP.

I DON'T HUNT FOR YOU. I HUNT FOR ME. I AM HUNGRY AND I DON'T WANT TO EAT THE THINGS FROM YOUR BOAT.

I THOUGHT YOU SAID YOU DON'T KNOW WHAT'S IN THESE WOODS.

I WILL FIND OUT. AND THEN I WILL KILL AND EAT WHATEVER IT IS.

GIVE HER SOME SPACE, BUT KEEP AN EYE ON HER, YORK.

YES, MASTER CLARK.

CAPTAIN CLARK!

I HOPE YOU HAVE A GOOD REASON FOR MISSING ASSEMBLY, MISTER COLLINS.

IT'S SHAW, CAPTAIN...

"HE THINKS HE'S FOUND A WAY BACK TO THE KEELBOAT!"

WHAT IF THE LINE SNAPS, SHAW?

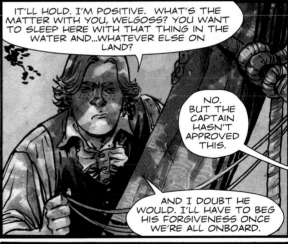

IT'LL HOLD. I'M POSITIVE. WHAT'S THE MATTER WITH YOU, WELGOSS? YOU WANT TO SLEEP HERE WITH THAT THING IN THE WATER AND...WHATEVER ELSE ON LAND?

NO. BUT THE CAPTAIN HASN'T APPROVED THIS.

AND I DOUBT HE WOULD. I'LL HAVE TO BEG HIS FORGIVENESS ONCE WE'RE ALL ONBOARD.

WHAT'S GOING ON OVER THERE, TUTTLE?

SHAW SAYS HE'S COMING ABOARD.

THAT FOOL.

SHAW! WHAT IN GOD'S NAME DO YOU THINK YOU'RE DOING!? COME DOWN THIS--

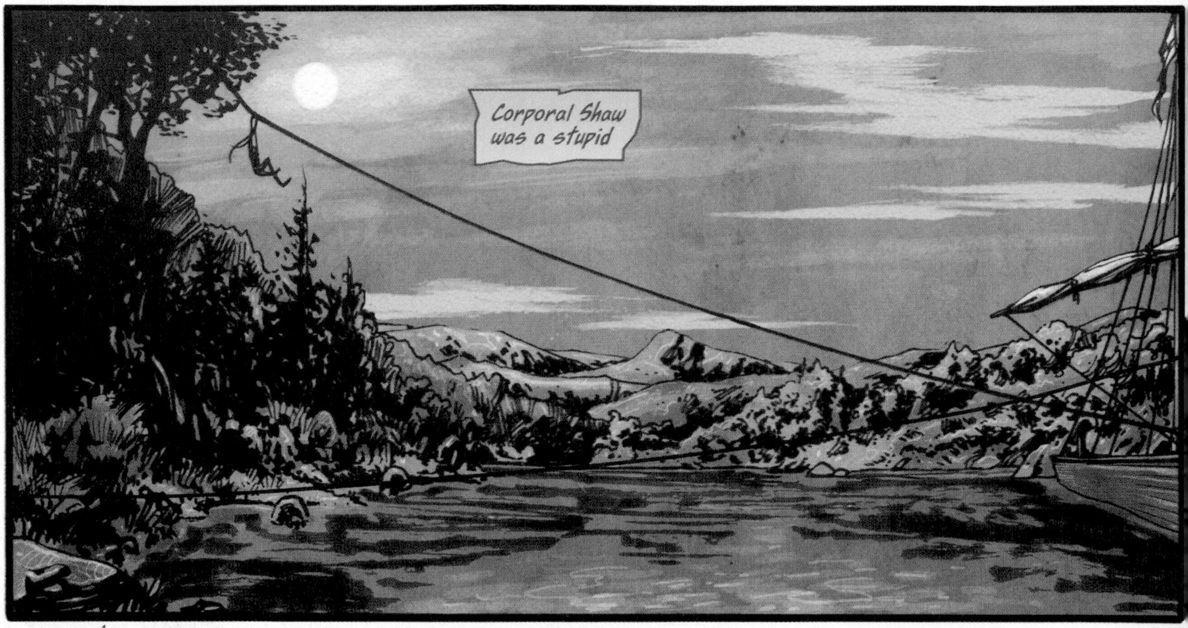
Corporal Shaw
was a stupid

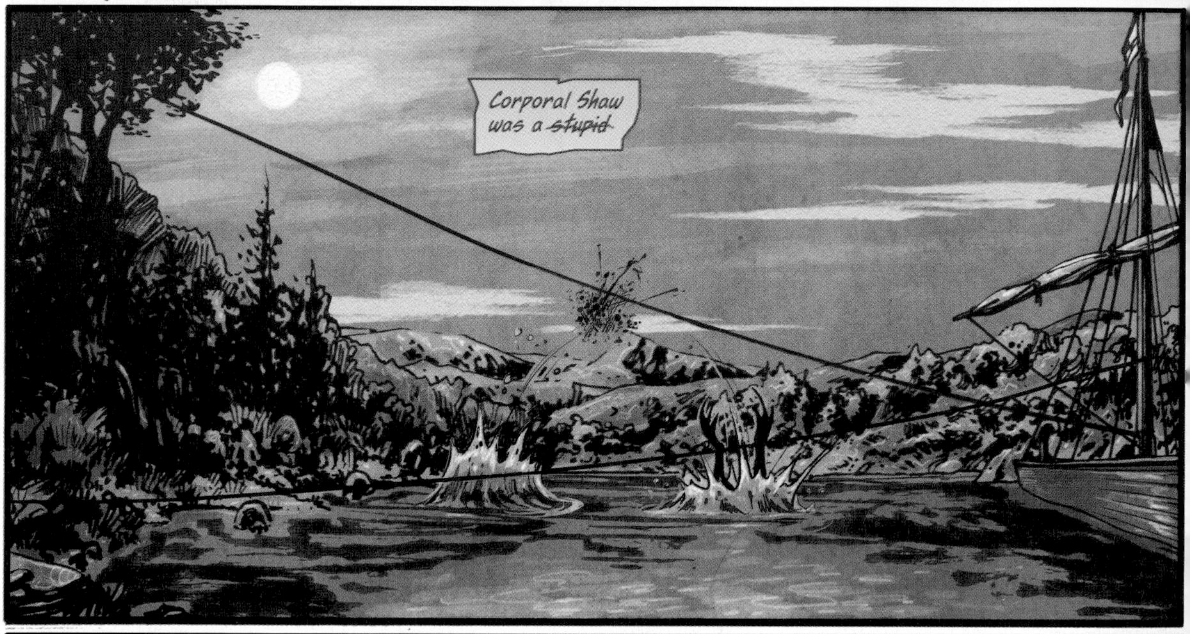
Corporal Shaw
was a ~~stupid~~

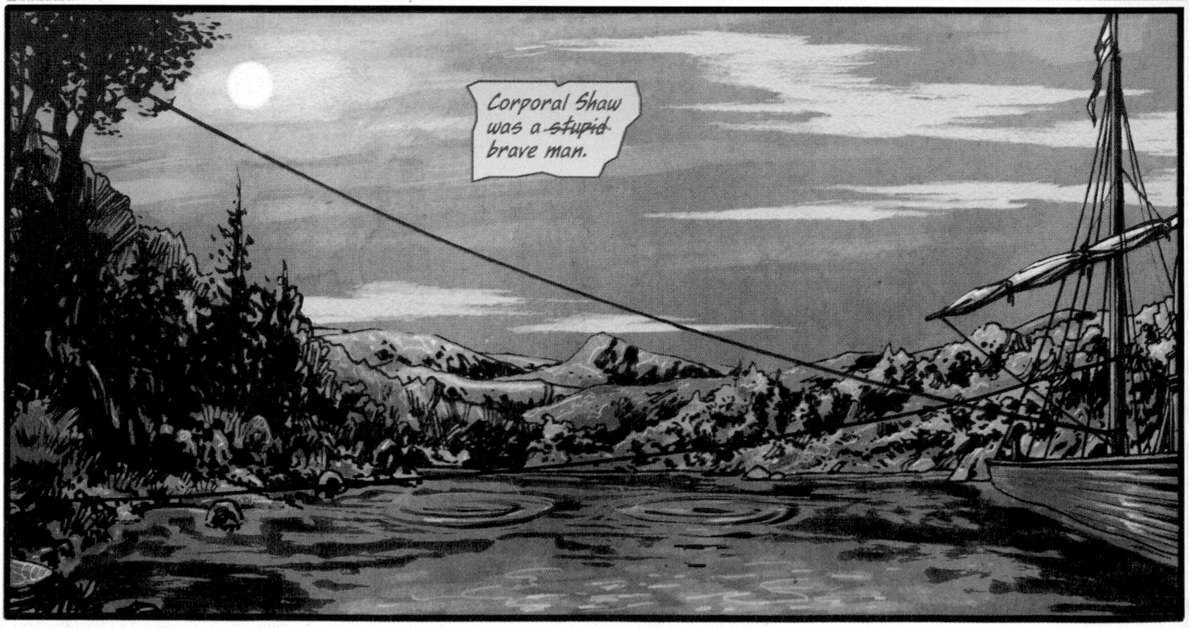
Corporal Shaw
was a ~~stupid~~
brave man.

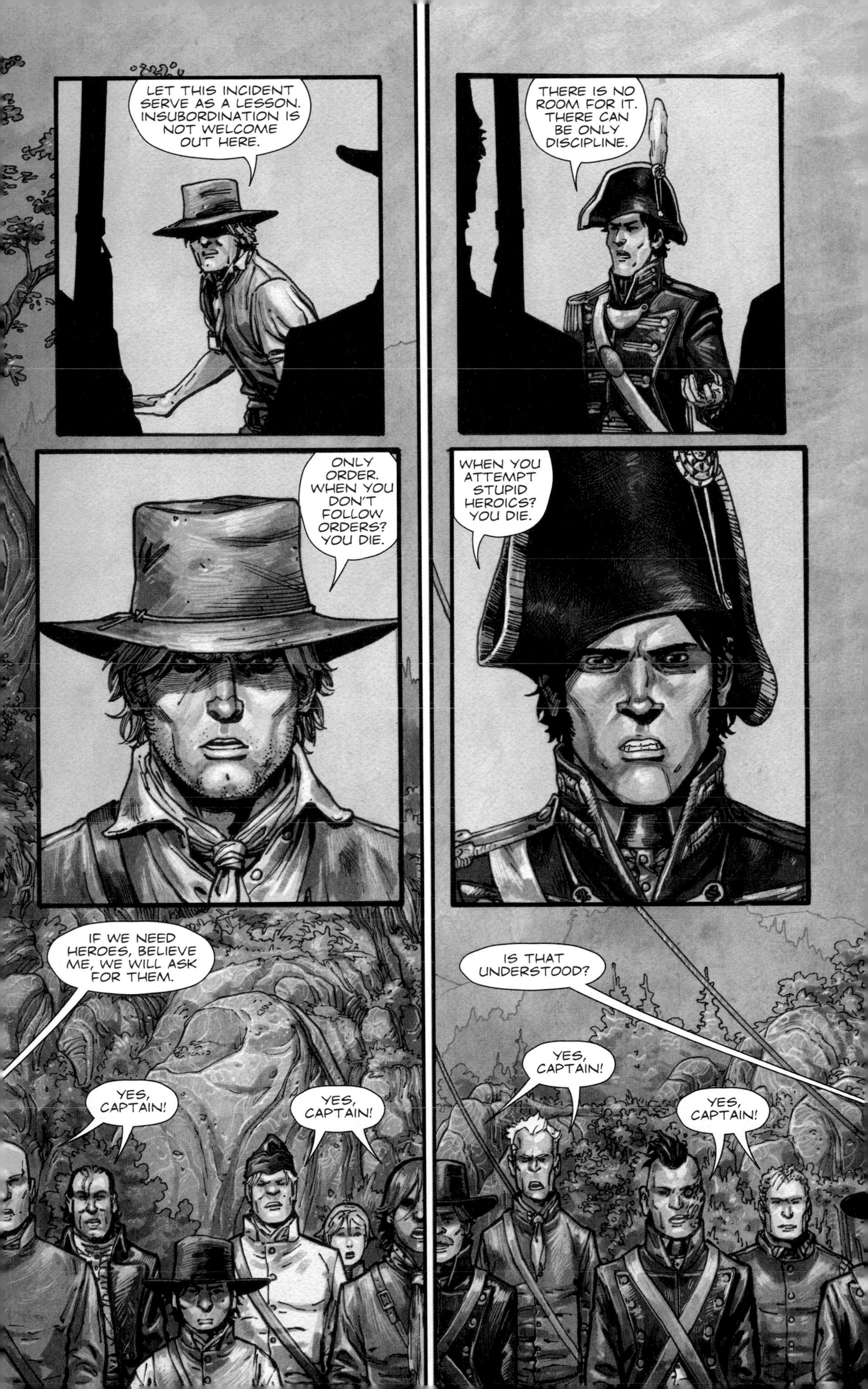
LET THIS INCIDENT SERVE AS A LESSON. INSUBORDINATION IS NOT WELCOME OUT HERE.
THERE IS NO ROOM FOR IT. THERE CAN BE ONLY DISCIPLINE.
ONLY ORDER. WHEN YOU DON'T FOLLOW ORDERS? YOU DIE.
WHEN YOU ATTEMPT STUPID HEROICS? YOU DIE.
IF WE NEED HEROES, BELIEVE ME, WE WILL ASK FOR THEM.
IS THAT UNDERSTOOD?
YES, CAPTAIN!
YES, CAPTAIN!
YES, CAPTAIN!
YES, CAPTAIN!

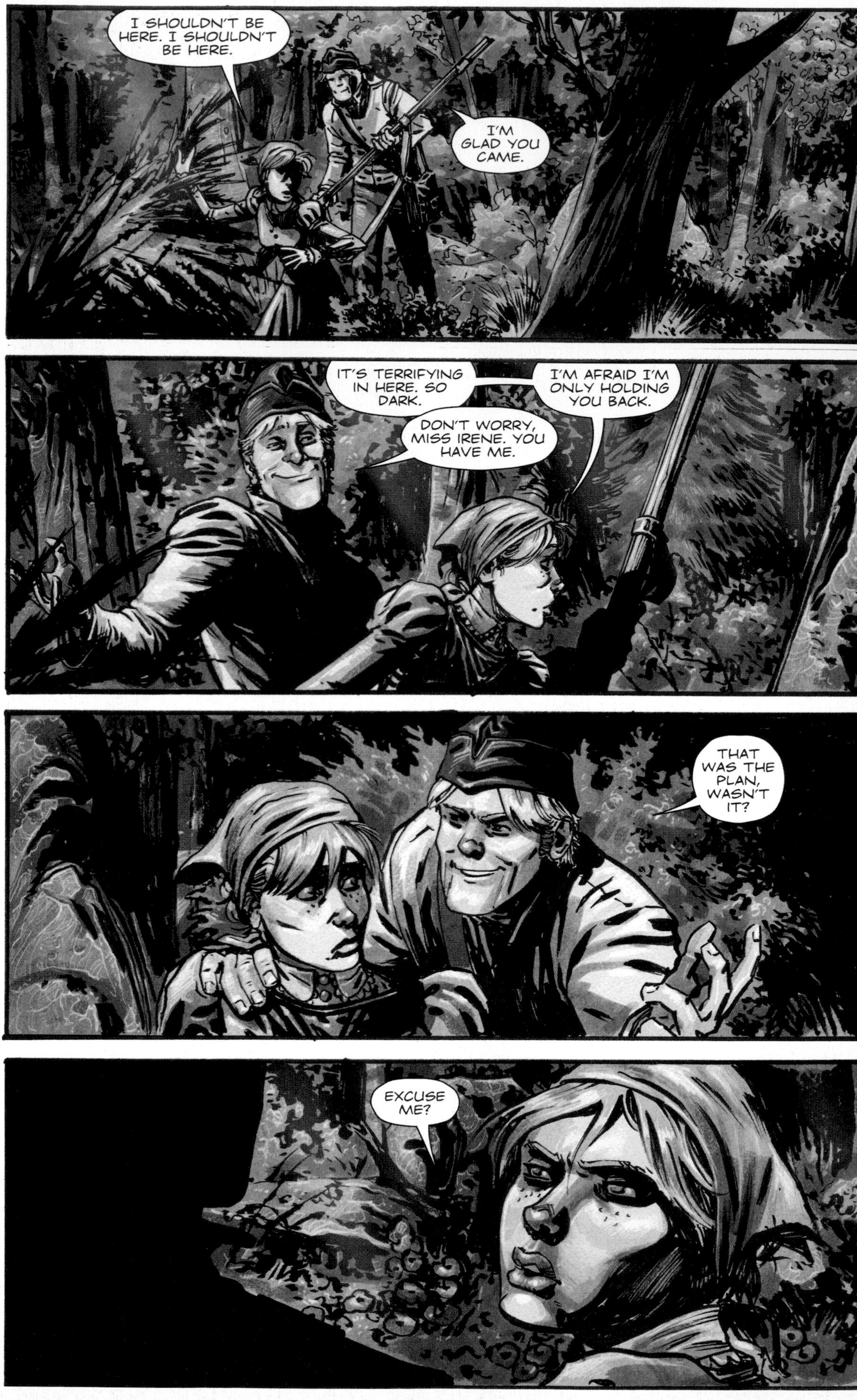
I SHOULDN'T BE HERE. I SHOULDN'T BE HERE.
I'M GLAD YOU CAME.
IT'S TERRIFYING IN HERE. SO DARK.
I'M AFRAID I'M ONLY HOLDING YOU BACK.
DON'T WORRY, MISS IRENE. YOU HAVE ME.
THAT WAS THE PLAN, WASN'T IT?
EXCUSE ME?

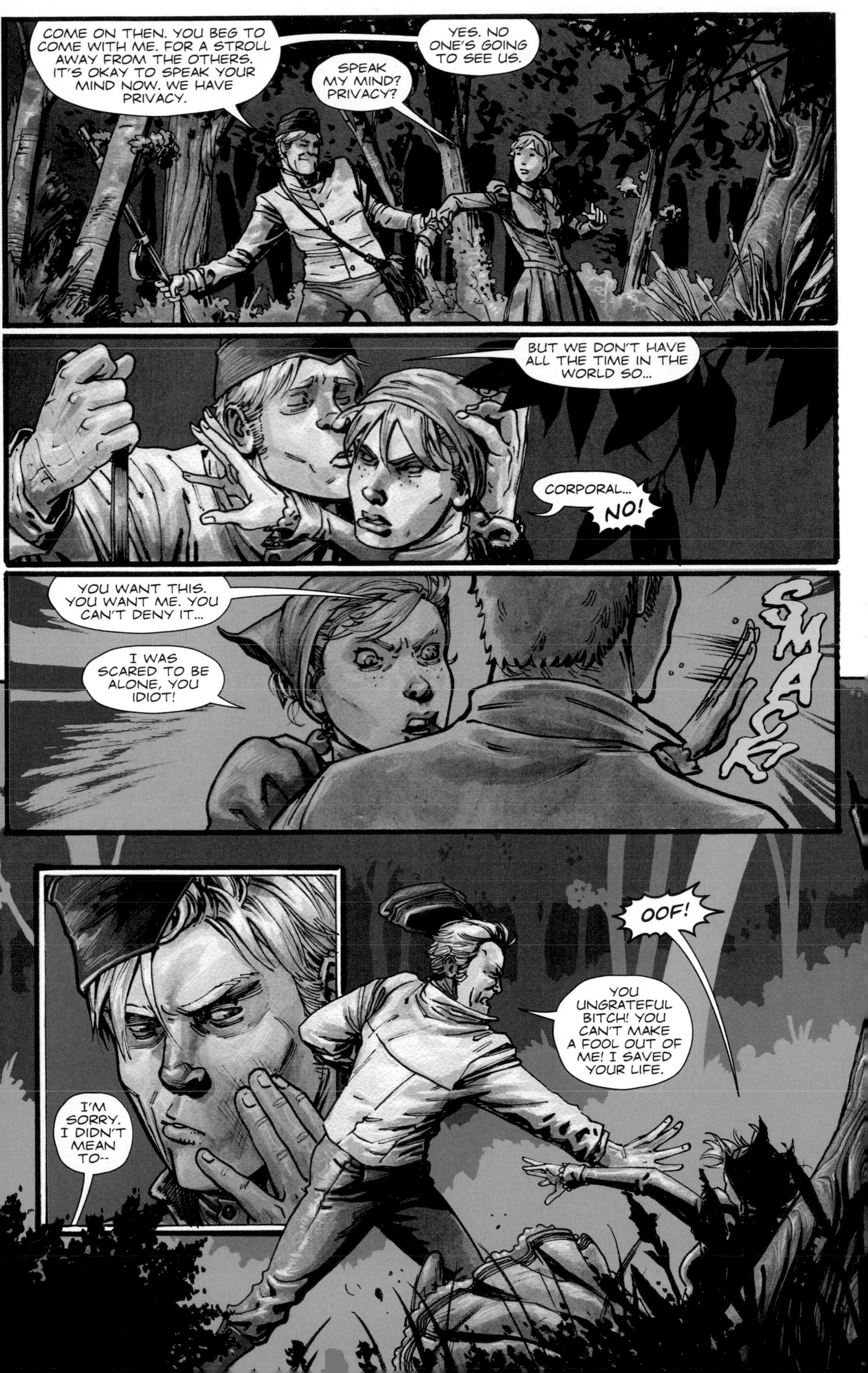
COME ON THEN. YOU BEG TO COME WITH ME. FOR A STROLL AWAY FROM THE OTHERS. IT'S OKAY TO SPEAK YOUR MIND NOW. WE HAVE PRIVACY.
SPEAK MY MIND? PRIVACY?
YES. NO ONE'S GOING TO SEE US.
BUT WE DON'T HAVE ALL THE TIME IN THE WORLD SO...
CORPORAL... NO!
YOU WANT THIS. YOU WANT ME. YOU CAN'T DENY IT...
I WAS SCARED TO BE ALONE, YOU IDIOT!
SMACK!
I'M SORRY. I DIDN'T MEAN TO--
YOU UNGRATEFUL BITCH! YOU CAN'T MAKE A FOOL OUT OF ME! I SAVED YOUR LIFE.
OOF!

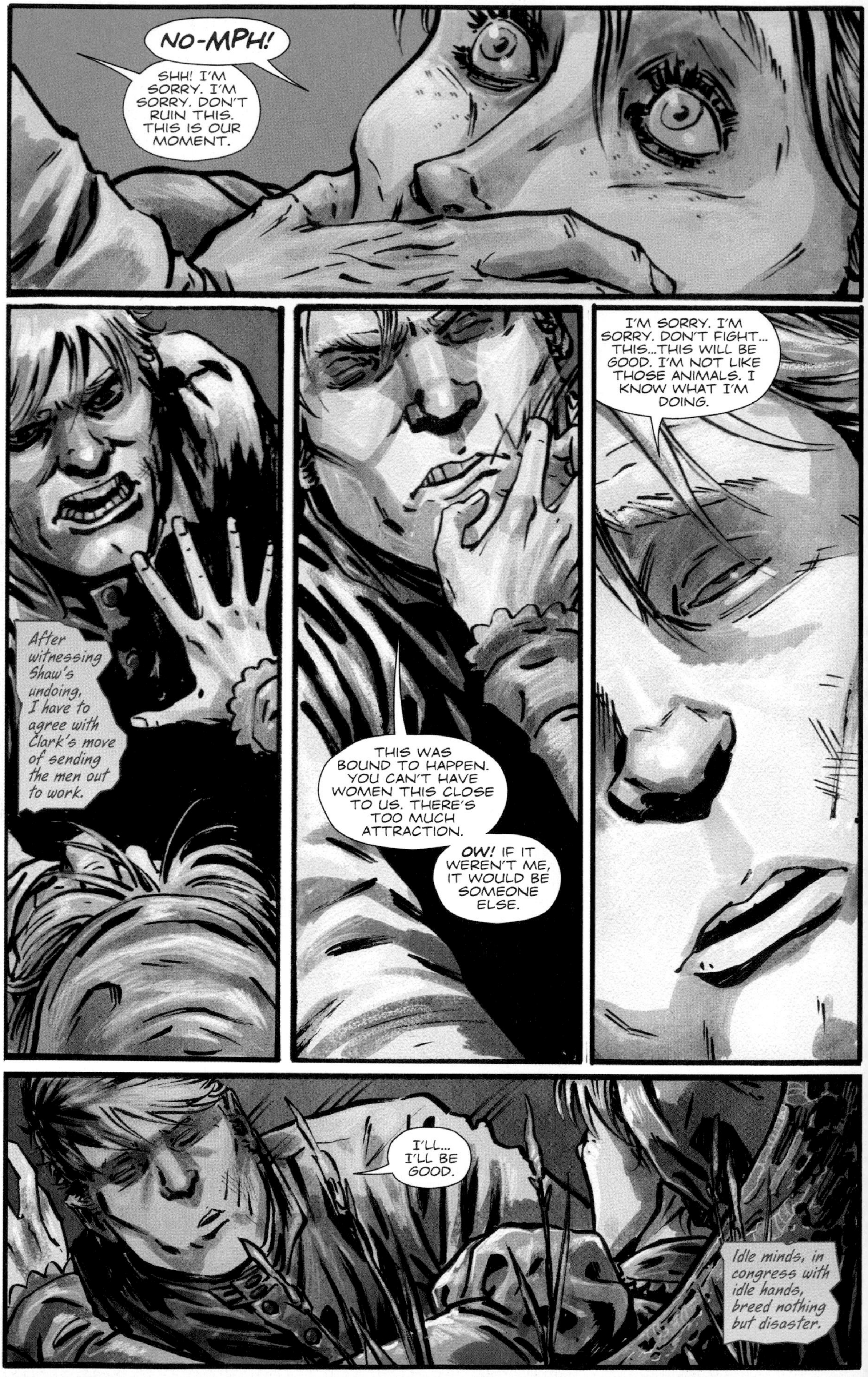
NO-MPH!
SHH! I'M SORRY. I'M SORRY. DON'T RUIN THIS. THIS IS OUR MOMENT.
After witnessing Shaw's undoing, I have to agree with Clark's move of sending the men out to work.
THIS WAS BOUND TO HAPPEN. YOU CAN'T HAVE WOMEN THIS CLOSE TO US. THERE'S TOO MUCH ATTRACTION.
OW! IF IT WEREN'T ME, IT WOULD BE SOMEONE ELSE.
I'M SORRY. I'M SORRY. DON'T FIGHT... THIS...THIS WILL BE GOOD. I'M NOT LIKE THOSE ANIMALS. I KNOW WHAT I'M DOING.
I'LL... I'LL BE GOOD.
Idle minds, in congress with idle hands, breed nothing but disaster.

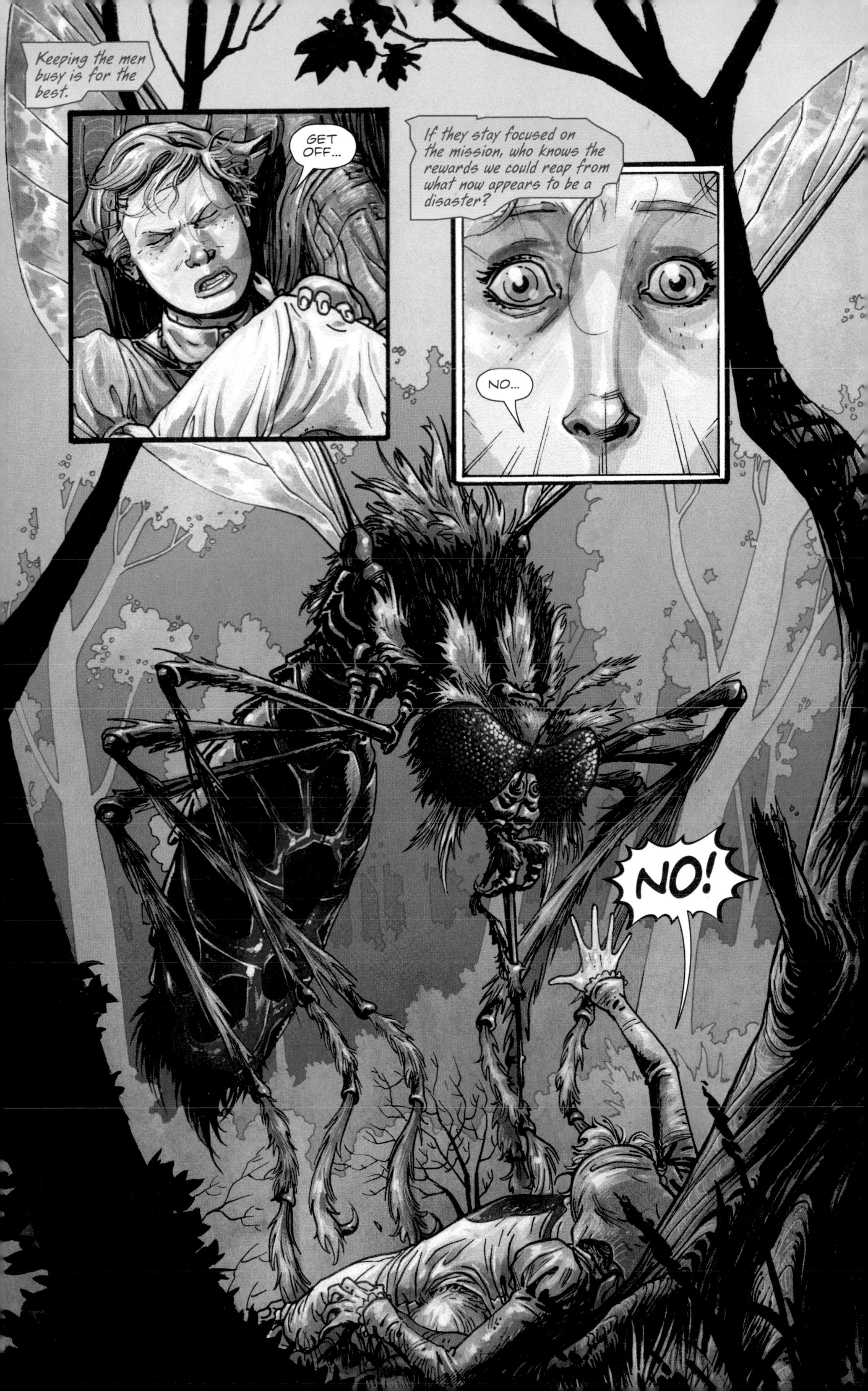
Keeping the men busy is for the best.
GET OFF...
If they stay focused on the mission, who knows the rewards we could reap from what now appears to be a disaster?
NO...
NO!

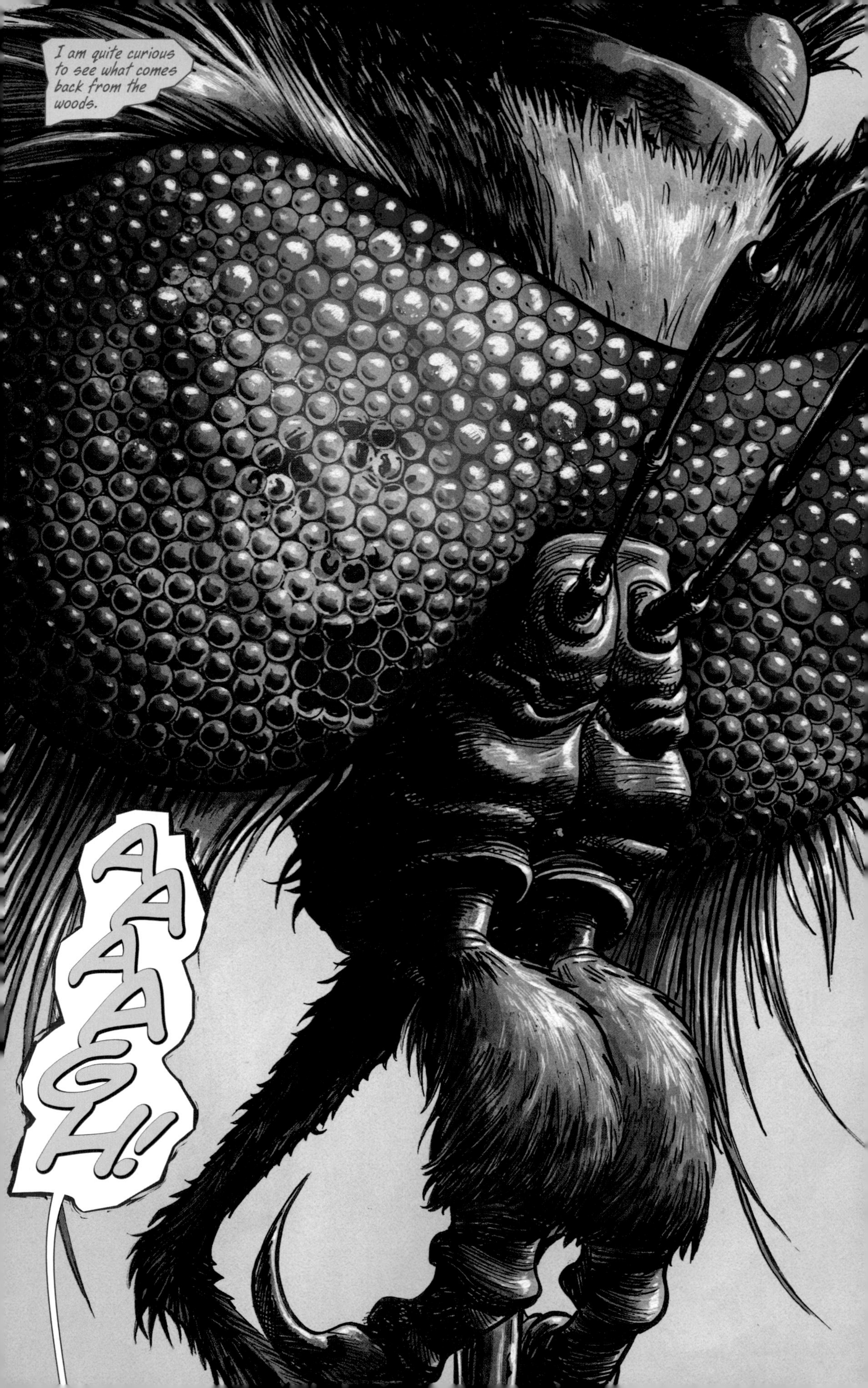
I am quite curious to see what comes back from the woods.
AAAAAGH!

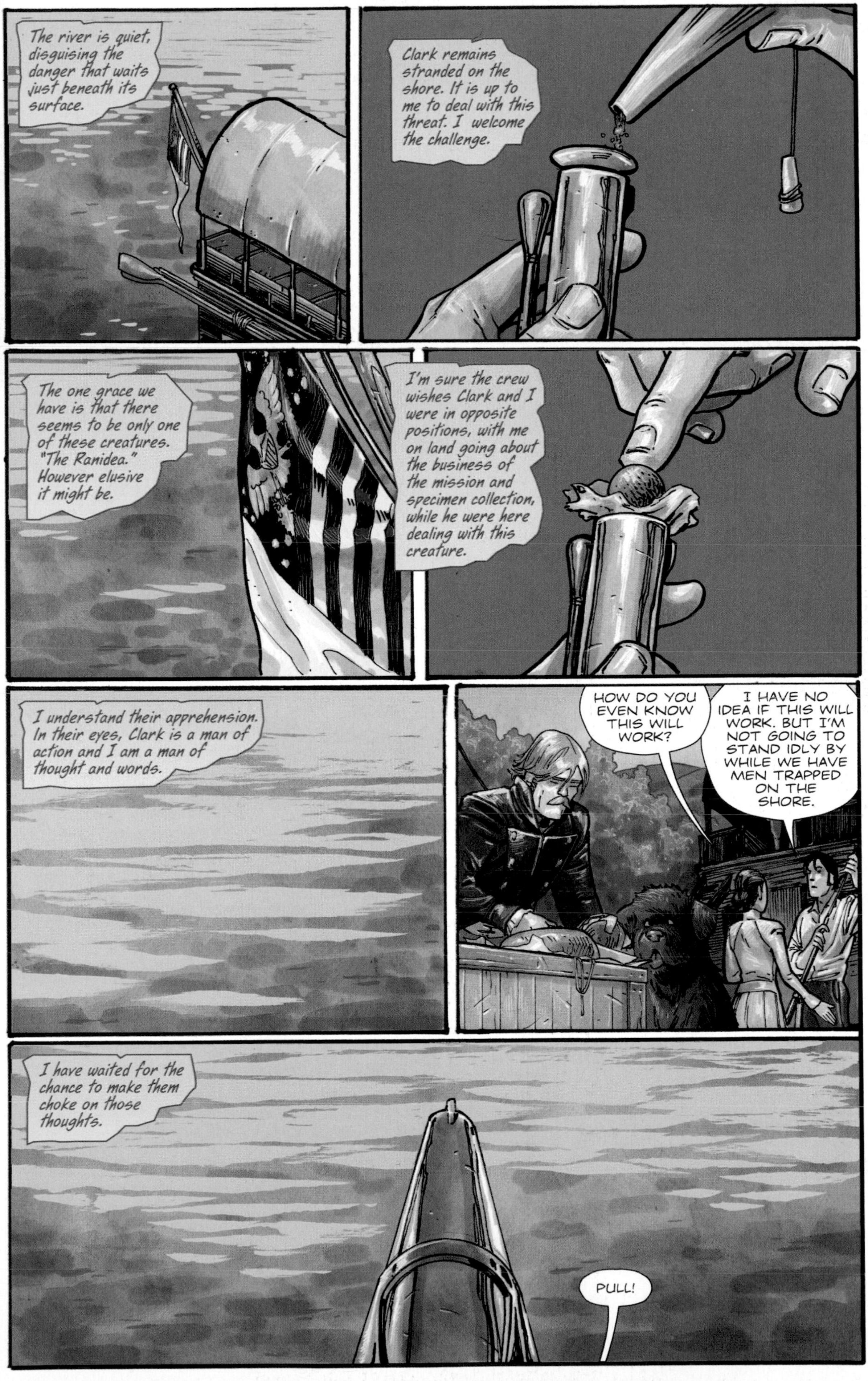
The river is quiet, disguising the danger that waits just beneath its surface.
Clark remains stranded on the shore. It is up to me to deal with this threat. I welcome the challenge.
The one grace we have is that there seems to be only one of these creatures. "The Ranidea." However elusive it might be.
I'm sure the crew wishes Clark and I were in opposite positions, with me on land going about the business of the mission and specimen collection, while he were here dealing with this creature.
I understand their apprehension. In their eyes, Clark is a man of action and I am a man of thought and words.
HOW DO YOU EVEN KNOW THIS WILL WORK?
I HAVE NO IDEA IF THIS WILL WORK. BUT I'M NOT GOING TO STAND IDLY BY WHILE WE HAVE MEN TRAPPED ON THE SHORE.
I have waited for the chance to make them choke on those thoughts.
PULL!

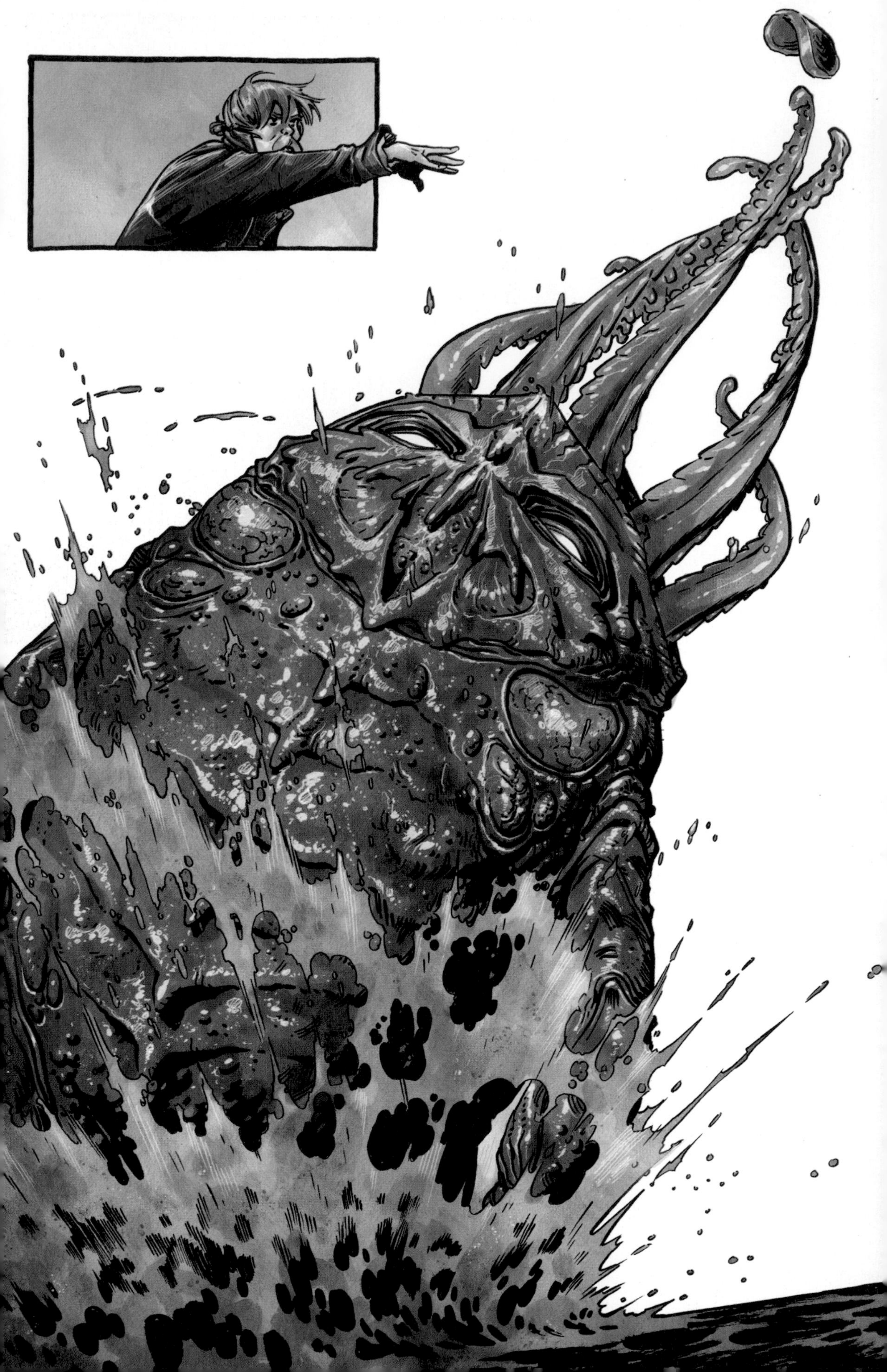

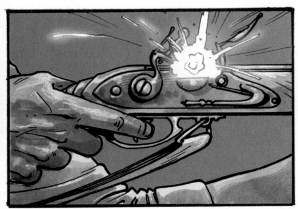

BOOM!

YOU MISSED.

YES. YES, I DID.

WHAT NOW?

I RELOAD AND TRY AGAIN.

WHY ONE RIFLE?

BECAUSE I DON'T WANT TO WASTE AMMUNITION. WE HAVE MUCH FARTHER TO GO ON THIS RIVER AND I AM POSITIVE THERE WILL BE PLENTY MORE CREATURES WE WILL HAVE TO SHOOT AT.

MAYBE YOU SHOULD AT LEAST LET SOMEONE ELSE TRY. SOMEONE WITH BETTER AIM.

I'LL HAVE YOU KNOW I HAPPEN TO BE AN EXCELLENT MARKSMAN. MY AIM IS IMPECCABLE!

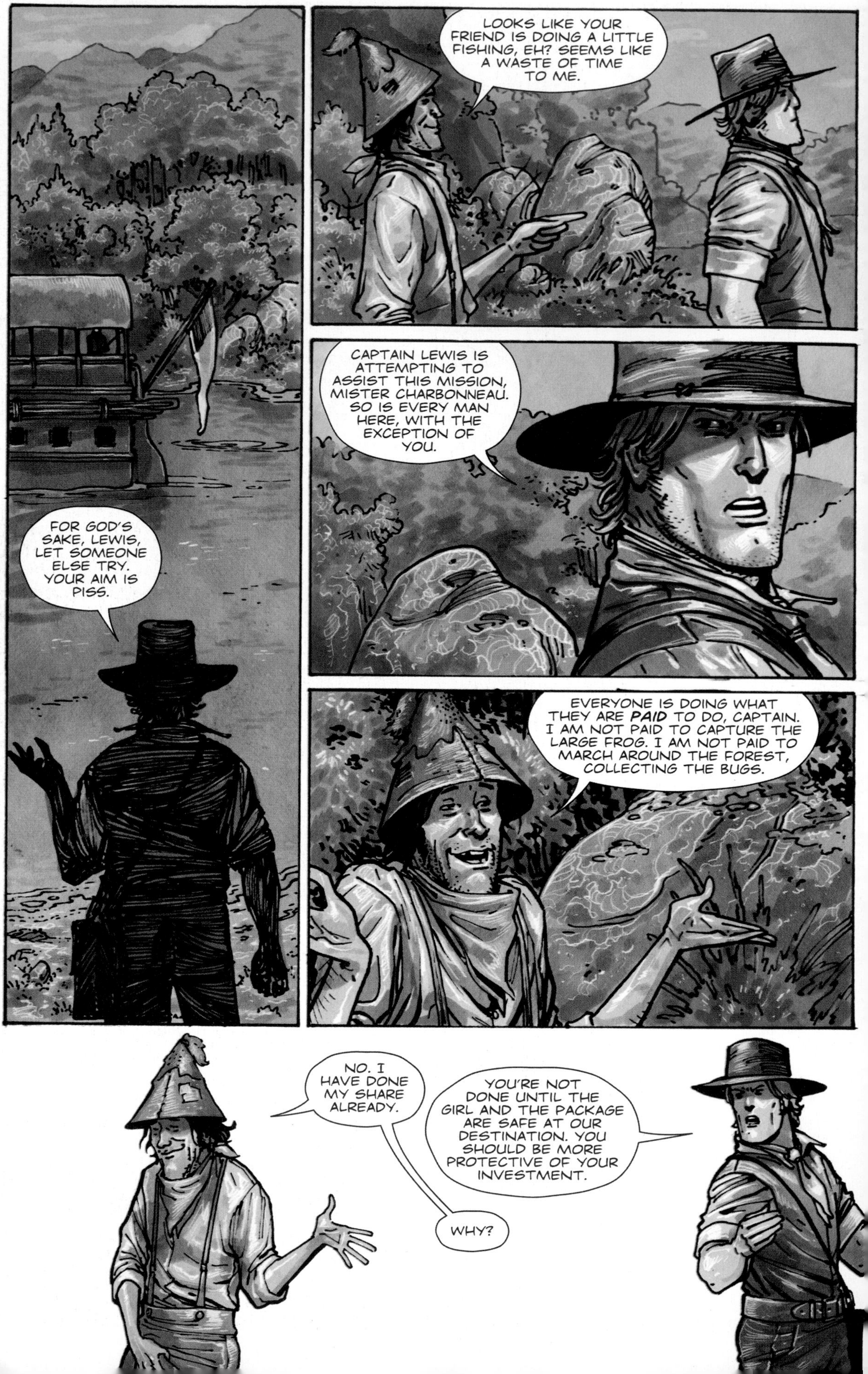
LOOKS LIKE YOUR FRIEND IS DOING A LITTLE FISHING, EH? SEEMS LIKE A WASTE OF TIME TO ME.
CAPTAIN LEWIS IS ATTEMPTING TO ASSIST THIS MISSION, MISTER CHARBONNEAU. SO IS EVERY MAN HERE, WITH THE EXCEPTION OF YOU.
FOR GOD'S SAKE, LEWIS, LET SOMEONE ELSE TRY. YOUR AIM IS PISS.
EVERYONE IS DOING WHAT THEY ARE *PAID* TO DO, CAPTAIN. I AM NOT PAID TO CAPTURE THE LARGE FROG. I AM NOT PAID TO MARCH AROUND THE FOREST, COLLECTING THE BUGS.
YOU'RE NOT DONE UNTIL THE GIRL AND THE PACKAGE ARE SAFE AT OUR DESTINATION. YOU SHOULD BE MORE PROTECTIVE OF YOUR INVESTMENT.
NO. I HAVE DONE MY SHARE ALREADY.
WHY?

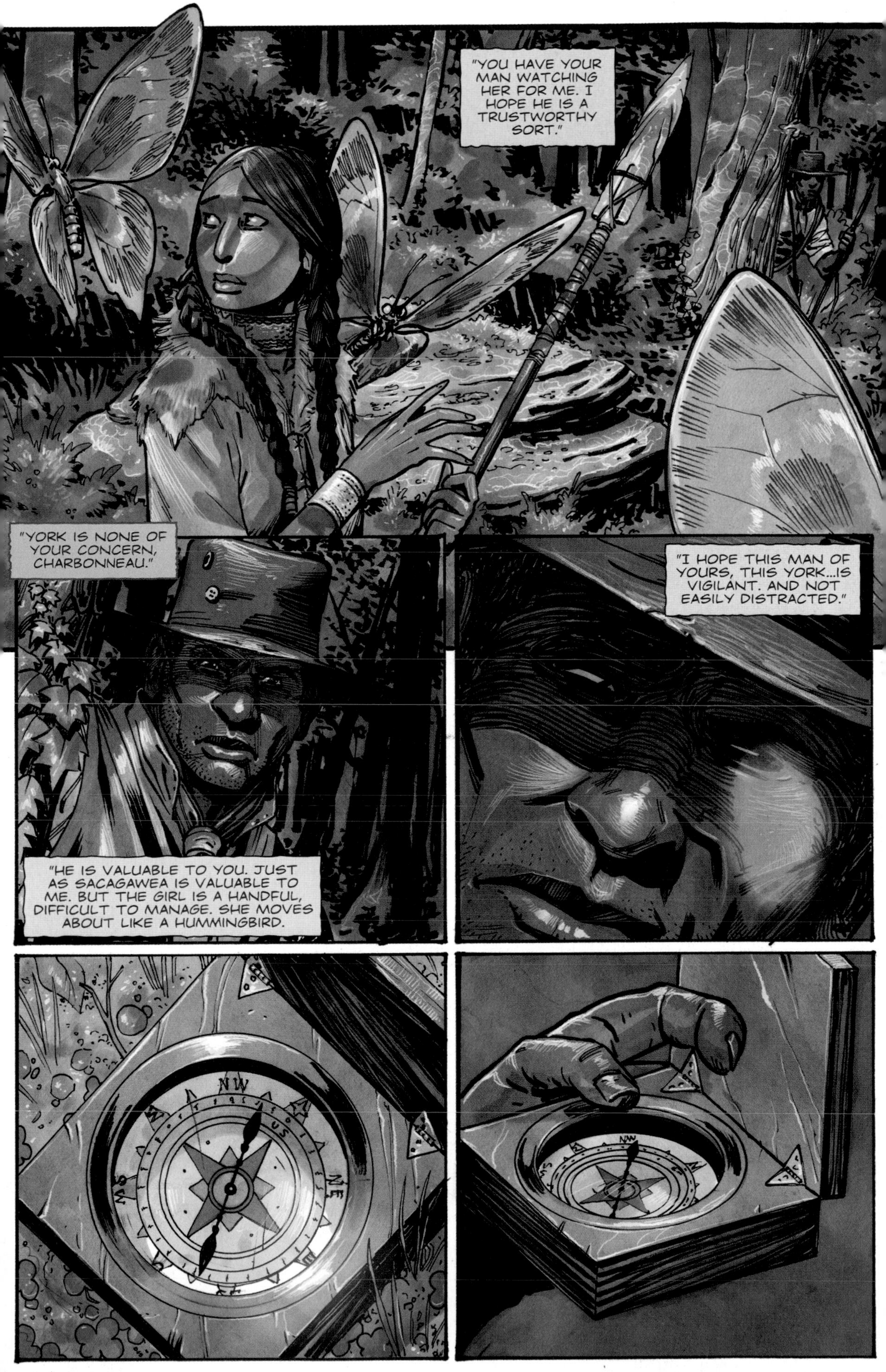
"YOU HAVE YOUR MAN WATCHING HER FOR ME. I HOPE HE IS A TRUSTWORTHY SORT."
"YORK IS NONE OF YOUR CONCERN, CHARBONNEAU."
"HE IS VALUABLE TO YOU. JUST AS SACAGAWEA IS VALUABLE TO ME. BUT THE GIRL IS A HANDFUL, DIFFICULT TO MANAGE. SHE MOVES ABOUT LIKE A HUMMINGBIRD.
"I HOPE THIS MAN OF YOURS, THIS YORK...IS VIGILANT. AND NOT EASILY DISTRACTED."

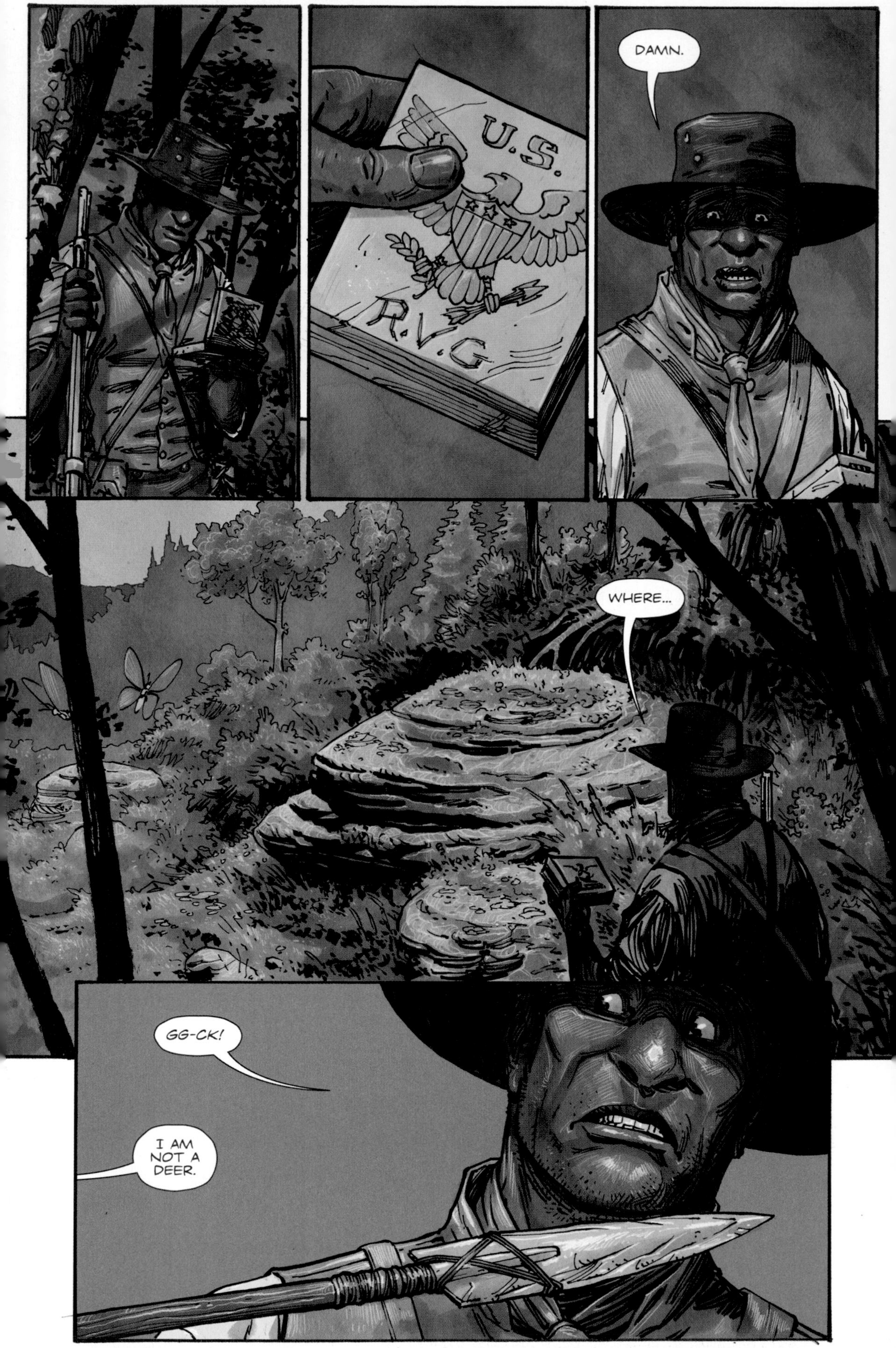
U.S.
R.V.G
DAMN.
WHERE...
GG-CK!
I AM NOT A DEER.

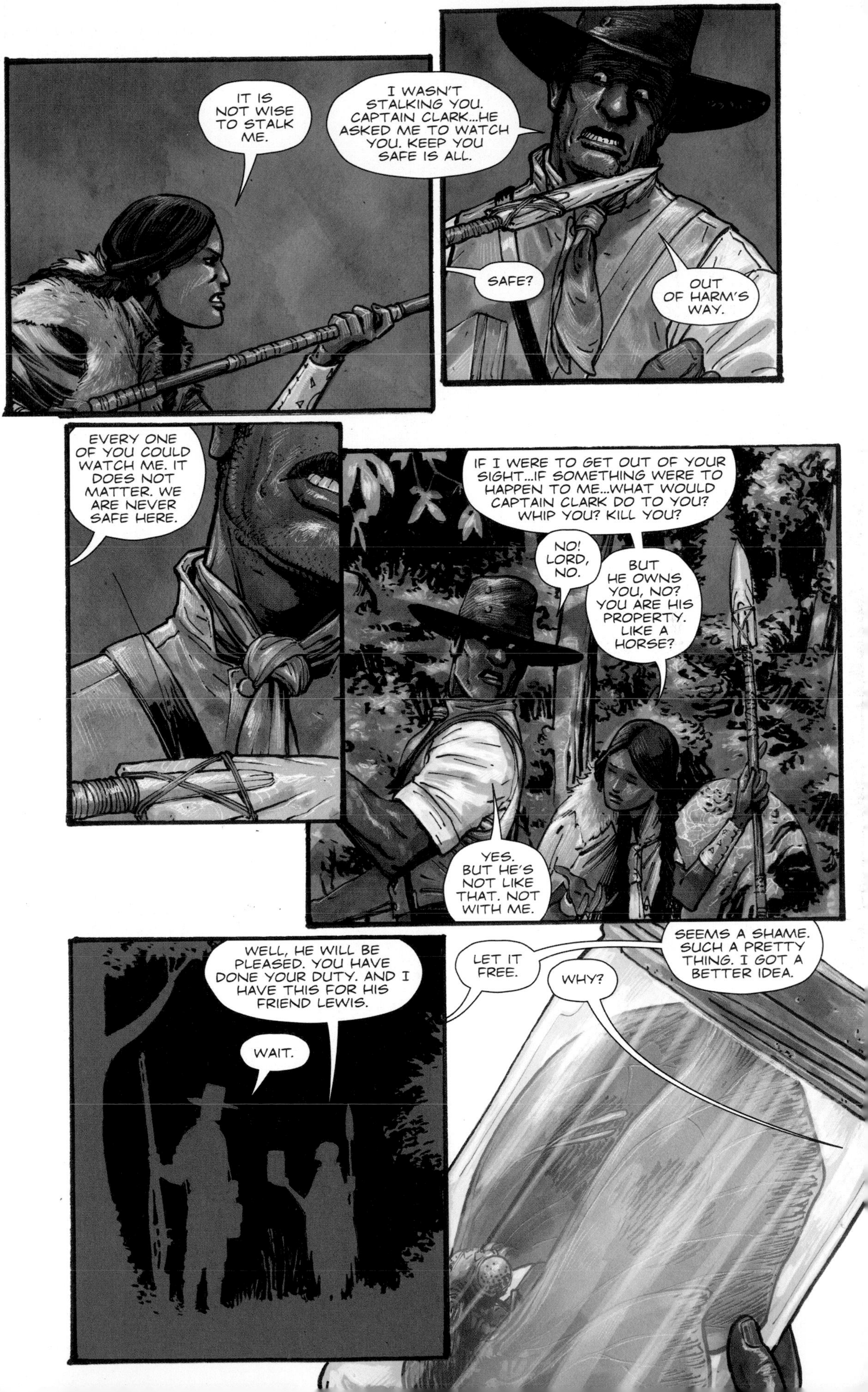
IT IS NOT WISE TO STALK ME.
I WASN'T STALKING YOU. CAPTAIN CLARK...HE ASKED ME TO WATCH YOU. KEEP YOU SAFE IS ALL.
SAFE?
OUT OF HARM'S WAY.
EVERY ONE OF YOU COULD WATCH ME. IT DOES NOT MATTER. WE ARE NEVER SAFE HERE.
IF I WERE TO GET OUT OF YOUR SIGHT...IF SOMETHING WERE TO HAPPEN TO ME...WHAT WOULD CAPTAIN CLARK DO TO YOU? WHIP YOU? KILL YOU?
NO! LORD, NO.
BUT HE OWNS YOU, NO? YOU ARE HIS PROPERTY. LIKE A HORSE?
YES. BUT HE'S NOT LIKE THAT. NOT WITH ME.
WELL, HE WILL BE PLEASED. YOU HAVE DONE YOUR DUTY. AND I HAVE THIS FOR HIS FRIEND LEWIS.
WAIT.
LET IT FREE.
WHY?
SEEMS A SHAME. SUCH A PRETTY THING. I GOT A BETTER IDEA.

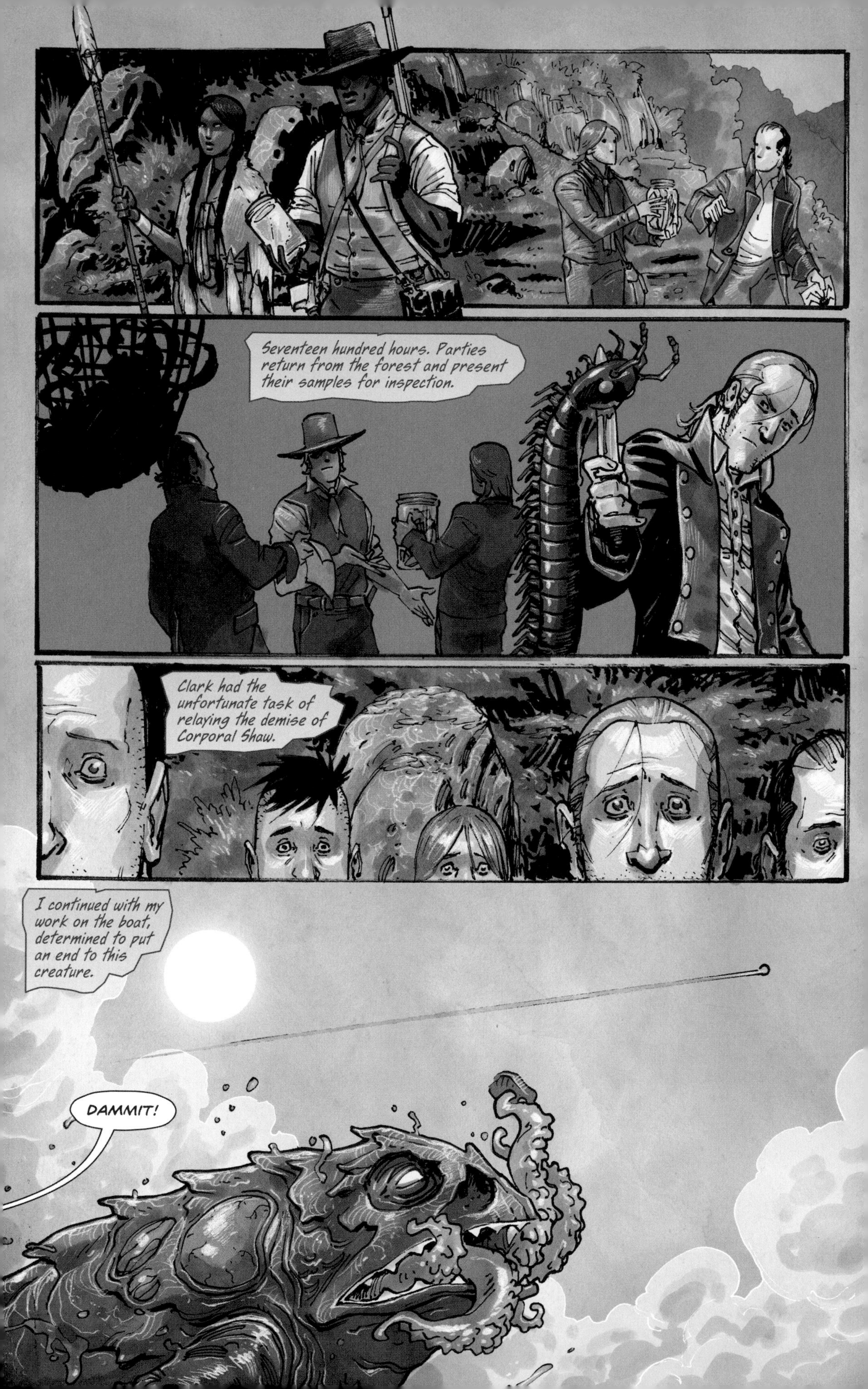
Seventeen hundred hours. Parties return from the forest and present their samples for inspection.
Clark had the unfortunate task of relaying the demise of Corporal Shaw.
I continued with my work on the boat, determined to put an end to this creature.
DAMMIT!

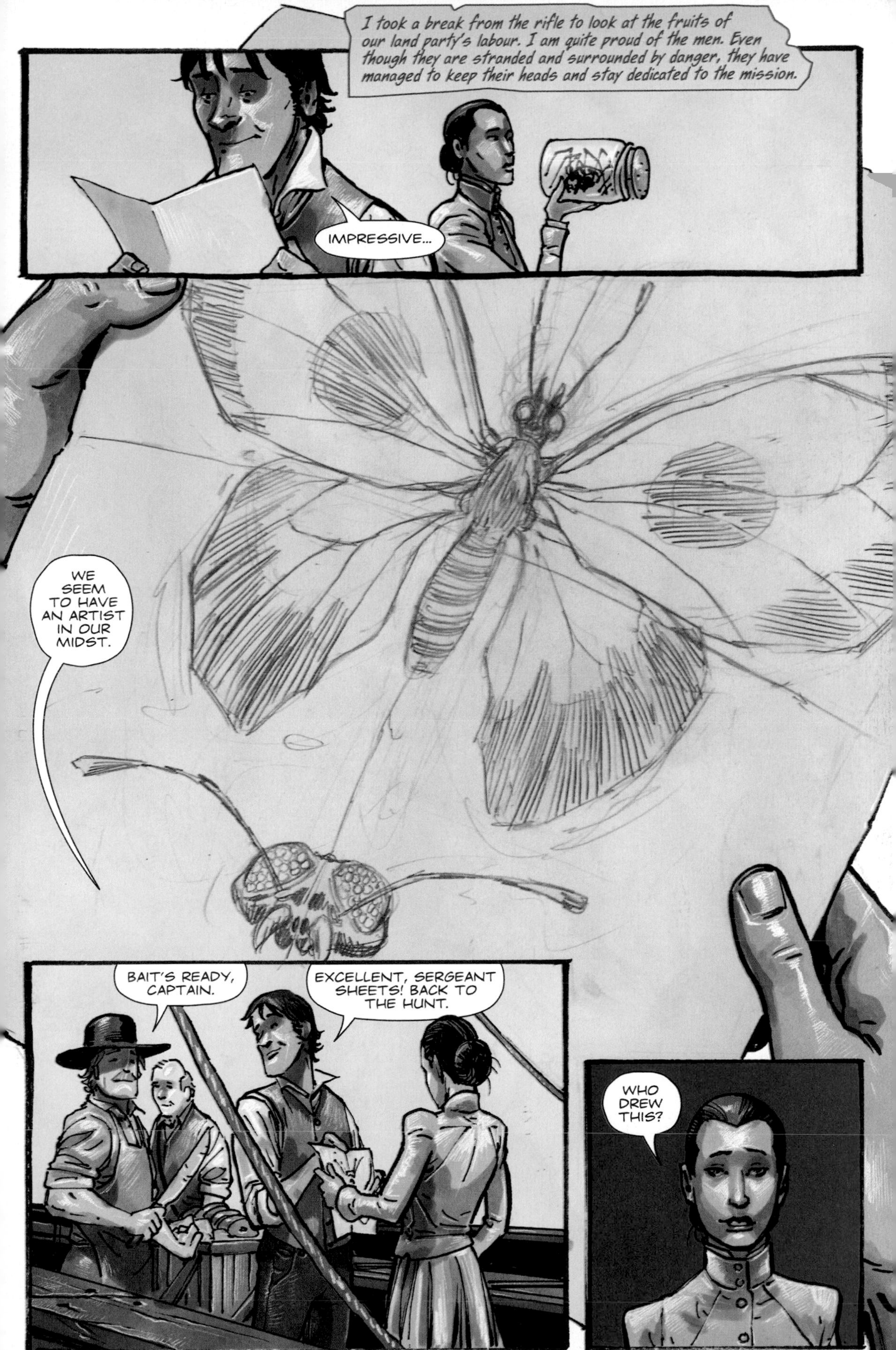
I took a break from the rifle to look at the fruits of our land party's labour. I am quite proud of the men. Even though they are stranded and surrounded by danger, they have managed to keep their heads and stay dedicated to the mission.
IMPRESSIVE...
WE SEEM TO HAVE AN ARTIST IN OUR MIDST.
BAIT'S READY, CAPTAIN.
EXCELLENT, SERGEANT SHEETS! BACK TO THE HUNT.
WHO DREW THIS?

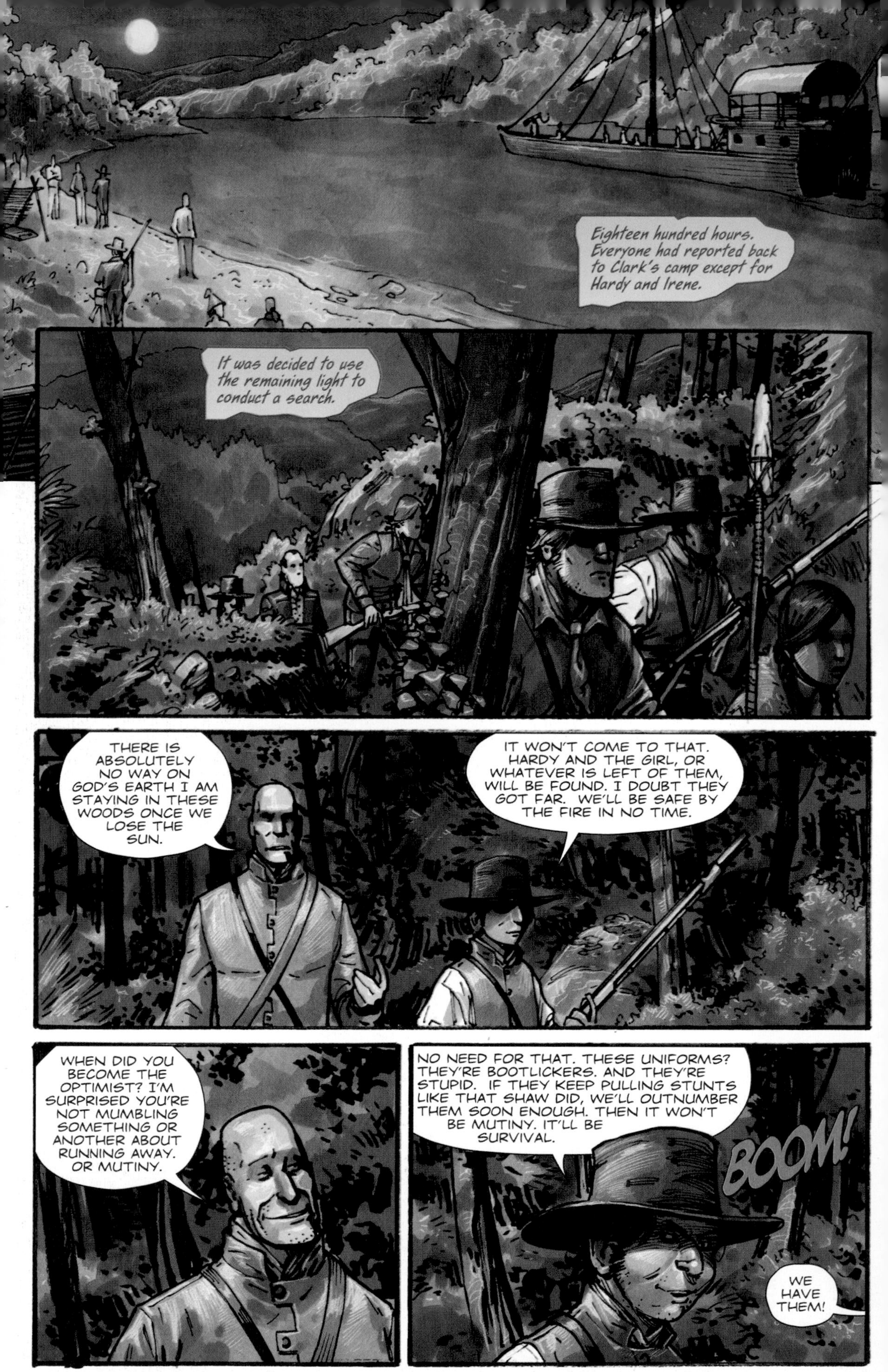
Eighteen hundred hours. Everyone had reported back to Clark's camp except for Hardy and Irene.
It was decided to use the remaining light to conduct a search.
THERE IS ABSOLUTELY NO WAY ON GOD'S EARTH I AM STAYING IN THESE WOODS ONCE WE LOSE THE SUN.
IT WON'T COME TO THAT. HARDY AND THE GIRL, OR WHATEVER IS LEFT OF THEM, WILL BE FOUND. I DOUBT THEY GOT FAR. WE'LL BE SAFE BY THE FIRE IN NO TIME.
WHEN DID YOU BECOME THE OPTIMIST? I'M SURPRISED YOU'RE NOT MUMBLING SOMETHING OR ANOTHER ABOUT RUNNING AWAY. OR MUTINY.
NO NEED FOR THAT. THESE UNIFORMS? THEY'RE BOOTLICKERS. AND THEY'RE STUPID. IF THEY KEEP PULLING STUNTS LIKE THAT SHAW DID, WE'LL OUTNUMBER THEM SOON ENOUGH. THEN IT WON'T BE MUTINY. IT'LL BE SURVIVAL.
BOOM!
WE HAVE THEM!

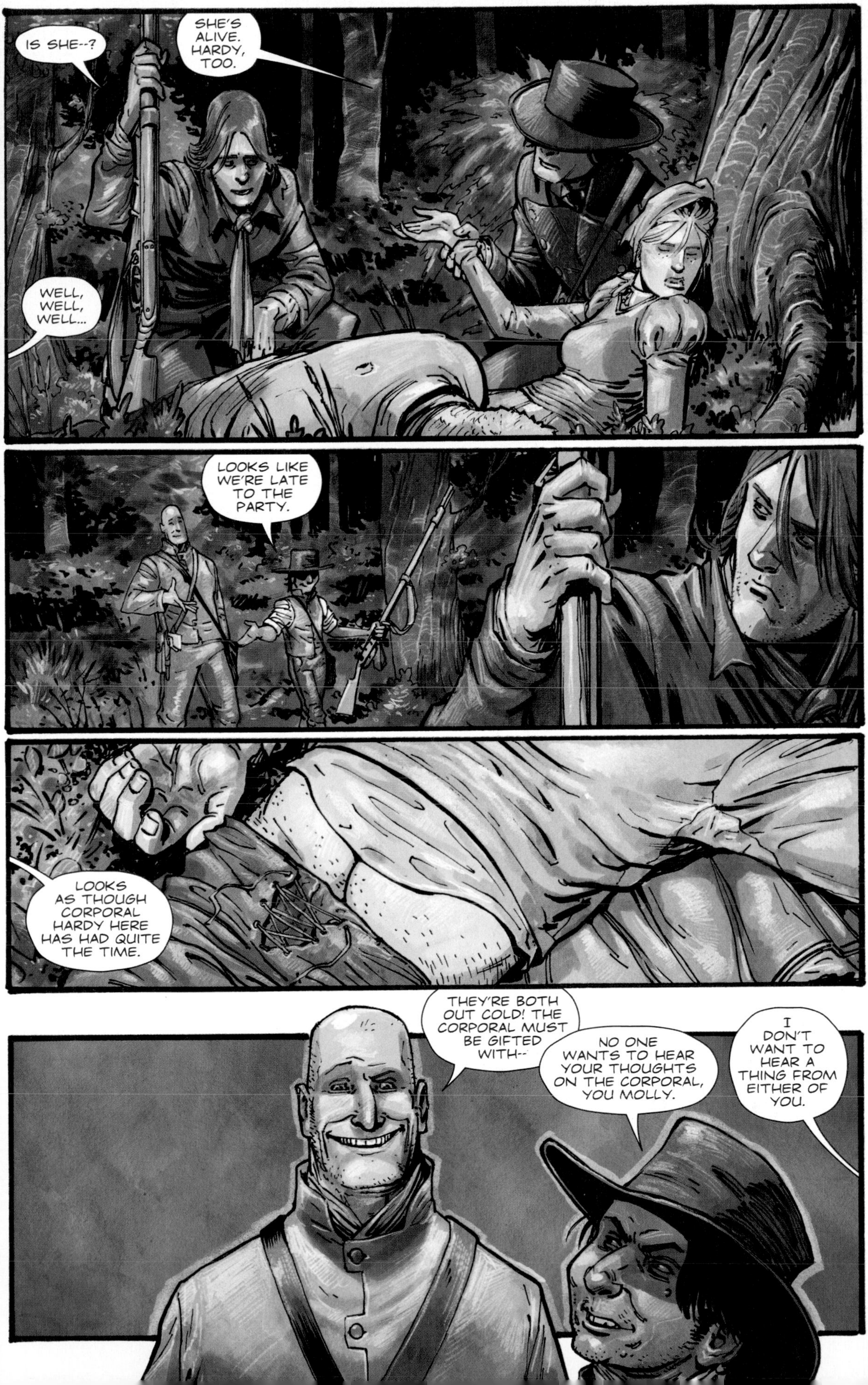
IS SHE--?
SHE'S ALIVE. HARDY, TOO.
WELL, WELL, WELL...
LOOKS LIKE WE'RE LATE TO THE PARTY.
LOOKS AS THOUGH CORPORAL HARDY HERE HAS HAD QUITE THE TIME.
THEY'RE BOTH OUT COLD! THE CORPORAL MUST BE GIFTED WITH--
NO ONE WANTS TO HEAR YOUR THOUGHTS ON THE CORPORAL, YOU MOLLY.
I DON'T WANT TO HEAR A THING FROM EITHER OF YOU.

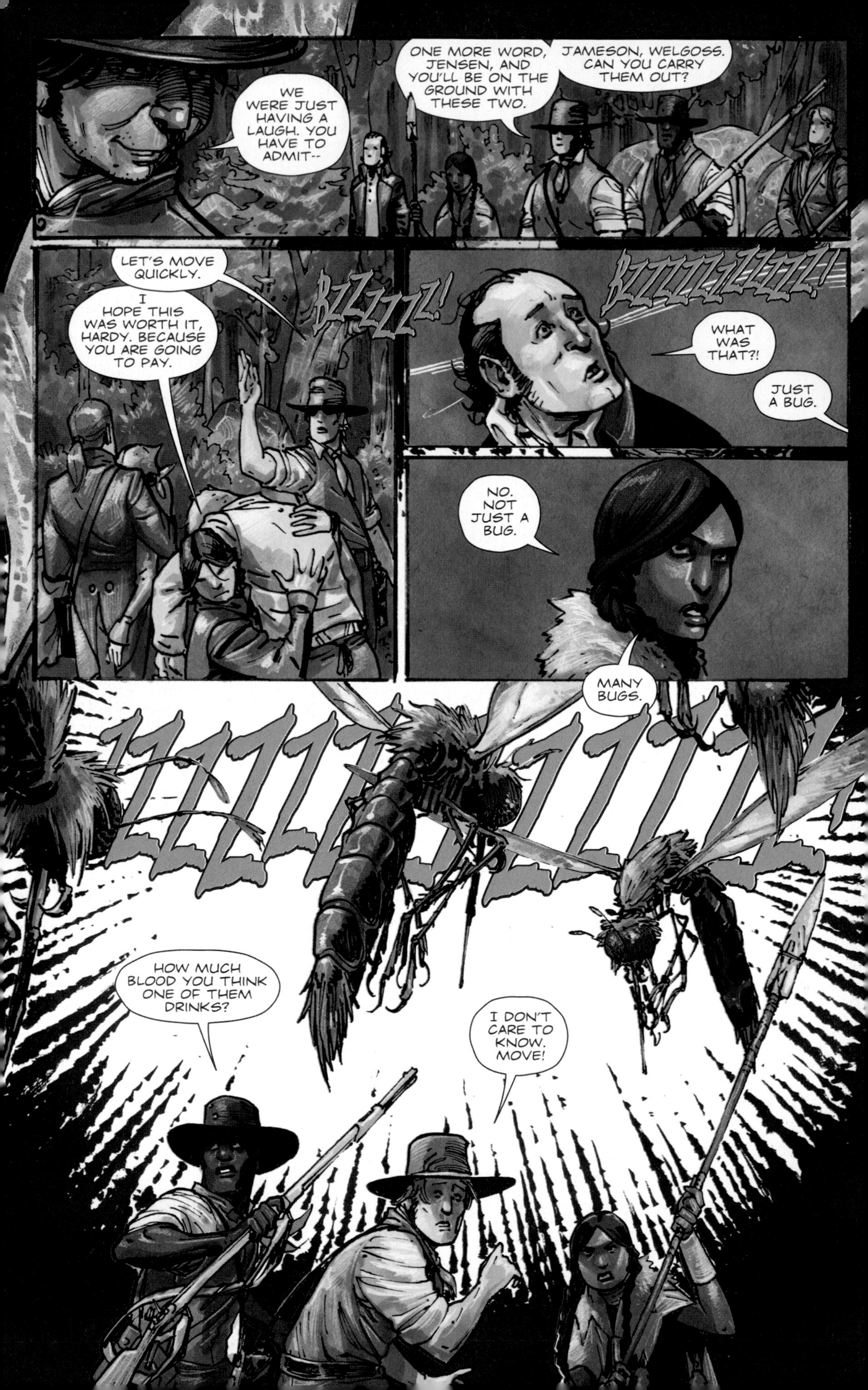
WE WERE JUST HAVING A LAUGH. YOU HAVE TO ADMIT--
ONE MORE WORD, JENSEN, AND YOU'LL BE ON THE GROUND WITH THESE TWO.
JAMESON, WELGOSS. CAN YOU CARRY THEM OUT?
LET'S MOVE QUICKLY.
I HOPE THIS WAS WORTH IT, HARDY. BECAUSE YOU ARE GOING TO PAY.
BZZZZZZ!
BZZZZZZZZZZZZZ!
WHAT WAS THAT?!
JUST A BUG.
NO. NOT JUST A BUG.
MANY BUGS.
ZZZZZZZZZZZZZZZ!
HOW MUCH BLOOD YOU THINK ONE OF THEM DRINKS?
I DON'T CARE TO KNOW. MOVE!

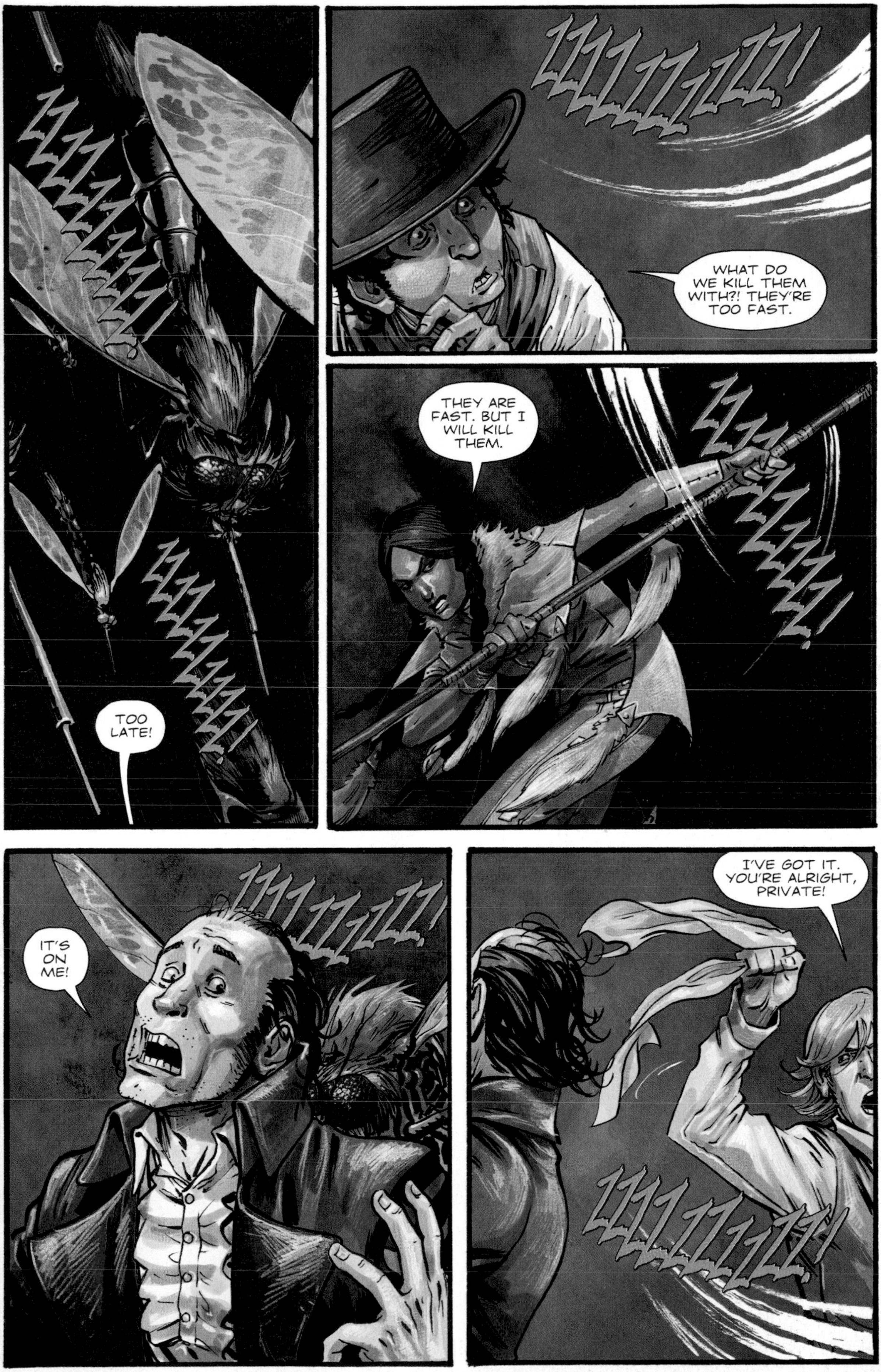
ZZZZZZZZZZZZ!
ZZZZZZZZZZZ!
ZZZZZZZZZZZZ!
WHAT DO WE KILL THEM WITH?! THEY'RE TOO FAST.
THEY ARE FAST. BUT I WILL KILL THEM.
ZZZZZZZZZZ!
ZZZZZZZZZZZ!
TOO LATE!
ZZZZZZZZZZZZ!
IT'S ON ME!
I'VE GOT IT. YOU'RE ALRIGHT, PRIVATE!
ZZZZZZZZZZZZ!

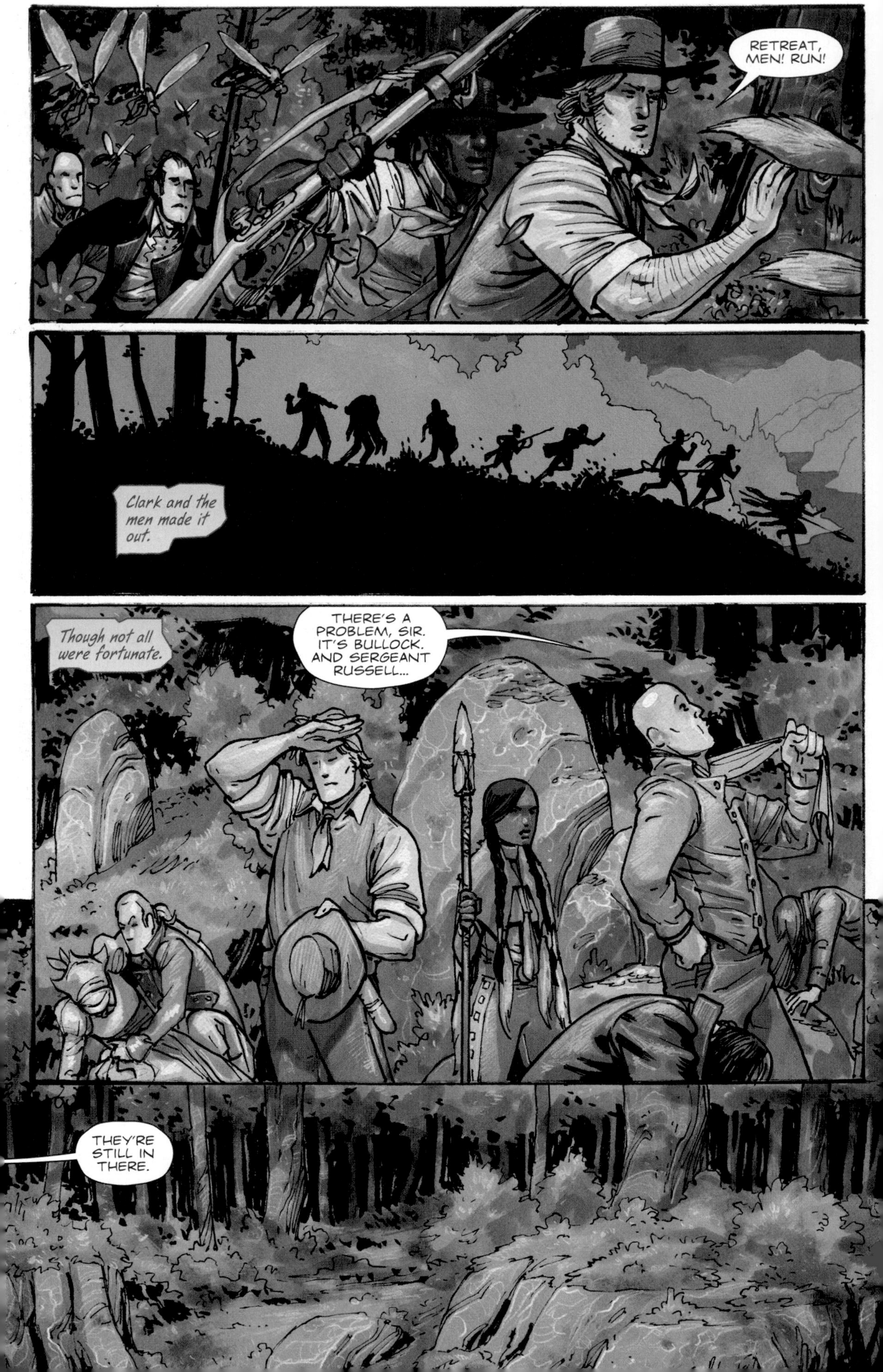
RETREAT, MEN! RUN!
Clark and the men made it out.
Though not all were fortunate.
THERE'S A PROBLEM, SIR. IT'S BULLOCK. AND SERGEANT RUSSELL...
THEY'RE STILL IN THERE.

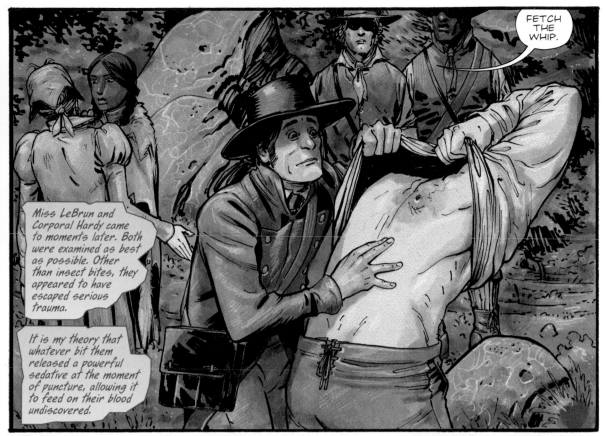

FETCH THE WHIP.

Miss LeBrun and Corporal Hardy came to moments later. Both were examined as best as possible. Other than insect bites, they appeared to have escaped serious trauma.

It is my theory that whatever bit them released a powerful sedative at the moment of puncture, allowing it to feed on their blood undiscovered.

Now they had to encounter something far more dangerous: Captain Clark's wrath.

FOOLISH, UNDISCIPLINED ASS! DO YOU REALIZE WHAT YOU'VE DONE? THE DANGER YOU'VE PUT US IN?!

WE HAVE TO GO BACK INTO THAT FOREST TO GET BULLOCK AND RUSSELL, MAYBE LOSE MORE MEN. SO YOU TWO COULD HAVE YOUR TRYST! WAS IT WORTH IT?! ANSWER ME!

AND YOU. AFTER THE KINDNESS WE'VE SHOWN. OUR PROTECTION, AND YOU TAKE ADVANTAGE AND--

I DIDN'T--

Clark is usually blind when he's in a fury. I don't know how he noticed--

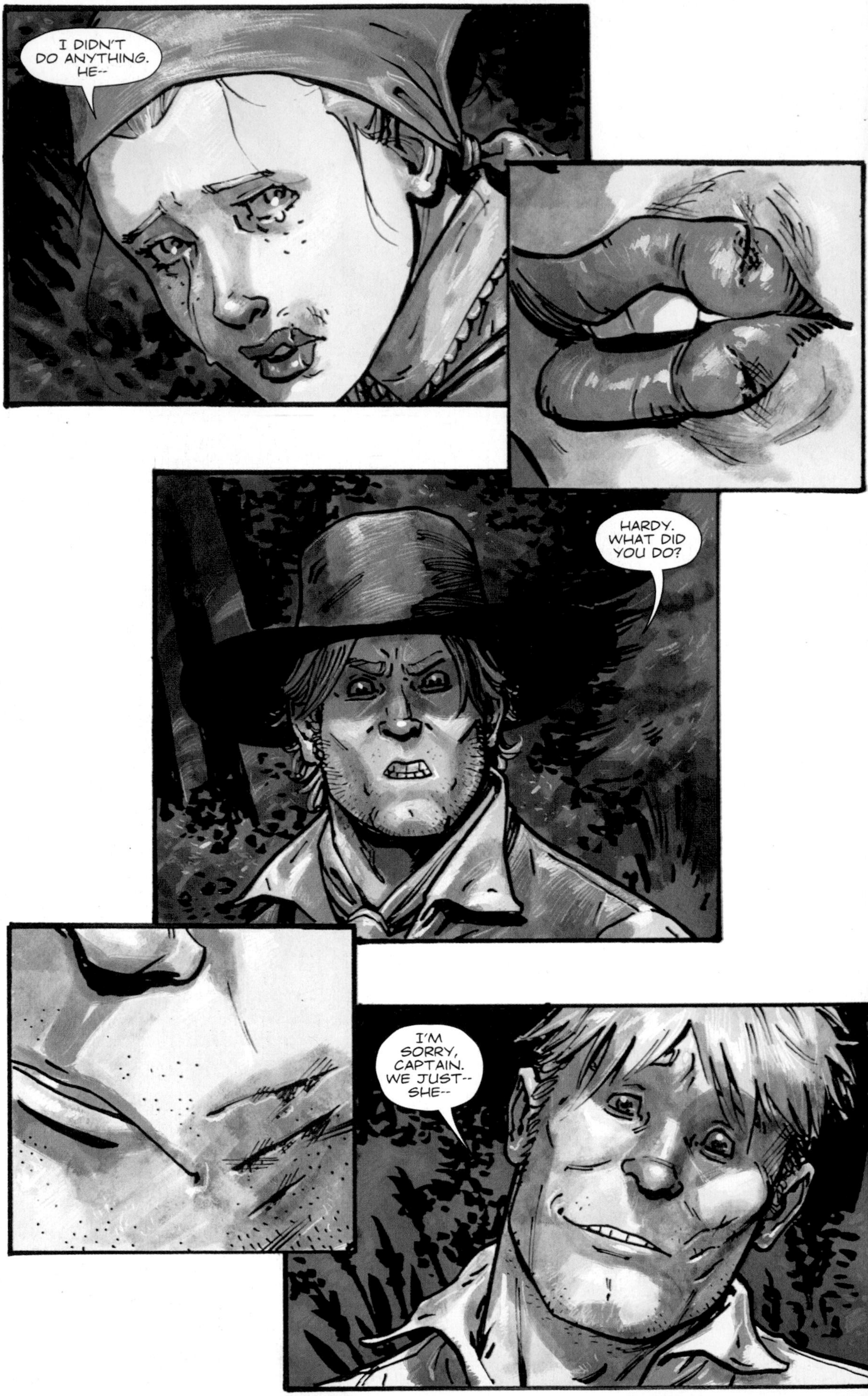
I DIDN'T DO ANYTHING. HE--
HARDY. WHAT DID YOU DO?
I'M SORRY, CAPTAIN. WE JUST-- SHE--

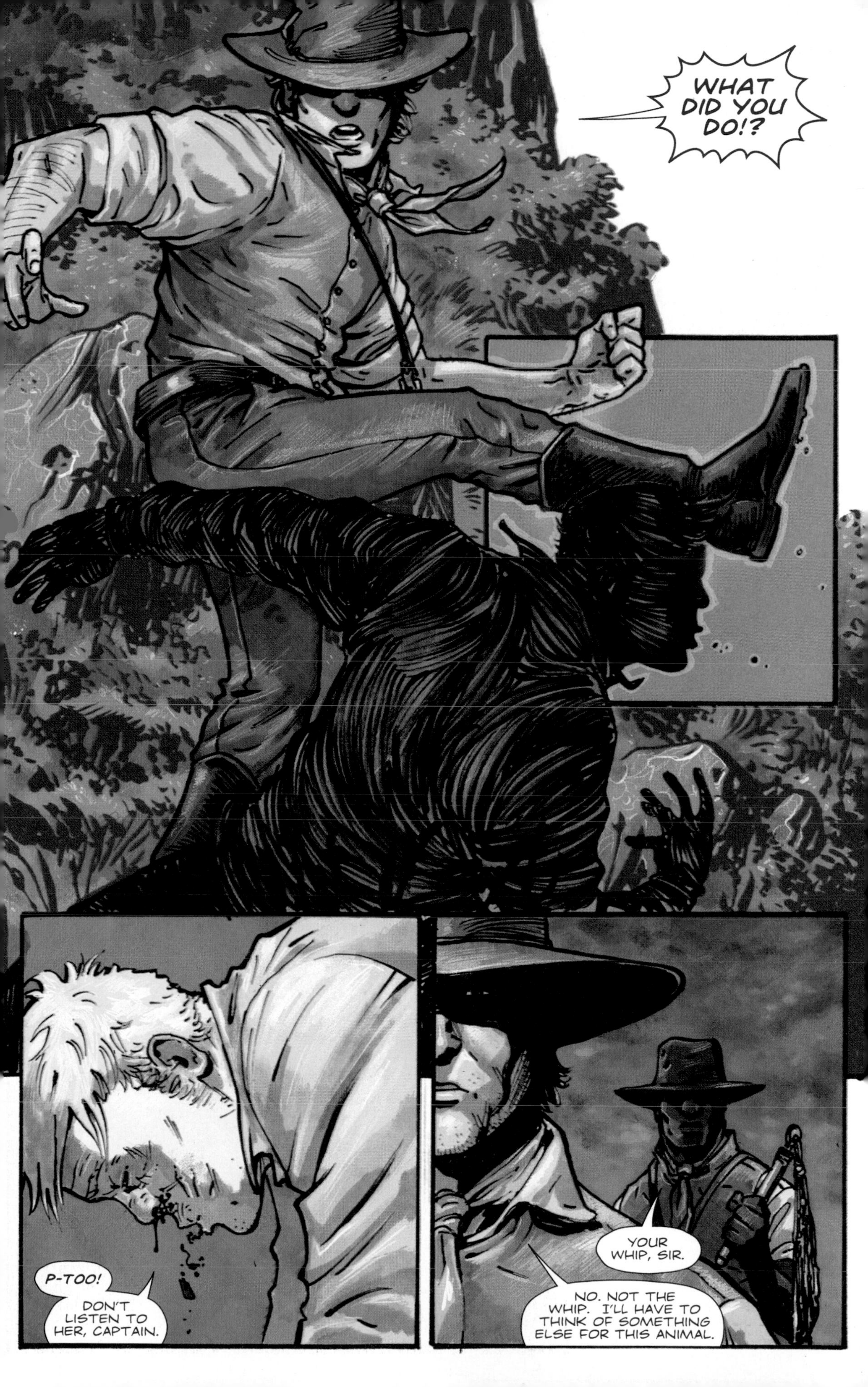
WHAT DID YOU DO!?
P-TOO!
DON'T LISTEN TO HER, CAPTAIN.
YOUR WHIP, SIR.
NO. NOT THE WHIP. I'LL HAVE TO THINK OF SOMETHING ELSE FOR THIS ANIMAL.

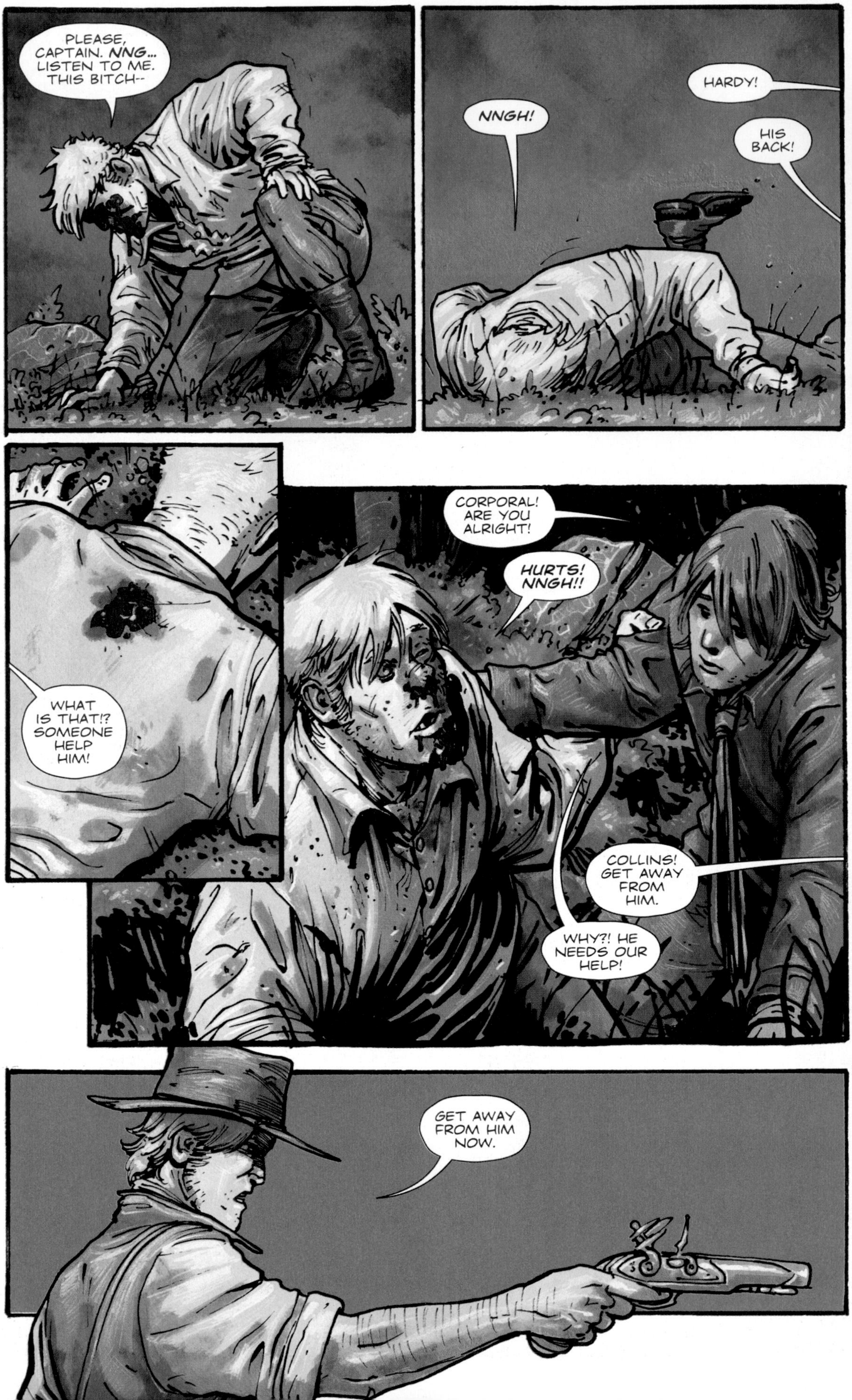
PLEASE, CAPTAIN. NNG... LISTEN TO ME. THIS BITCH--
HARDY!
NNGH!
HIS BACK!
WHAT IS THAT!? SOMEONE HELP HIM!
CORPORAL! ARE YOU ALRIGHT!
HURTS! NNGH!!
COLLINS! GET AWAY FROM HIM.
WHY?! HE NEEDS OUR HELP!
GET AWAY FROM HIM NOW.

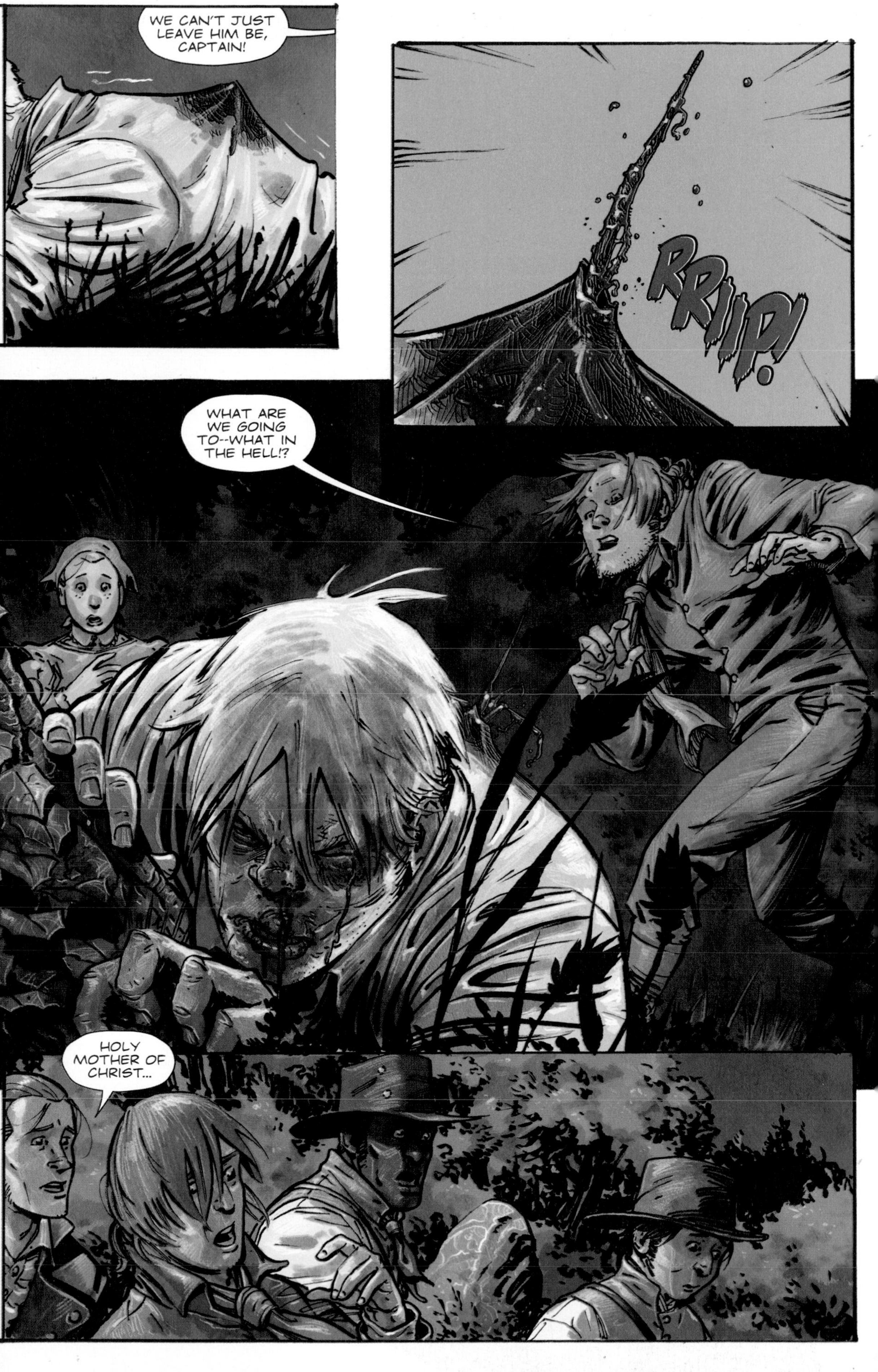
WE CAN'T JUST LEAVE HIM BE, CAPTAIN!
RRIIP!
WHAT ARE WE GOING TO--WHAT IN THE HELL!?
HOLY MOTHER OF CHRIST...

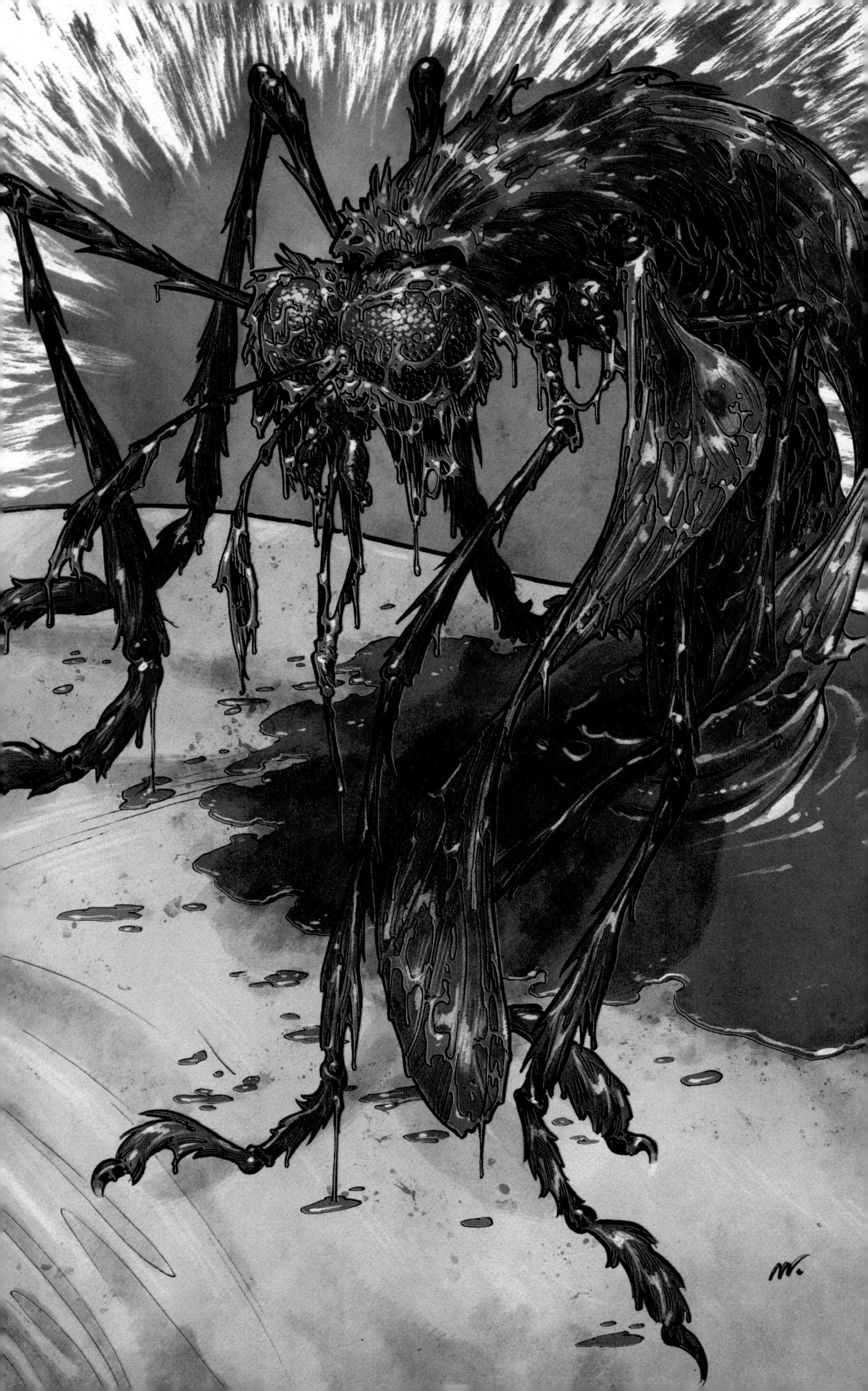

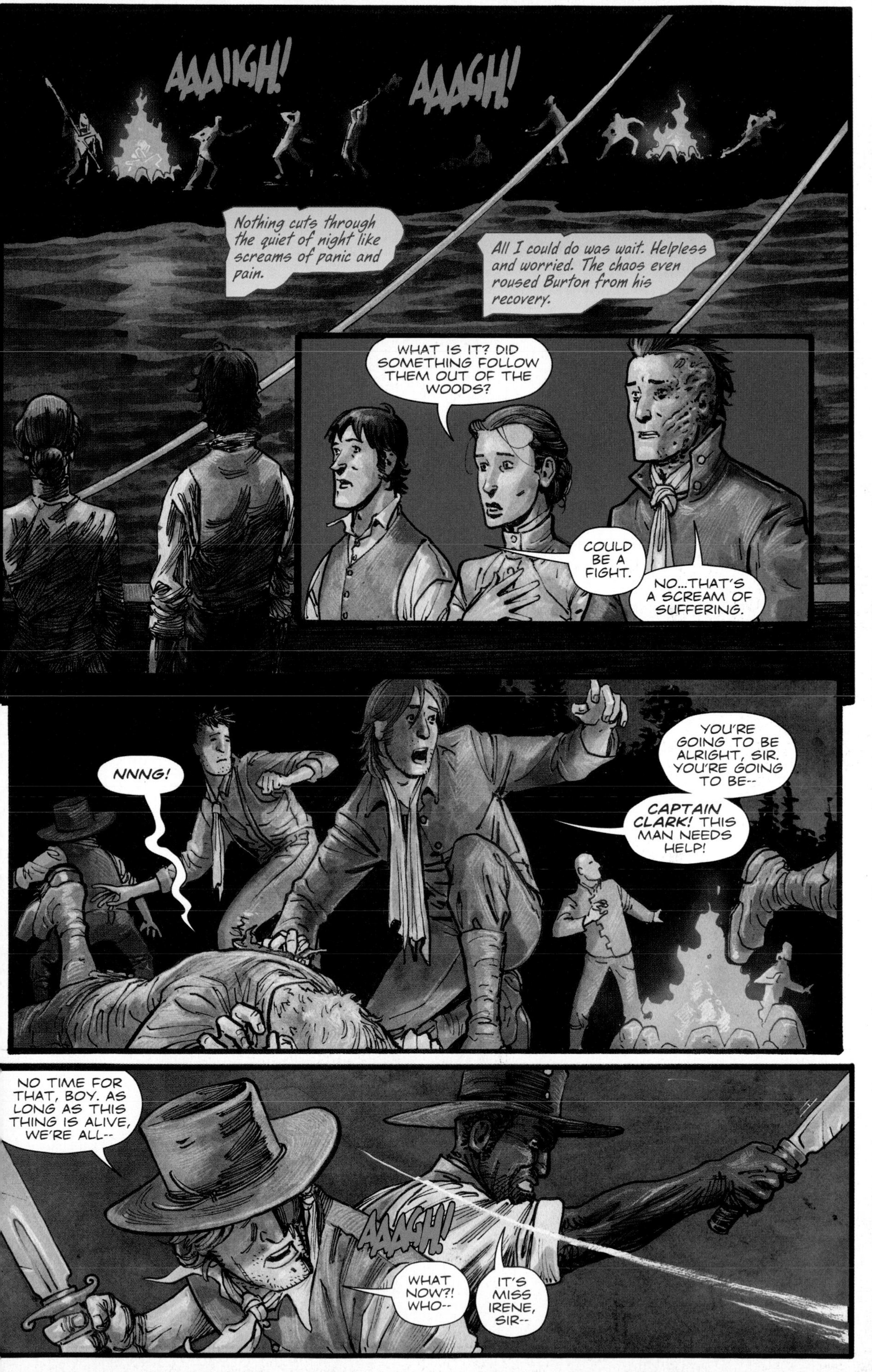
AAAIIGH!
AAAGH!
Nothing cuts through the quiet of night like screams of panic and pain.
All I could do was wait. Helpless and worried. The chaos even roused Burton from his recovery.
WHAT IS IT? DID SOMETHING FOLLOW THEM OUT OF THE WOODS?
COULD BE A FIGHT.
NO...THAT'S A SCREAM OF SUFFERING.
NNNG!
YOU'RE GOING TO BE ALRIGHT, SIR. YOU'RE GOING TO BE--
CAPTAIN CLARK! THIS MAN NEEDS HELP!
NO TIME FOR THAT, BOY. AS LONG AS THIS THING IS ALIVE, WE'RE ALL--
AAAGH!
WHAT NOW?! WHO--
IT'S MISS IRENE, SIR--

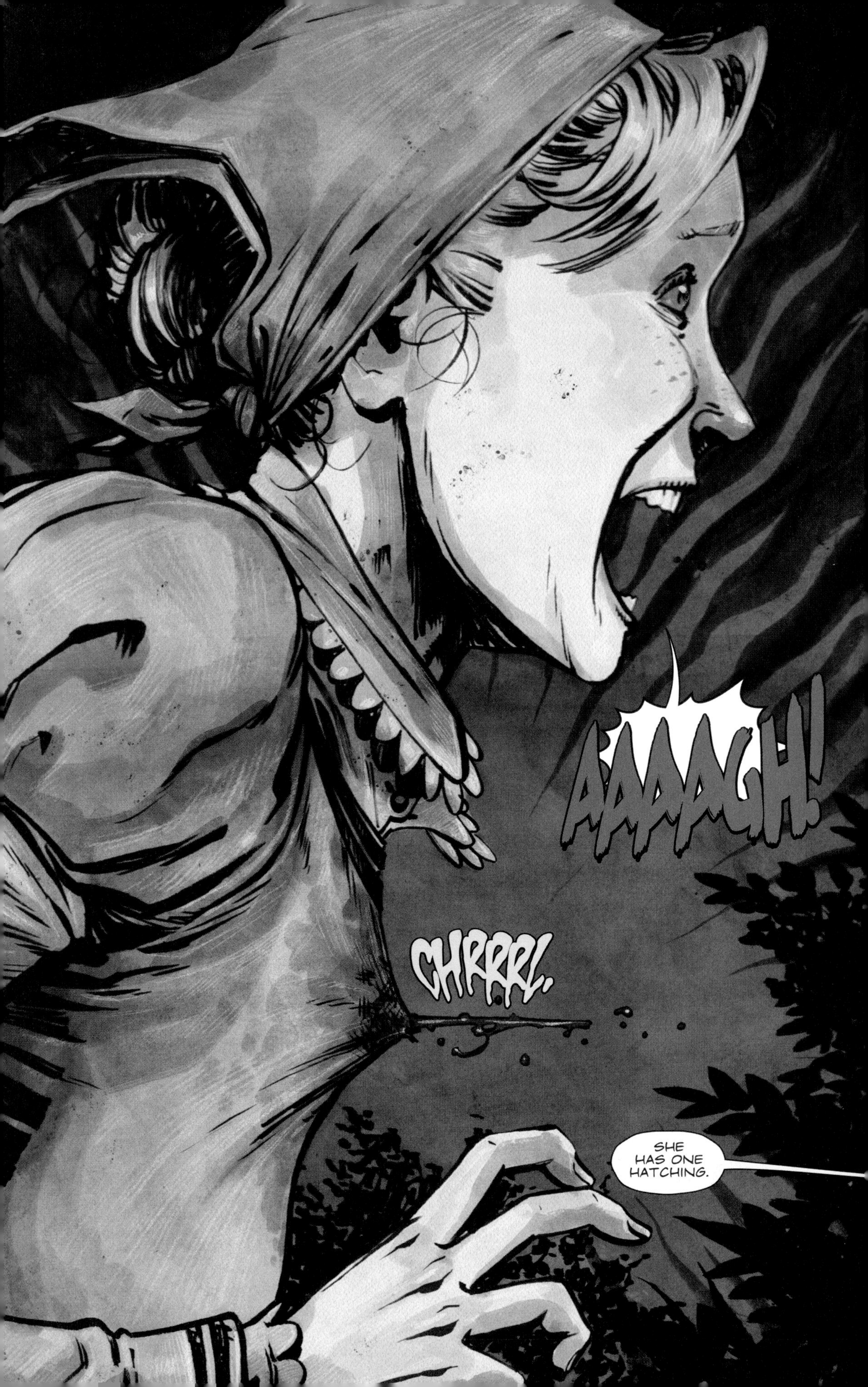
AAAAGH!
CHRRRL.
SHE HAS ONE HATCHING.

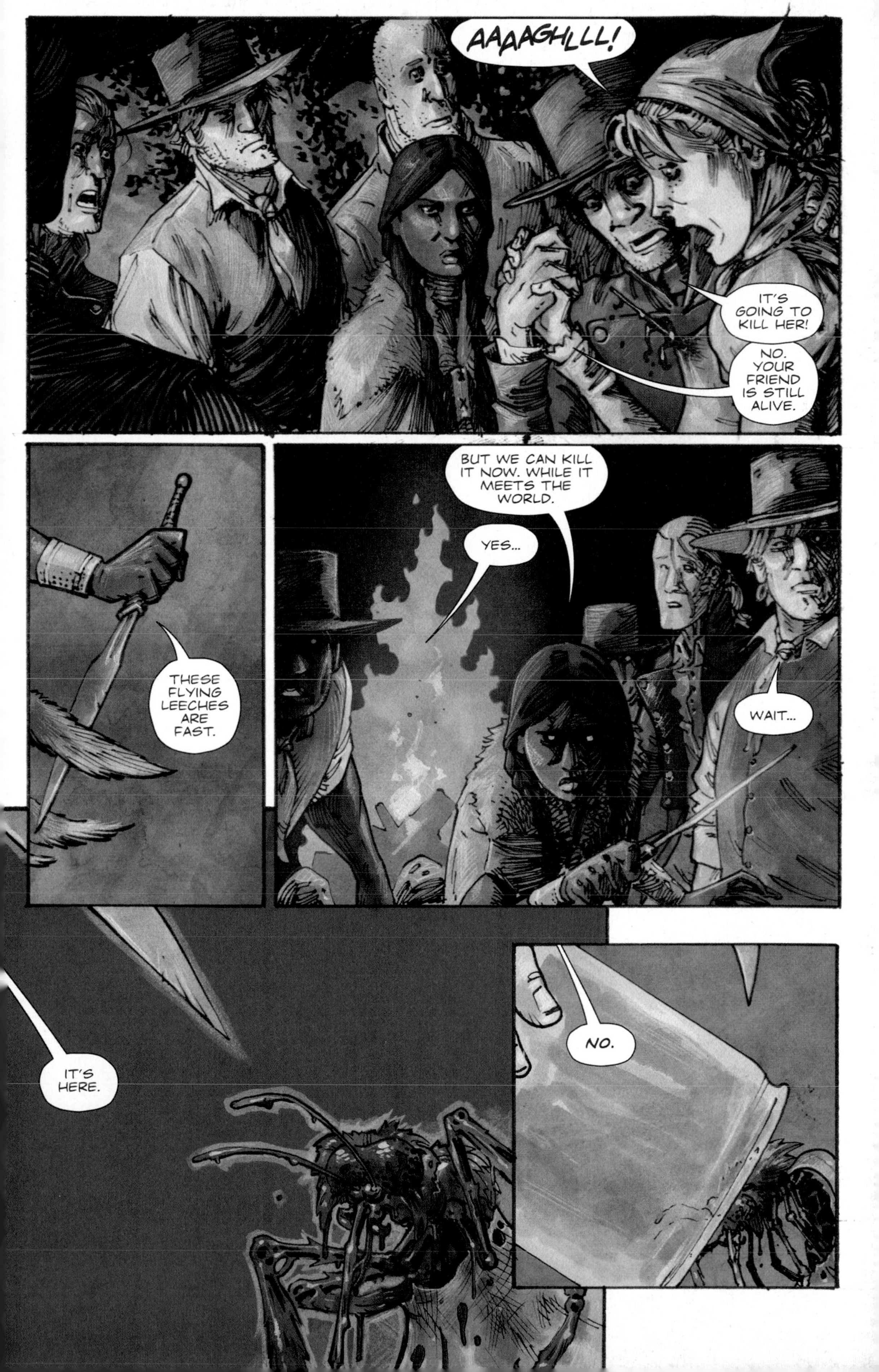
AAAAGHLLL!
IT'S GOING TO KILL HER!
NO. YOUR FRIEND IS STILL ALIVE.
THESE FLYING LEECHES ARE FAST.
BUT WE CAN KILL IT NOW. WHILE IT MEETS THE WORLD.
YES...
WAIT...
IT'S HERE.
NO.

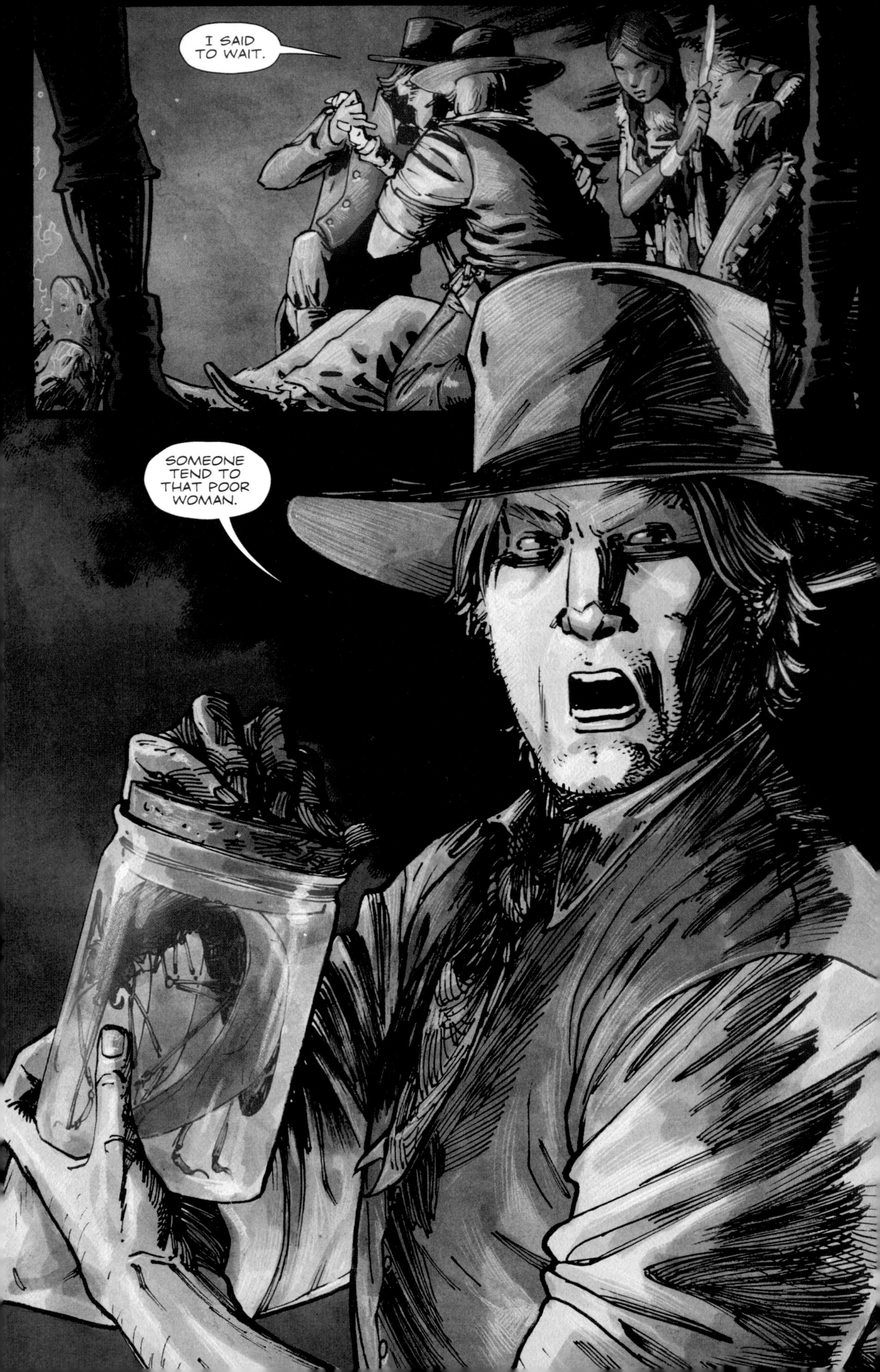
I SAID TO WAIT.
SOMEONE TEND TO THAT POOR WOMAN.

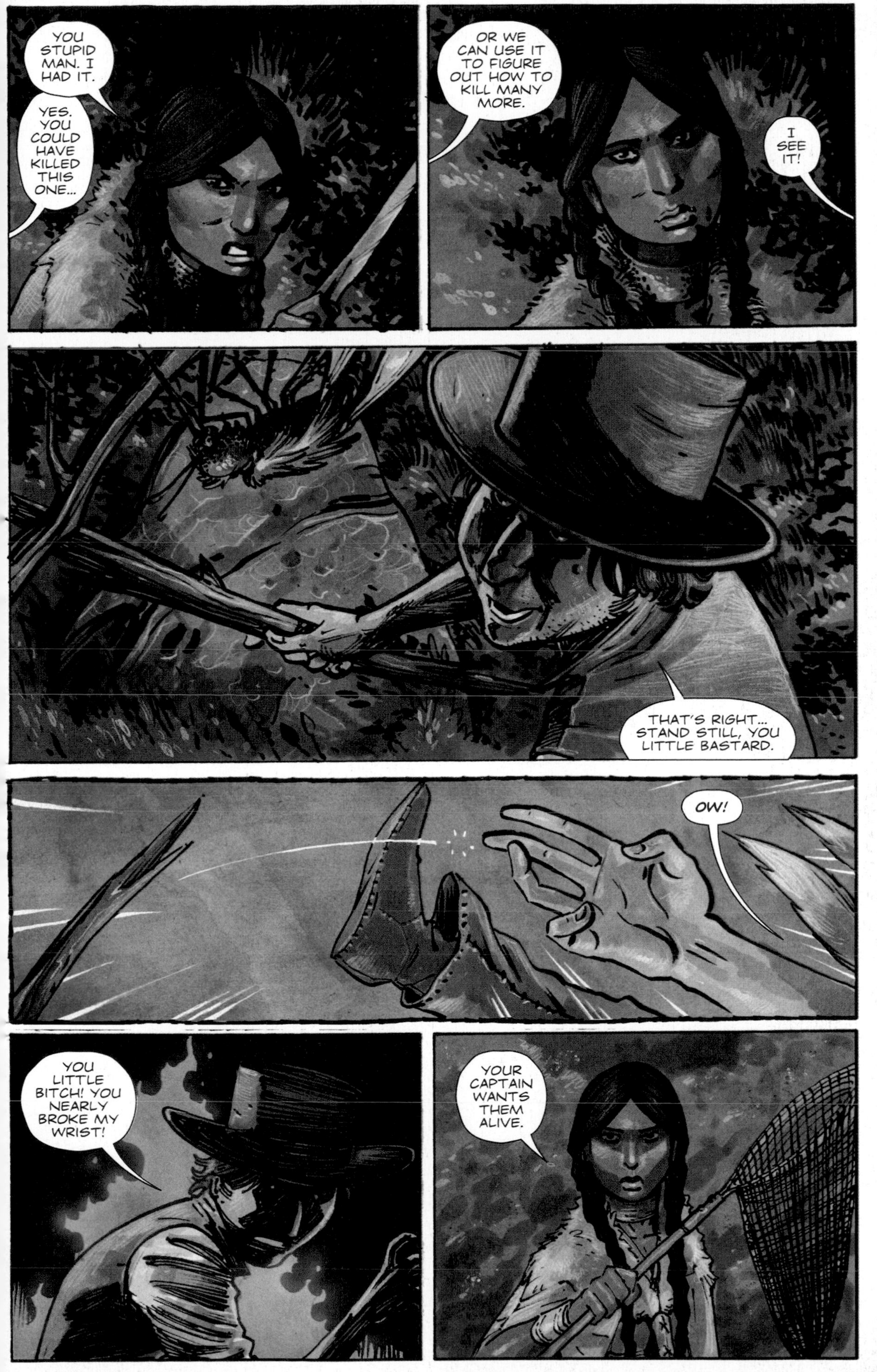
YOU STUPID MAN. I HAD IT.
YES. YOU COULD HAVE KILLED THIS ONE...
OR WE CAN USE IT TO FIGURE OUT HOW TO KILL MANY MORE.
I SEE IT!
THAT'S RIGHT... STAND STILL, YOU LITTLE BASTARD.
OW!
YOU LITTLE BITCH! YOU NEARLY BROKE MY WRIST!
YOUR CAPTAIN WANTS THEM ALIVE.

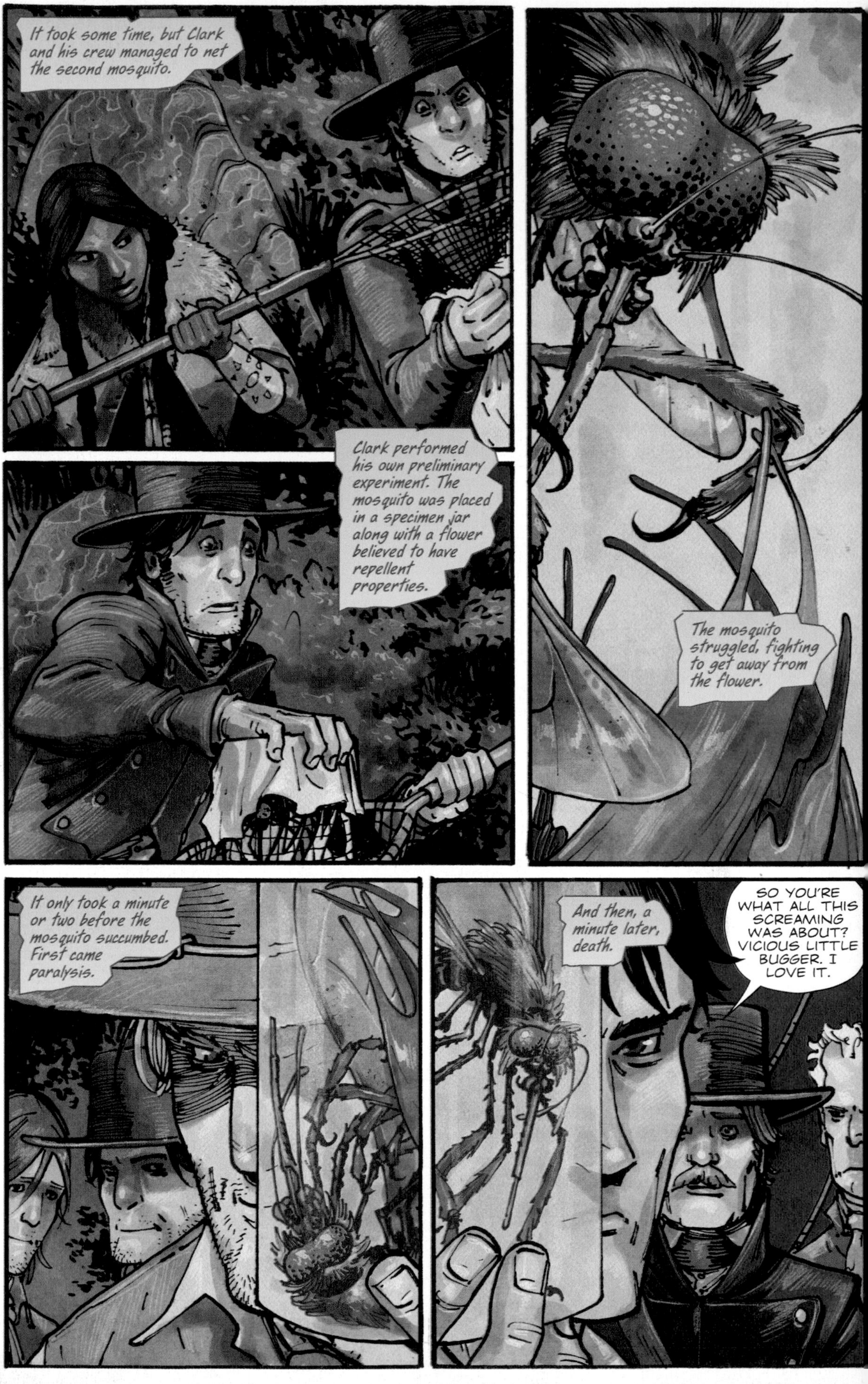
It took some time, but Clark and his crew managed to net the second mosquito.
Clark performed his own preliminary experiment. The mosquito was placed in a specimen jar along with a flower believed to have repellent properties.
The mosquito struggled, fighting to get away from the flower.
It only took a minute or two before the mosquito succumbed. First came paralysis.
And then, a minute later, death.
SO YOU'RE WHAT ALL THIS SCREAMING WAS ABOUT? VICIOUS LITTLE BUGGER. I LOVE IT.

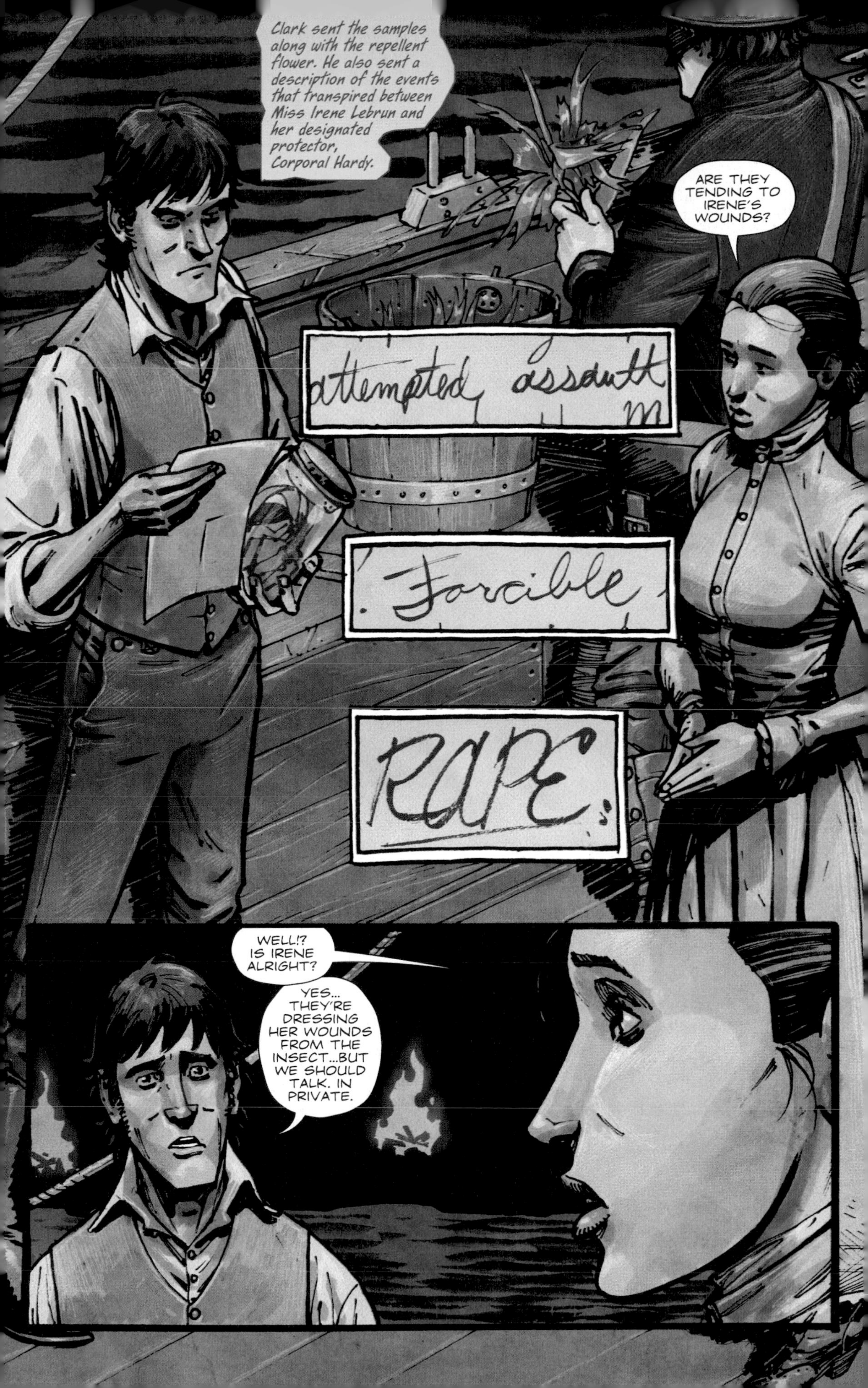
Clark sent the samples along with the repellent flower. He also sent a description of the events that transpired between Miss Irene Lebrun and her designated protector, Corporal Hardy.
ARE THEY TENDING TO IRENE'S WOUNDS?
attempted assault
Forcible
RAPE
WELL!? IS IRENE ALRIGHT?
YES... THEY'RE DRESSING HER WOUNDS FROM THE INSECT...BUT WE SHOULD TALK. IN PRIVATE.

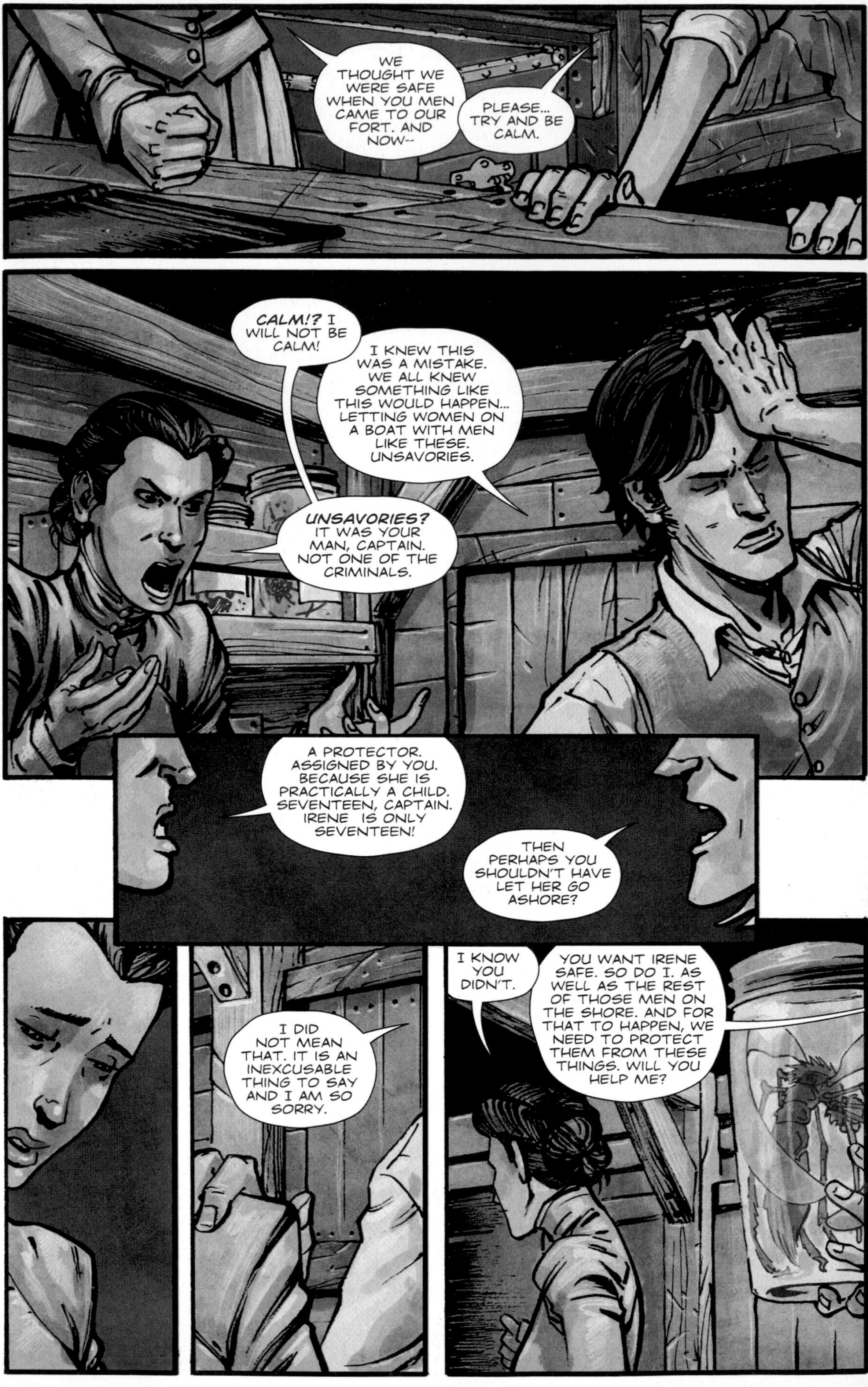
WE THOUGHT WE WERE SAFE WHEN YOU MEN CAME TO OUR FORT. AND NOW--
PLEASE... TRY AND BE CALM.
CALM!? I WILL NOT BE CALM!
I KNEW THIS WAS A MISTAKE. WE ALL KNEW SOMETHING LIKE THIS WOULD HAPPEN... LETTING WOMEN ON A BOAT WITH MEN LIKE THESE. UNSAVORIES.
UNSAVORIES? IT WAS YOUR MAN, CAPTAIN. NOT ONE OF THE CRIMINALS.
A PROTECTOR. ASSIGNED BY YOU. BECAUSE SHE IS PRACTICALLY A CHILD. SEVENTEEN, CAPTAIN. IRENE IS ONLY SEVENTEEN!
THEN PERHAPS YOU SHOULDN'T HAVE LET HER GO ASHORE?
I DID NOT MEAN THAT. IT IS AN INEXCUSABLE THING TO SAY AND I AM SO SORRY.
I KNOW YOU DIDN'T.
YOU WANT IRENE SAFE. SO DO I. AS WELL AS THE REST OF THOSE MEN ON THE SHORE. AND FOR THAT TO HAPPEN, WE NEED TO PROTECT THEM FROM THESE THINGS. WILL YOU HELP ME?

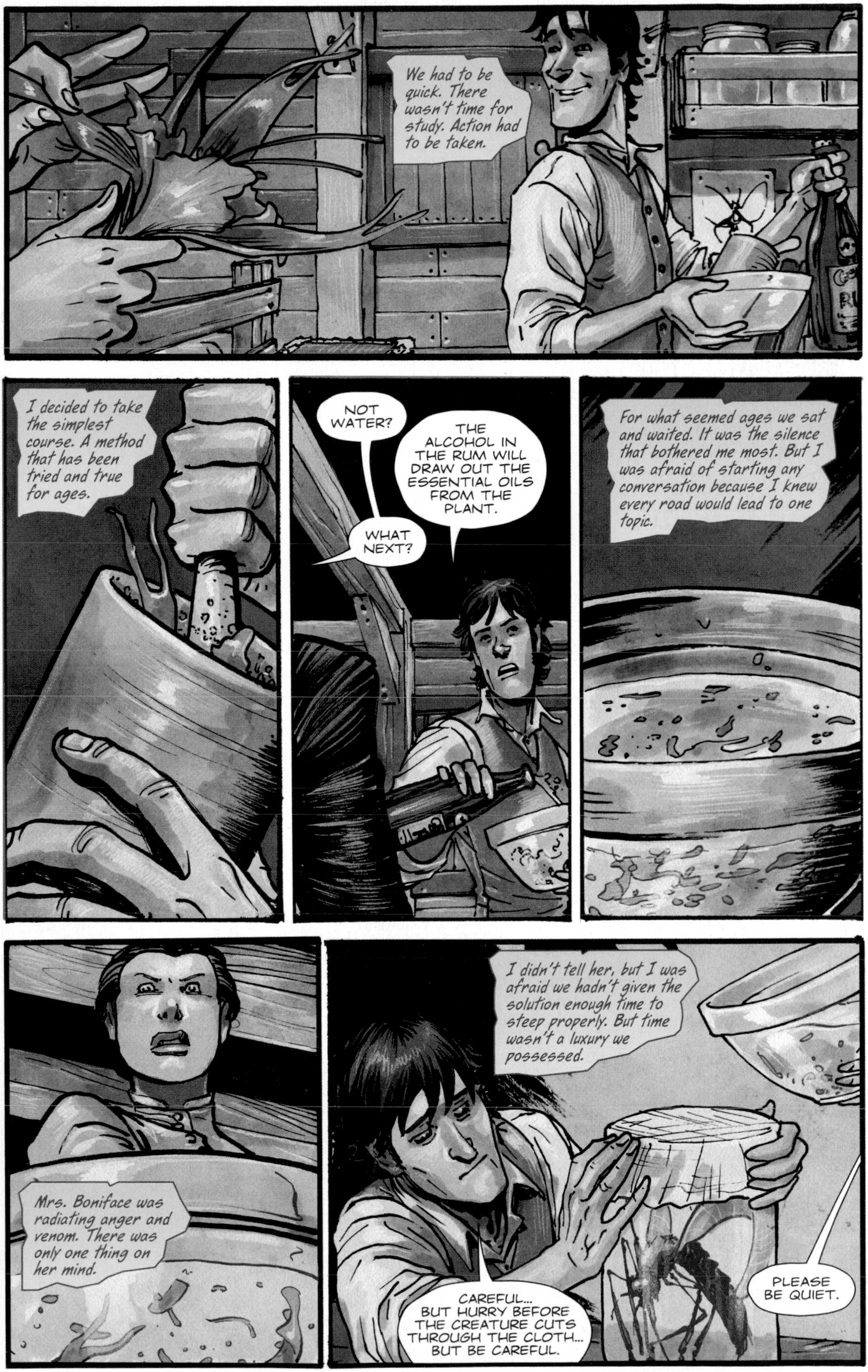
We had to be quick. There wasn't time for study. Action had to be taken.
I decided to take the simplest course. A method that has been tried and true for ages.
NOT WATER?
THE ALCOHOL IN THE RUM WILL DRAW OUT THE ESSENTIAL OILS FROM THE PLANT.
WHAT NEXT?
For what seemed ages we sat and waited. It was the silence that bothered me most. But I was afraid of starting any conversation because I knew every road would lead to one topic.
Mrs. Boniface was radiating anger and venom. There was only one thing on her mind.
I didn't tell her, but I was afraid we hadn't given the solution enough time to steep properly. But time wasn't a luxury we possessed.
CAREFUL... BUT HURRY BEFORE THE CREATURE CUTS THROUGH THE CLOTH... BUT BE CAREFUL.
PLEASE BE QUIET.

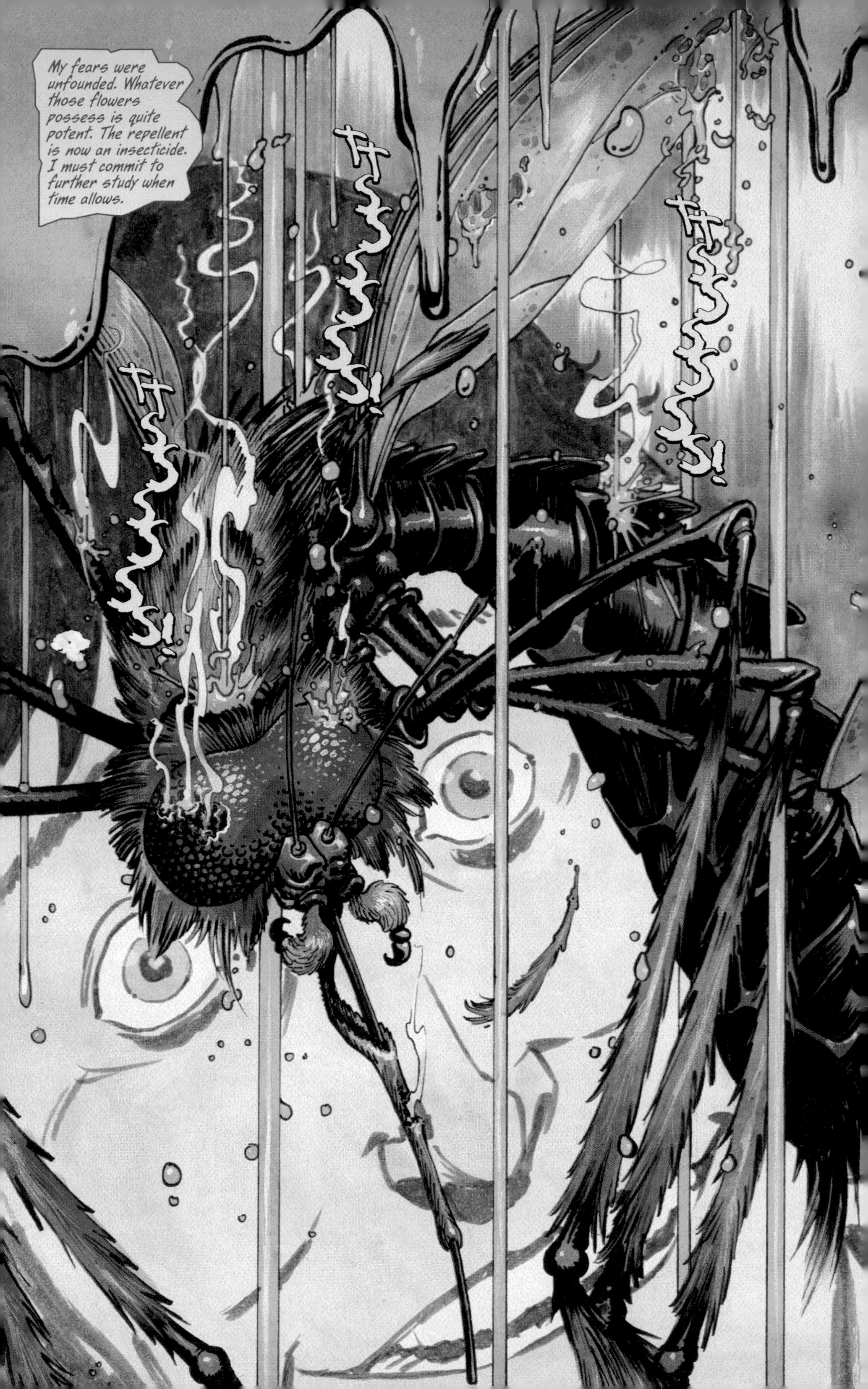
My fears were unfounded. Whatever those flowers possess is quite potent. The repellent is now an insecticide. I must commit to further study when time allows.
TTSSSSSS!
TTSSSSSS!
TTSSSSSS!

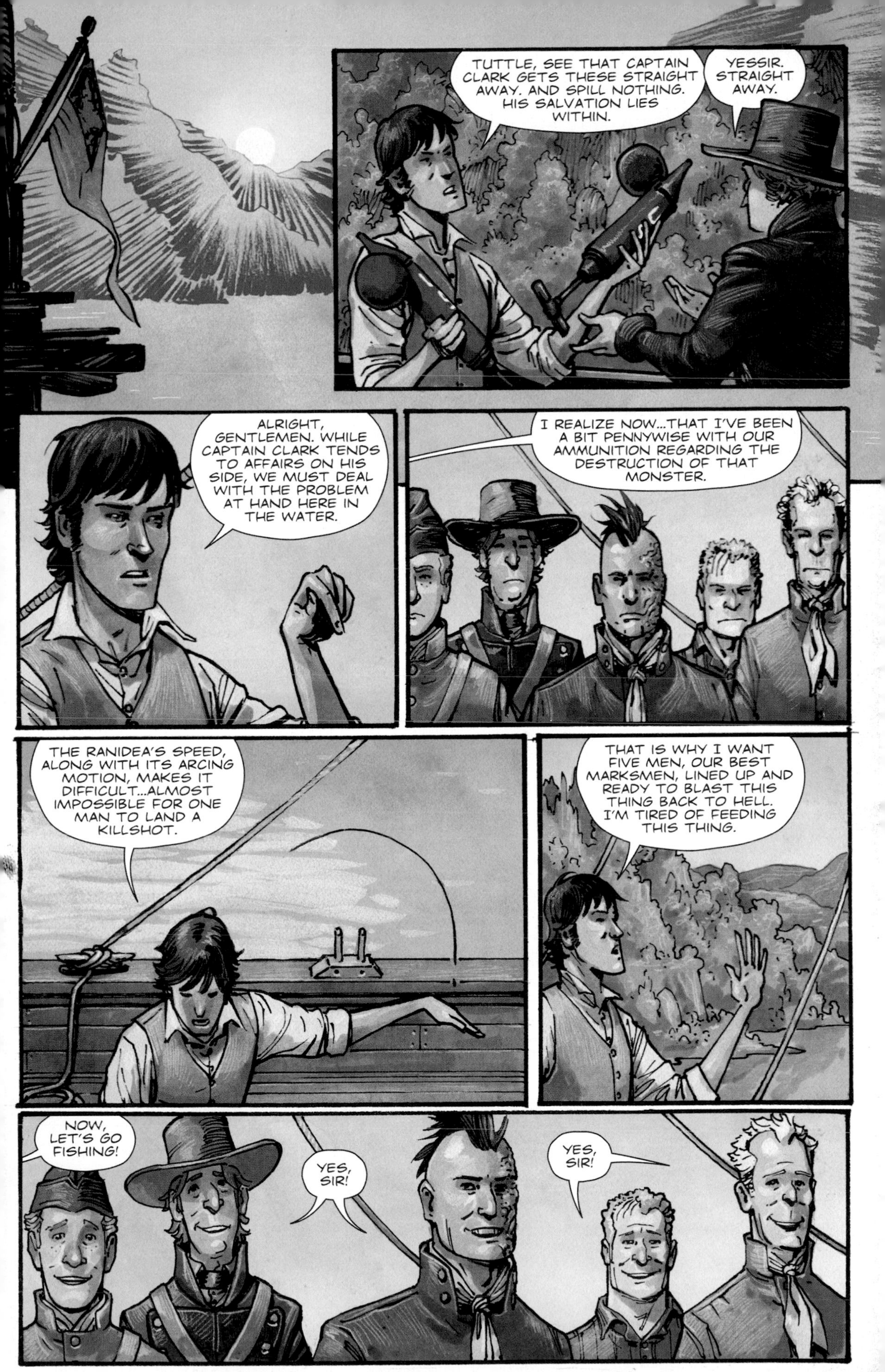
TUTTLE, SEE THAT CAPTAIN CLARK GETS THESE STRAIGHT AWAY. AND SPILL NOTHING. HIS SALVATION LIES WITHIN.
YESSIR. STRAIGHT AWAY.
ALRIGHT, GENTLEMEN. WHILE CAPTAIN CLARK TENDS TO AFFAIRS ON HIS SIDE, WE MUST DEAL WITH THE PROBLEM AT HAND HERE IN THE WATER.
I REALIZE NOW...THAT I'VE BEEN A BIT PENNYWISE WITH OUR AMMUNITION REGARDING THE DESTRUCTION OF THAT MONSTER.
THE RANIDEA'S SPEED, ALONG WITH ITS ARCING MOTION, MAKES IT DIFFICULT...ALMOST IMPOSSIBLE FOR ONE MAN TO LAND A KILLSHOT.
THAT IS WHY I WANT FIVE MEN, OUR BEST MARKSMEN, LINED UP AND READY TO BLAST THIS THING BACK TO HELL. I'M TIRED OF FEEDING THIS THING.
NOW, LET'S GO FISHING!
YES, SIR!
YES, SIR!

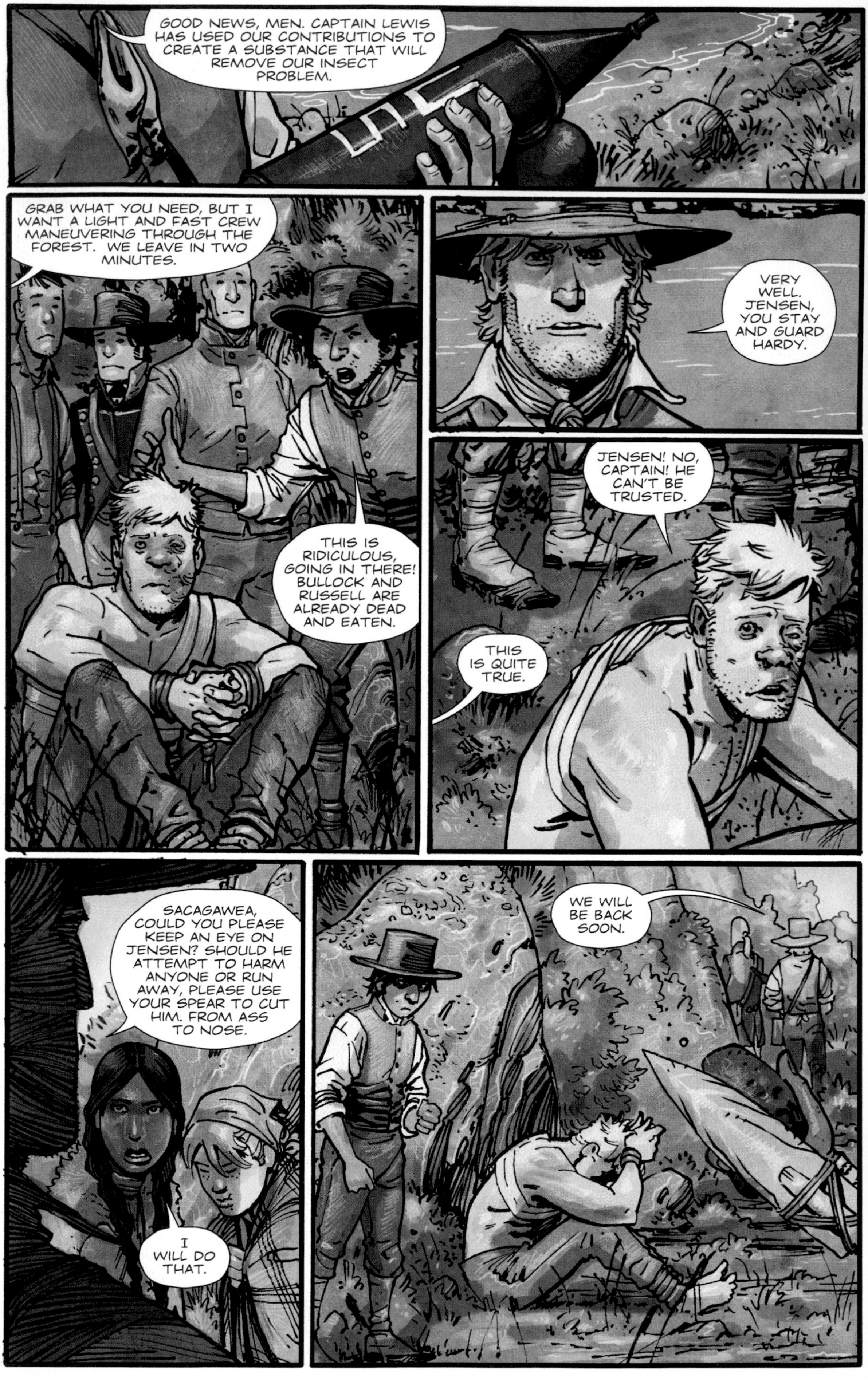
GOOD NEWS, MEN. CAPTAIN LEWIS HAS USED OUR CONTRIBUTIONS TO CREATE A SUBSTANCE THAT WILL REMOVE OUR INSECT PROBLEM.
GRAB WHAT YOU NEED, BUT I WANT A LIGHT AND FAST CREW MANEUVERING THROUGH THE FOREST. WE LEAVE IN TWO MINUTES.
THIS IS RIDICULOUS, GOING IN THERE! BULLOCK AND RUSSELL ARE ALREADY DEAD AND EATEN.
VERY WELL. JENSEN, YOU STAY AND GUARD HARDY.
JENSEN! NO, CAPTAIN! HE CAN'T BE TRUSTED.
THIS IS QUITE TRUE.
SACAGAWEA, COULD YOU PLEASE KEEP AN EYE ON JENSEN? SHOULD HE ATTEMPT TO HARM ANYONE OR RUN AWAY, PLEASE USE YOUR SPEAR TO CUT HIM. FROM ASS TO NOSE.
I WILL DO THAT.
WE WILL BE BACK SOON.

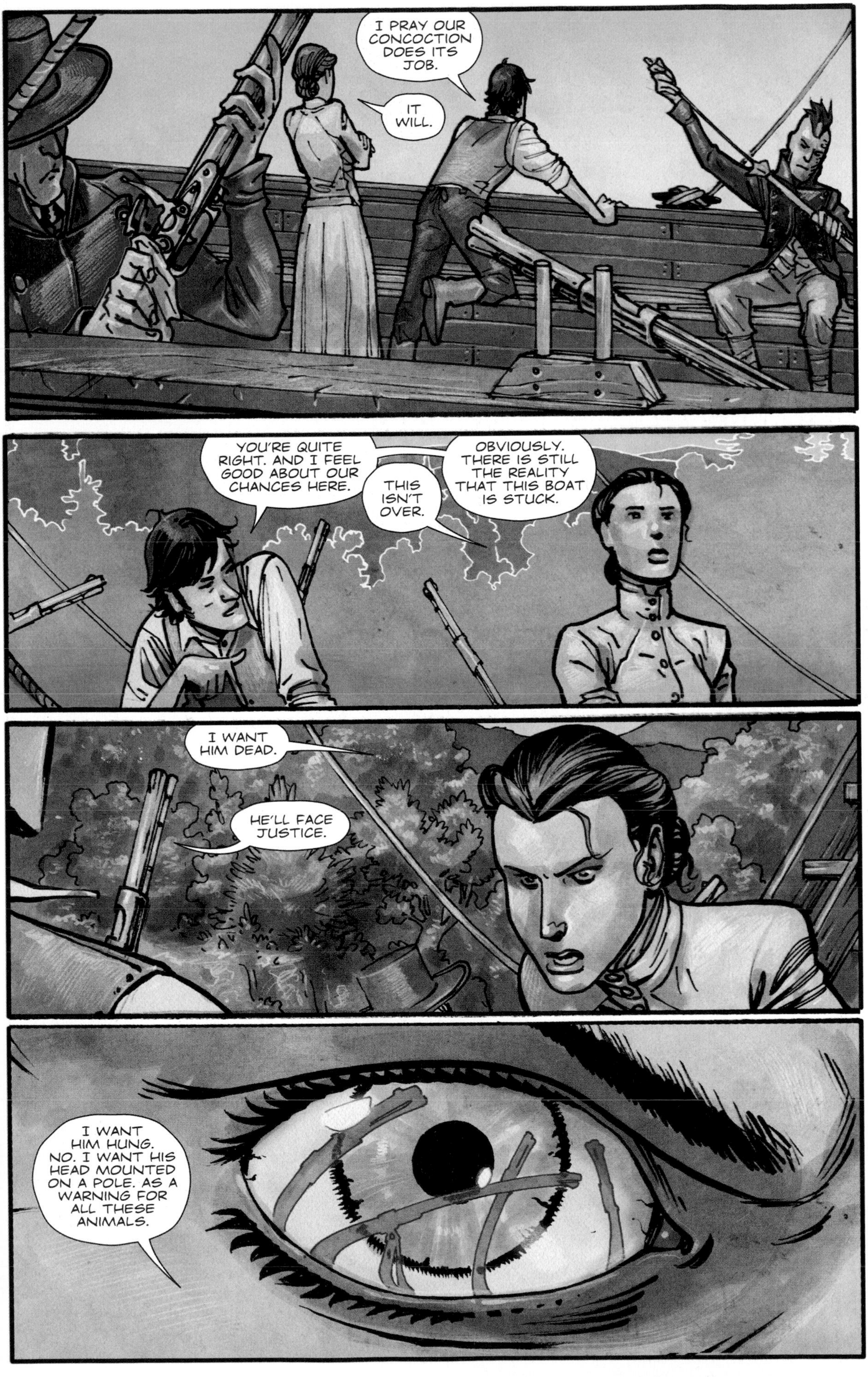
I PRAY OUR CONCOCTION DOES ITS JOB.
IT WILL.
YOU'RE QUITE RIGHT. AND I FEEL GOOD ABOUT OUR CHANCES HERE.
THIS ISN'T OVER.
OBVIOUSLY. THERE IS STILL THE REALITY THAT THIS BOAT IS STUCK.
I WANT HIM DEAD.
HE'LL FACE JUSTICE.
I WANT HIM HUNG. NO. I WANT HIS HEAD MOUNTED ON A POLE. AS A WARNING FOR ALL THESE ANIMALS.

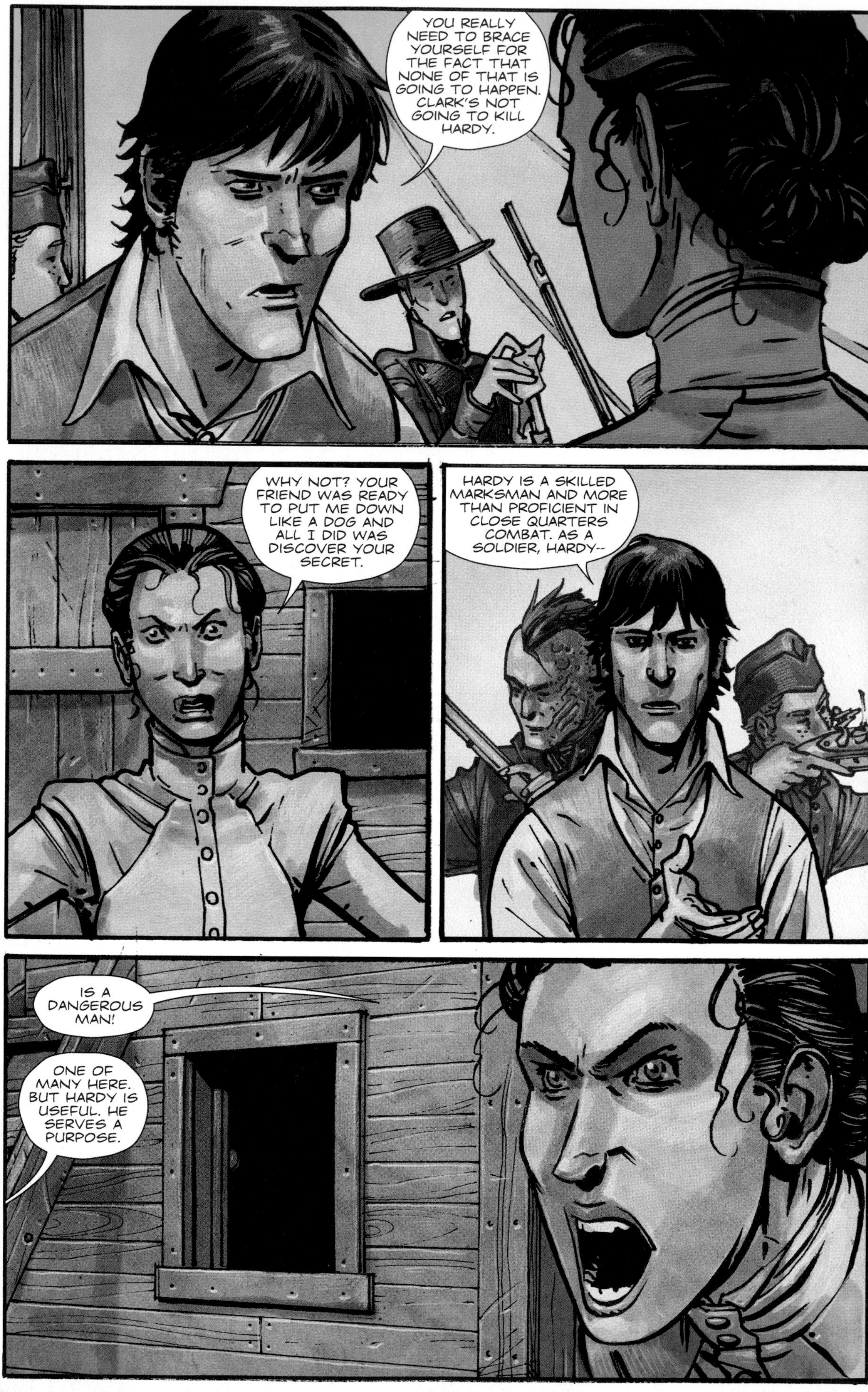
YOU REALLY NEED TO BRACE YOURSELF FOR THE FACT THAT NONE OF THAT IS GOING TO HAPPEN. CLARK'S NOT GOING TO KILL HARDY.
WHY NOT? YOUR FRIEND WAS READY TO PUT ME DOWN LIKE A DOG AND ALL I DID WAS DISCOVER YOUR SECRET.
HARDY IS A SKILLED MARKSMAN AND MORE THAN PROFICIENT IN CLOSE QUARTERS COMBAT. AS A SOLDIER, HARDY--
IS A DANGEROUS MAN!
ONE OF MANY HERE. BUT HARDY IS USEFUL. HE SERVES A PURPOSE.

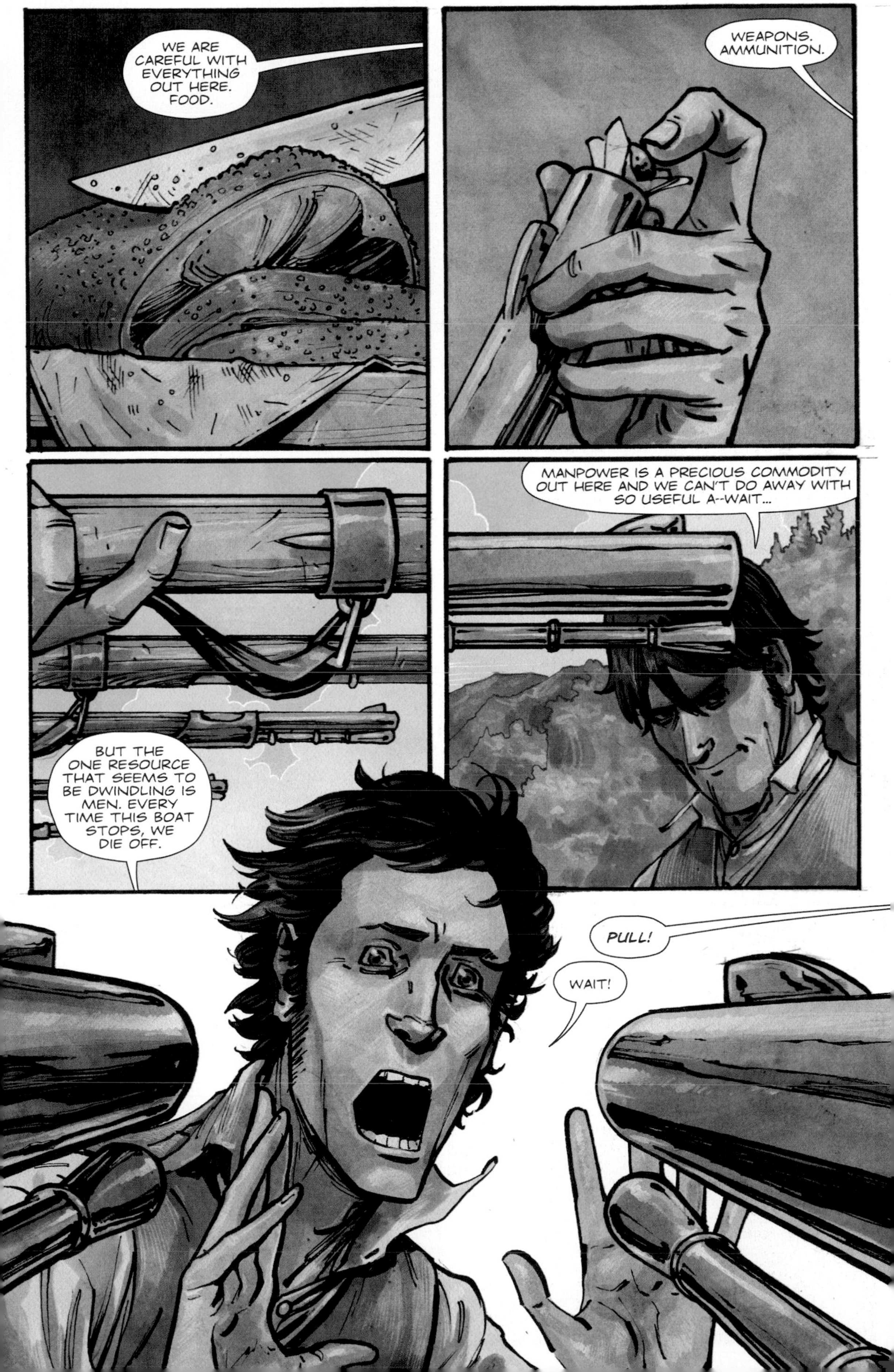
WE ARE CAREFUL WITH EVERYTHING OUT HERE. FOOD.
WEAPONS. AMMUNITION.
BUT THE ONE RESOURCE THAT SEEMS TO BE DWINDLING IS MEN. EVERY TIME THIS BOAT STOPS, WE DIE OFF.
MANPOWER IS A PRECIOUS COMMODITY OUT HERE AND WE CAN'T DO AWAY WITH SO USEFUL A--WAIT...
PULL!
WAIT!

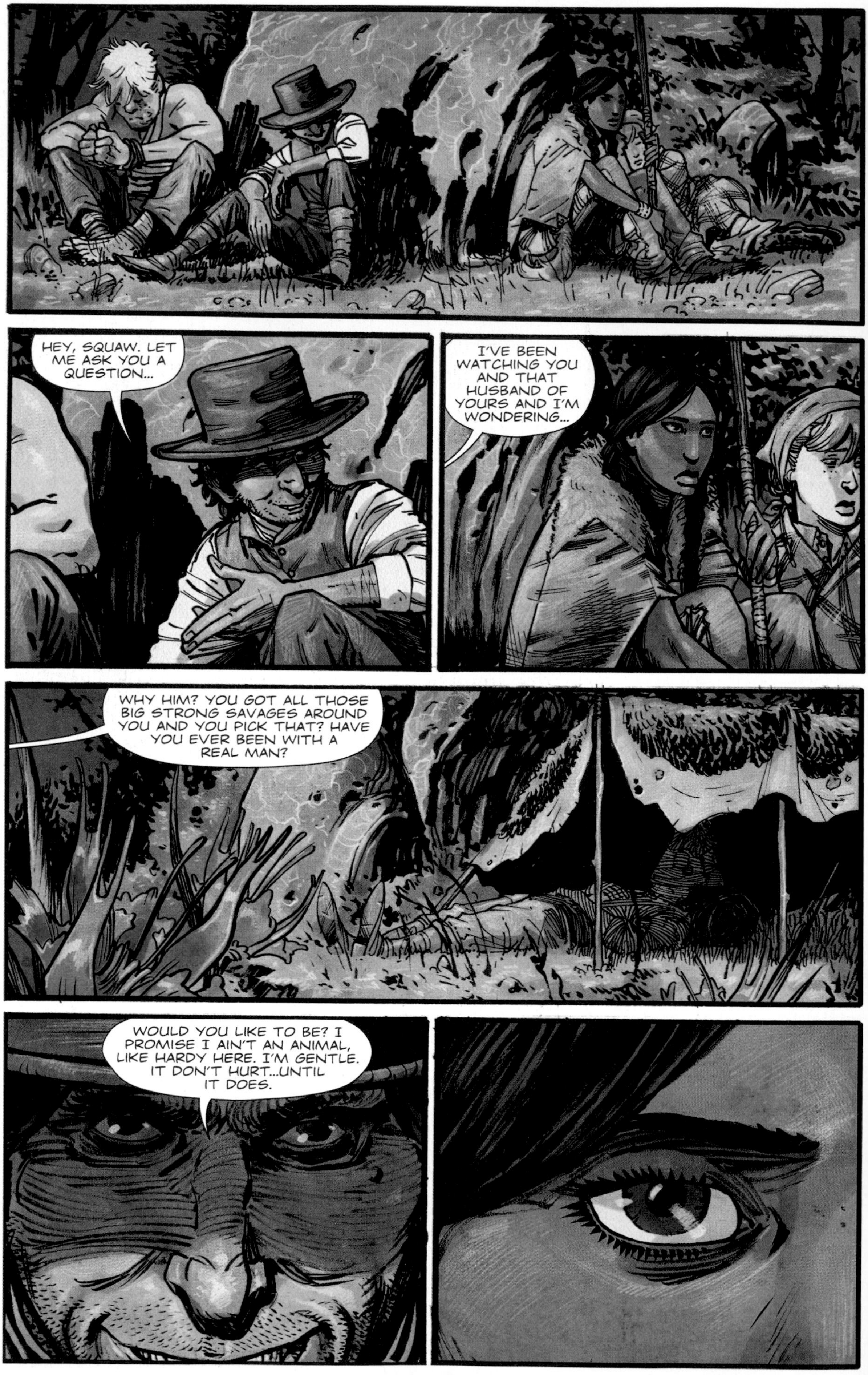
HEY, SQUAW. LET ME ASK YOU A QUESTION...
I'VE BEEN WATCHING YOU AND THAT HUSBAND OF YOURS AND I'M WONDERING...
WHY HIM? YOU GOT ALL THOSE BIG STRONG SAVAGES AROUND YOU AND YOU PICK THAT? HAVE YOU EVER BEEN WITH A REAL MAN?
WOULD YOU LIKE TO BE? I PROMISE I AIN'T AN ANIMAL, LIKE HARDY HERE. I'M GENTLE. IT DON'T HURT...UNTIL IT DOES.

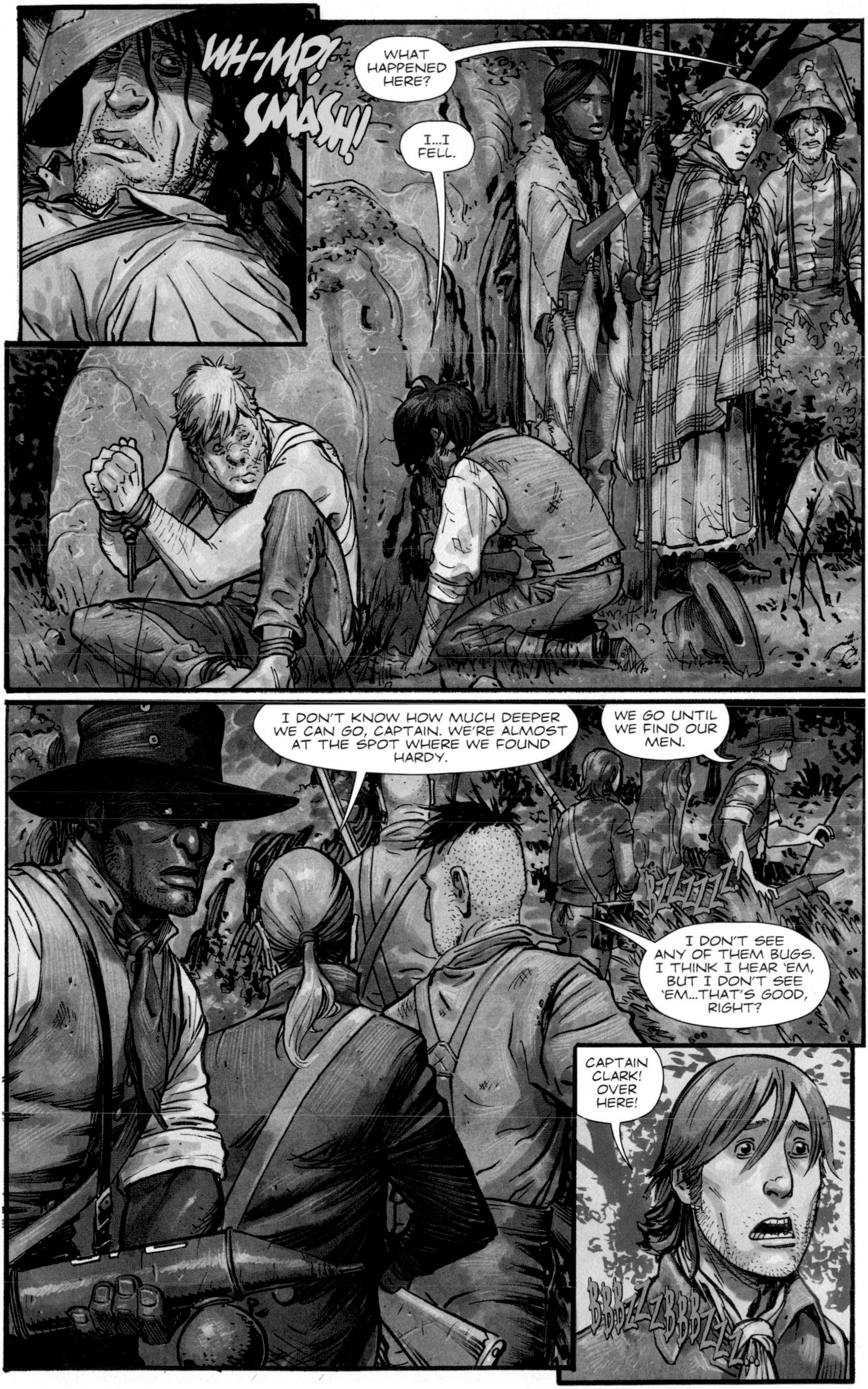
WH-MP!
SMASH!
WHAT HAPPENED HERE?
I...I FELL.
I DON'T KNOW HOW MUCH DEEPER WE CAN GO, CAPTAIN. WE'RE ALMOST AT THE SPOT WHERE WE FOUND HARDY.
WE GO UNTIL WE FIND OUR MEN.
BZZZZZ
I DON'T SEE ANY OF THEM BUGS. I THINK I HEAR 'EM, BUT I DON'T SEE 'EM...THAT'S GOOD, RIGHT?
CAPTAIN CLARK! OVER HERE!
BBBZZZBBBZZZ

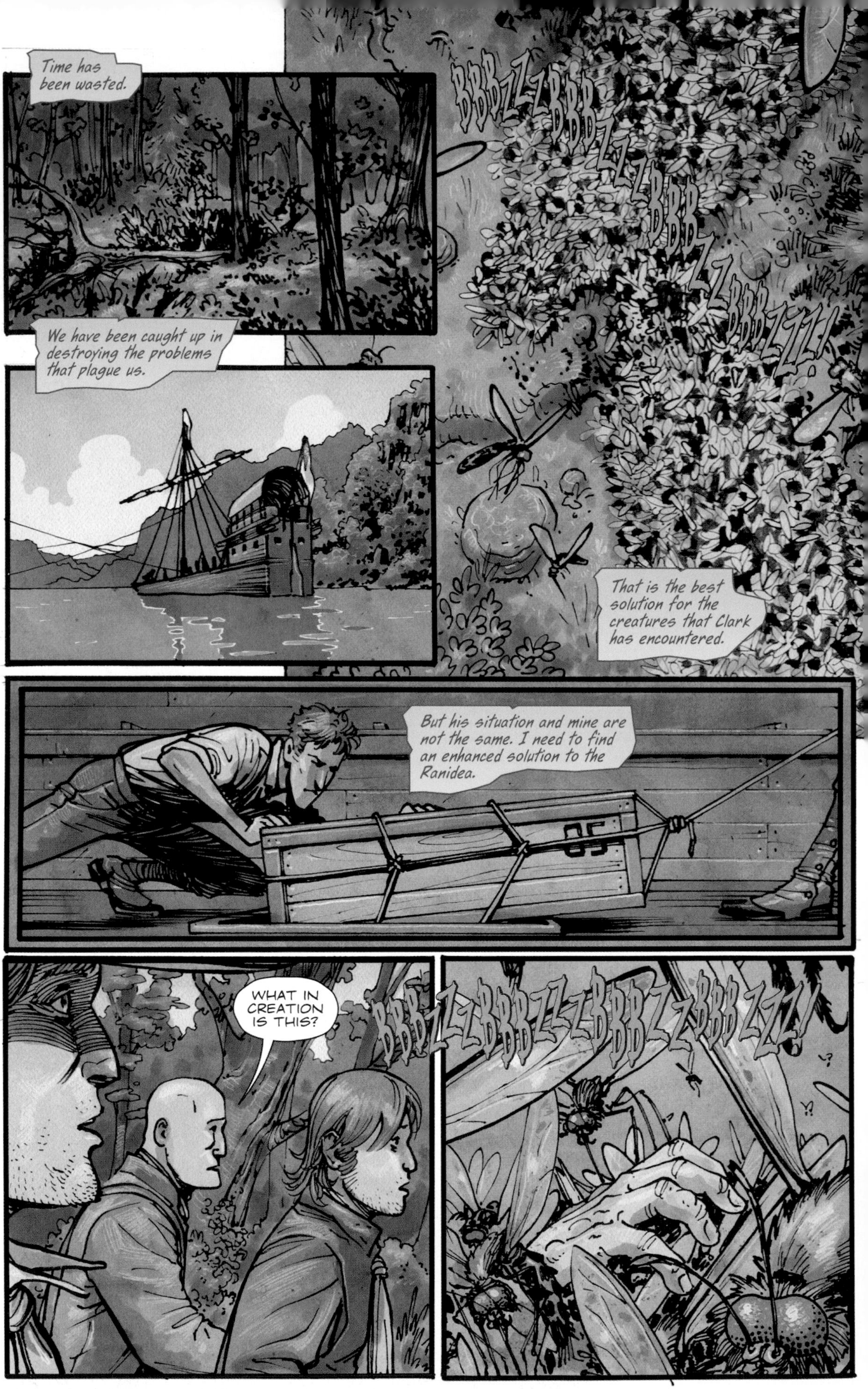
Time has been wasted.
We have been caught up in destroying the problems that plague us.
BBBZZZBBBZZZBBBZZBBBZZZ!
That is the best solution for the creatures that Clark has encountered.
But his situation and mine are not the same. I need to find an enhanced solution to the Ranidea.
WHAT IN CREATION IS THIS?
BBBZZZBBBZZZBBBZZBBBZZZ!

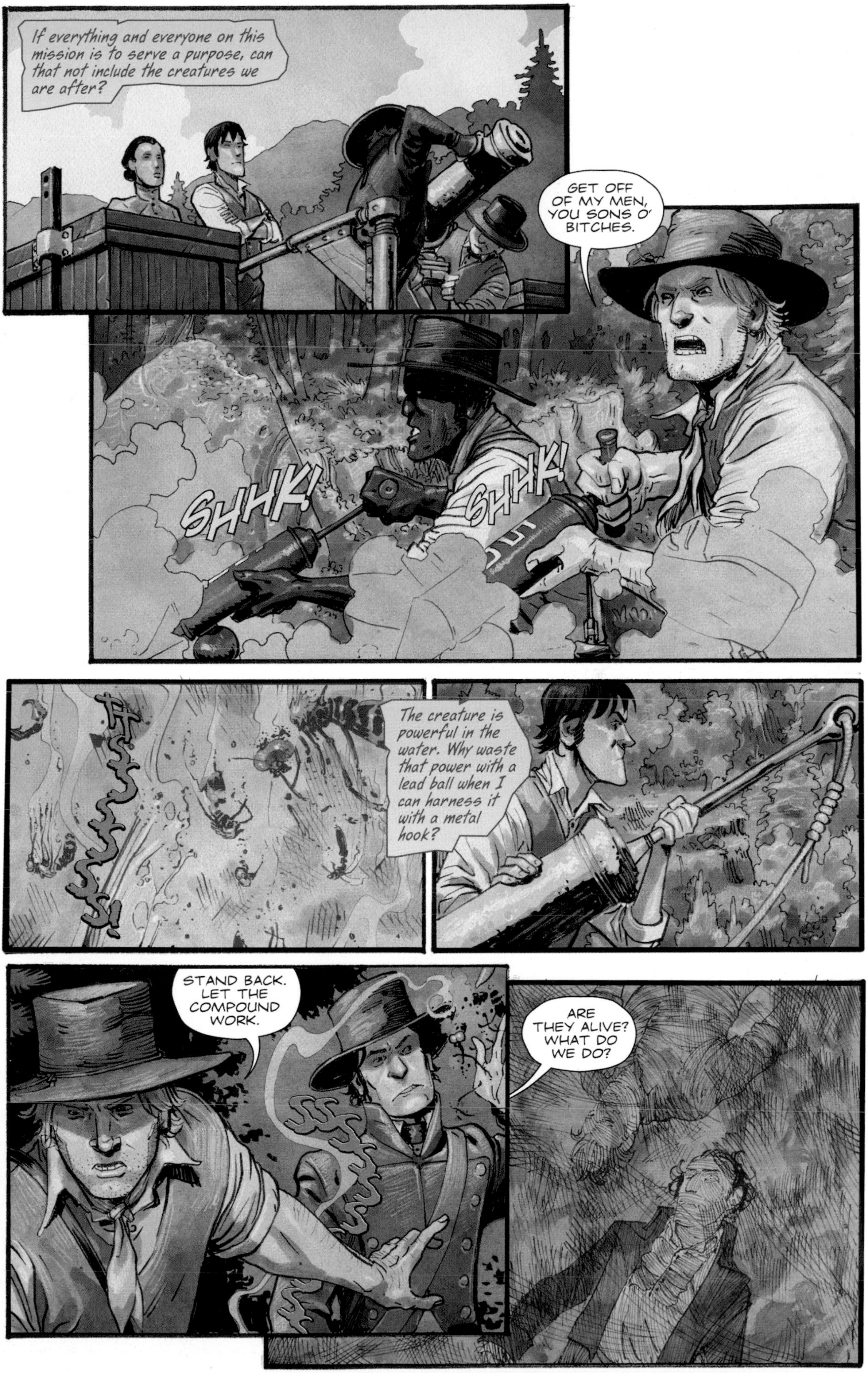
If everything and everyone on this mission is to serve a purpose, can that not include the creatures we are after?
GET OFF OF MY MEN, YOU SONS O' BITCHES.
SHHK!
SHHK!
HSSSSSS!
The creature is powerful in the water. Why waste that power with a lead ball when I can harness it with a metal hook?
STAND BACK. LET THE COMPOUND WORK.
ARE THEY ALIVE? WHAT DO WE DO?

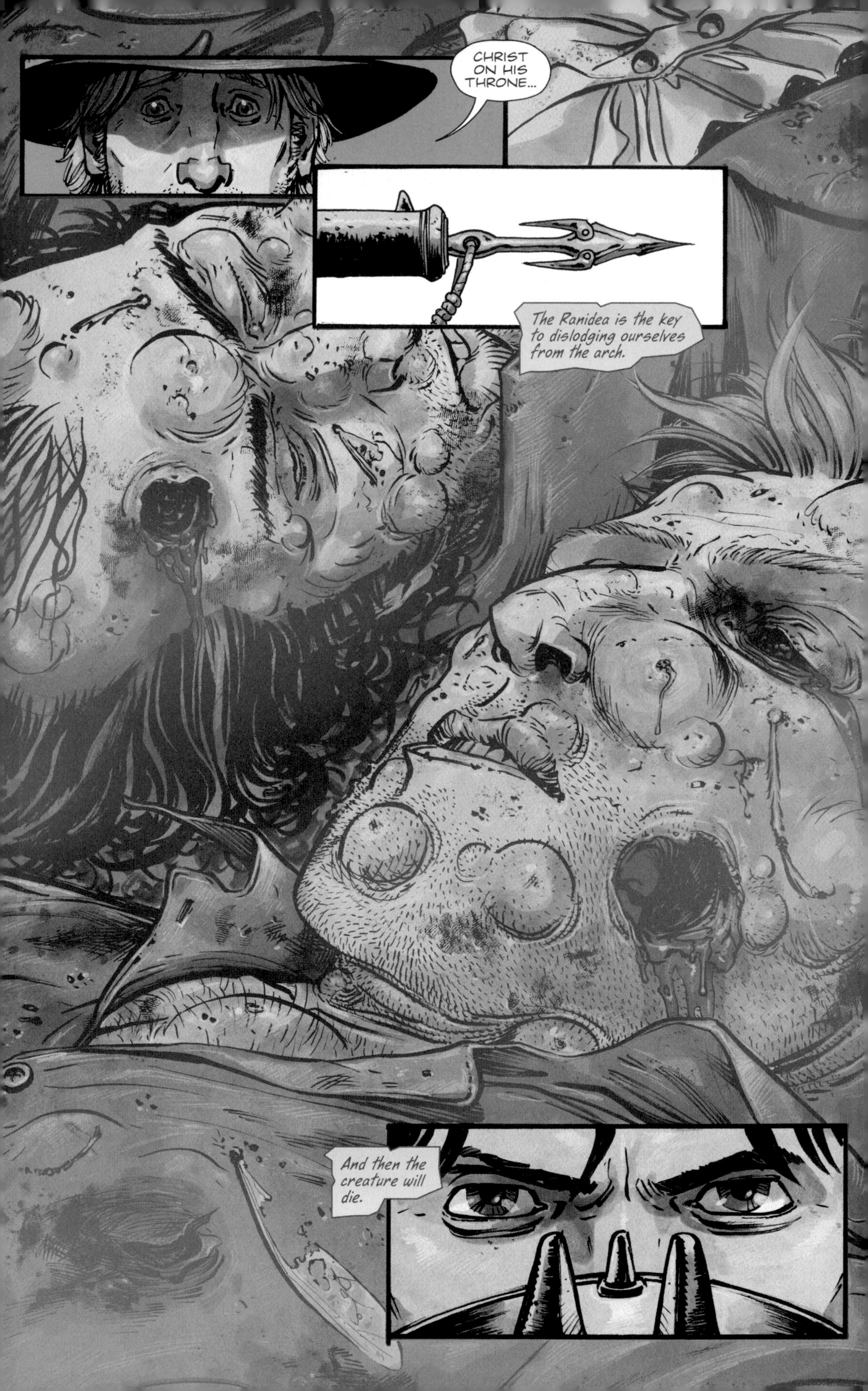
CHRIST ON HIS THRONE...
The Ranidea is the key to dislodging ourselves from the arch.
And then the creature will die.

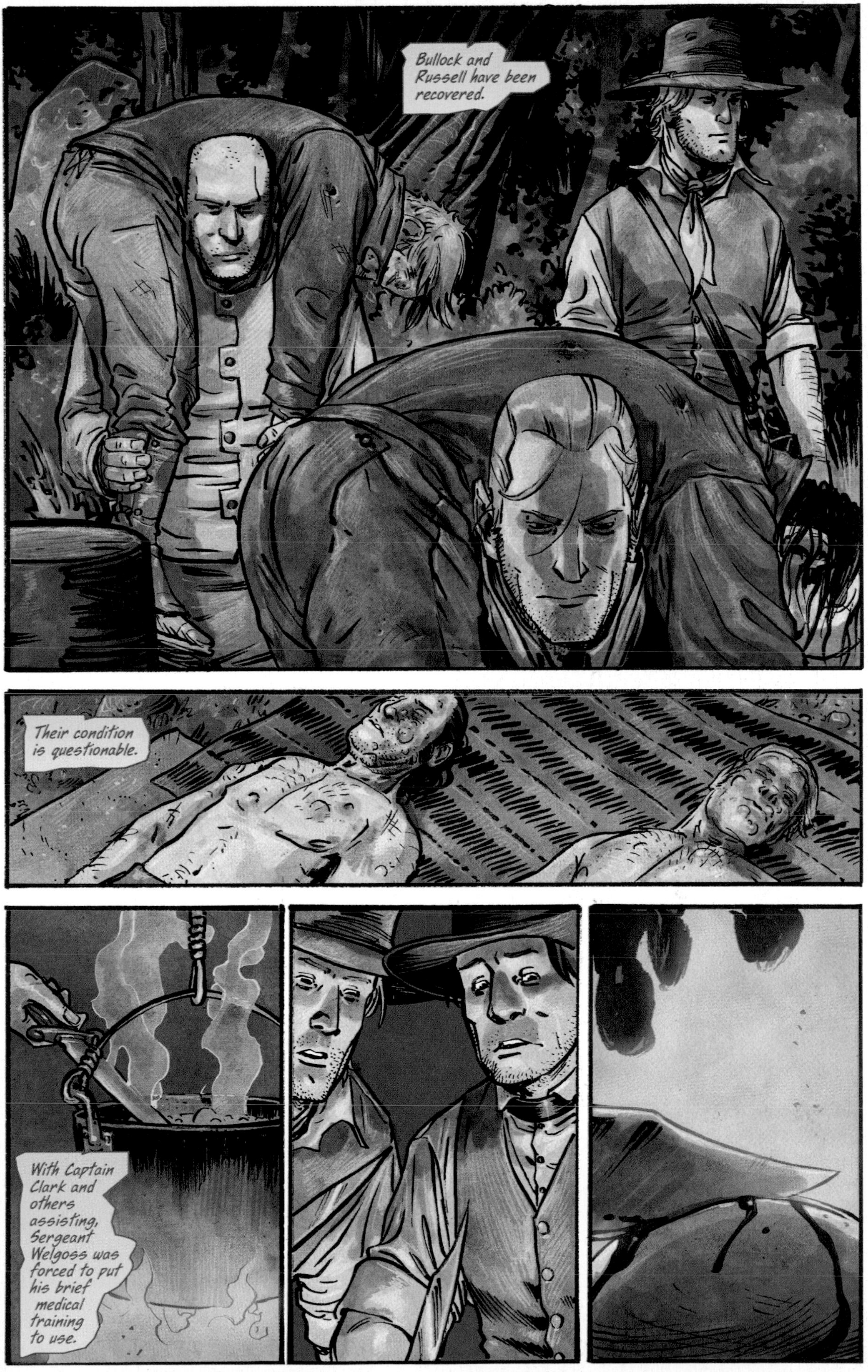
Bullock and Russell have been recovered.
Their condition is questionable.
With Captain Clark and others assisting, Sergeant Welgoss was forced to put his brief medical training to use.

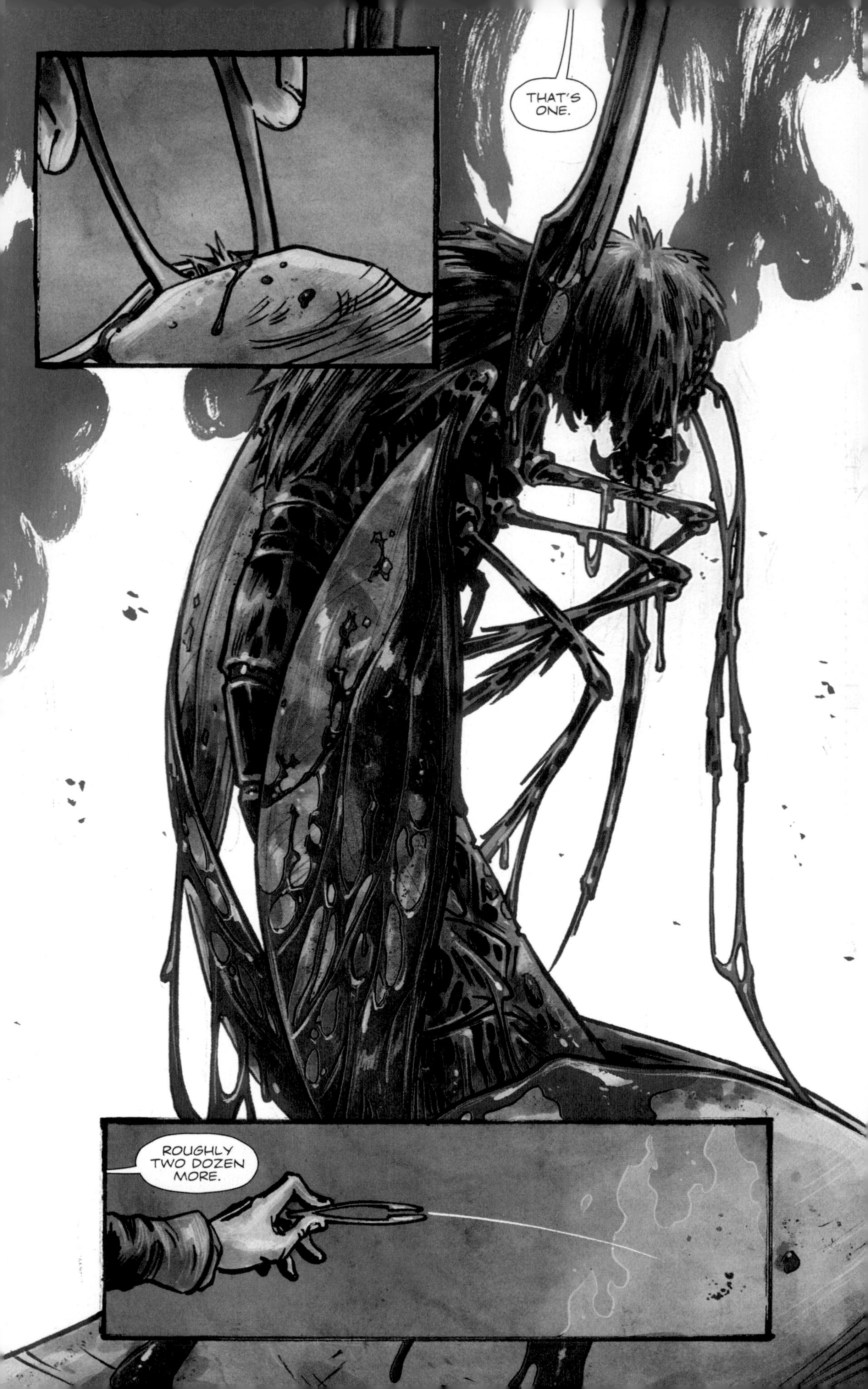
THAT'S ONE.
ROUGHLY TWO DOZEN MORE.

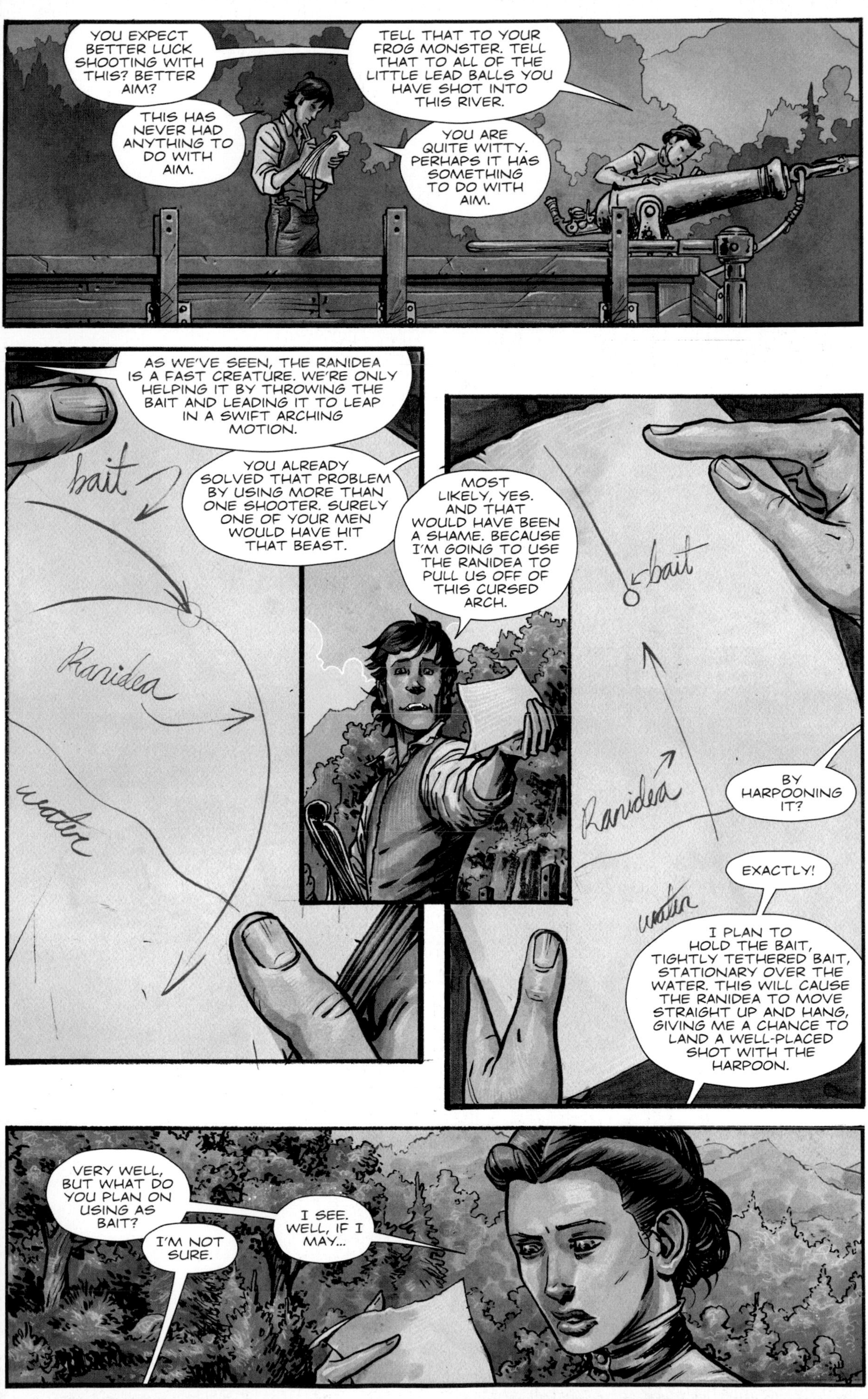
YOU EXPECT BETTER LUCK SHOOTING WITH THIS? BETTER AIM?
THIS HAS NEVER HAD ANYTHING TO DO WITH AIM.
TELL THAT TO YOUR FROG MONSTER. TELL THAT TO ALL OF THE LITTLE LEAD BALLS YOU HAVE SHOT INTO THIS RIVER.
YOU ARE QUITE WITTY. PERHAPS IT HAS SOMETHING TO DO WITH AIM.
AS WE'VE SEEN, THE RANIDEA IS A FAST CREATURE. WE'RE ONLY HELPING IT BY THROWING THE BAIT AND LEADING IT TO LEAP IN A SWIFT ARCHING MOTION.
bait
Ranidea
water
YOU ALREADY SOLVED THAT PROBLEM BY USING MORE THAN ONE SHOOTER. SURELY ONE OF YOUR MEN WOULD HAVE HIT THAT BEAST.
MOST LIKELY, YES. AND THAT WOULD HAVE BEEN A SHAME. BECAUSE I'M GOING TO USE THE RANIDEA TO PULL US OFF OF THIS CURSED ARCH.
bait
Ranidea
water
BY HARPOONING IT?
EXACTLY!
I PLAN TO HOLD THE BAIT, TIGHTLY TETHERED BAIT, STATIONARY OVER THE WATER. THIS WILL CAUSE THE RANIDEA TO MOVE STRAIGHT UP AND HANG, GIVING ME A CHANCE TO LAND A WELL-PLACED SHOT WITH THE HARPOON.
VERY WELL, BUT WHAT DO YOU PLAN ON USING AS BAIT?
I'M NOT SURE.
I SEE. WELL, IF I MAY...

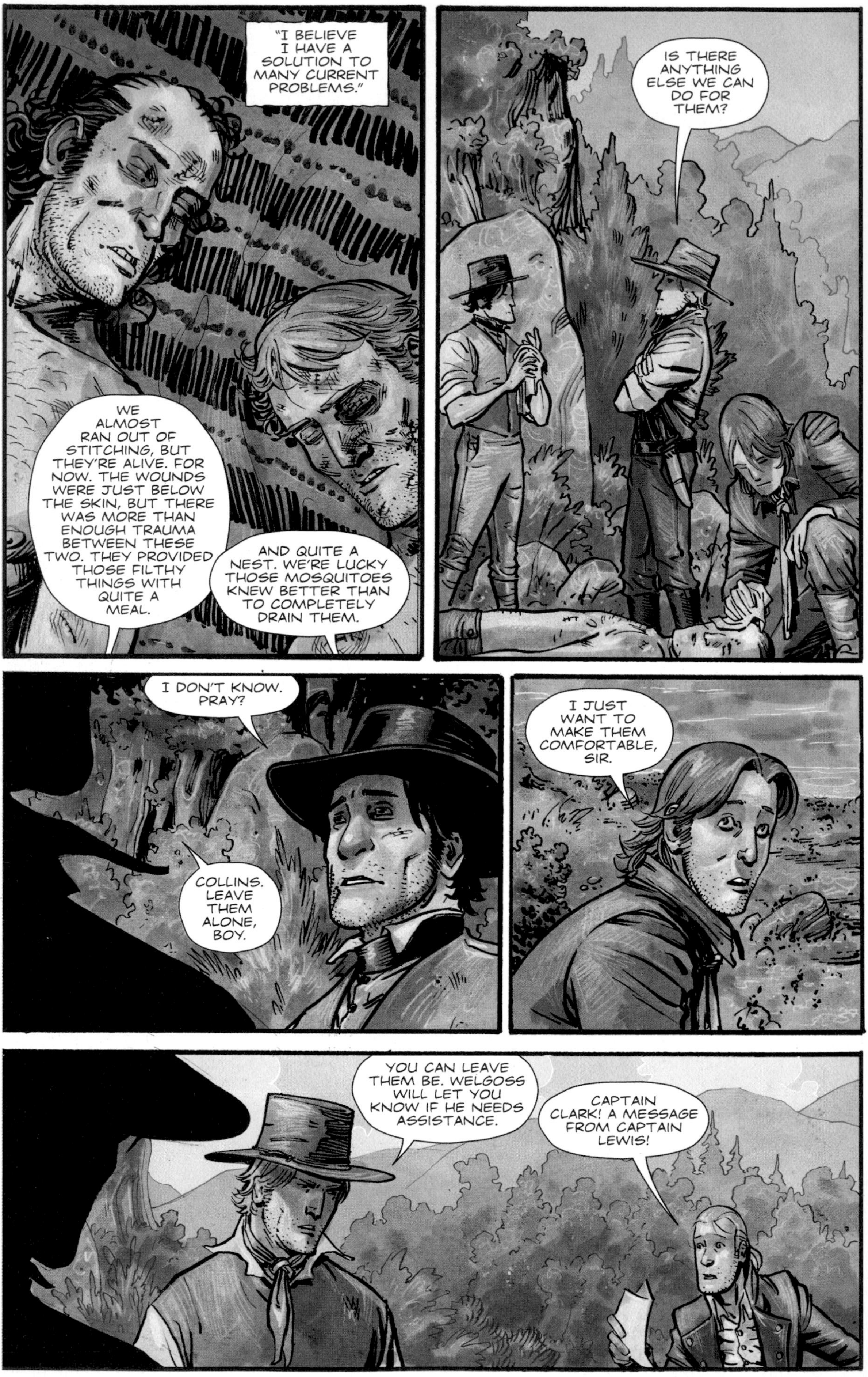
"I BELIEVE I HAVE A SOLUTION TO MANY CURRENT PROBLEMS."
WE ALMOST RAN OUT OF STITCHING, BUT THEY'RE ALIVE. FOR NOW. THE WOUNDS WERE JUST BELOW THE SKIN, BUT THERE WAS MORE THAN ENOUGH TRAUMA BETWEEN THESE TWO. THEY PROVIDED THOSE FILTHY THINGS WITH QUITE A MEAL.
AND QUITE A NEST. WE'RE LUCKY THOSE MOSQUITOES KNEW BETTER THAN TO COMPLETELY DRAIN THEM.
IS THERE ANYTHING ELSE WE CAN DO FOR THEM?
I DON'T KNOW. PRAY?
COLLINS. LEAVE THEM ALONE, BOY.
I JUST WANT TO MAKE THEM COMFORTABLE, SIR.
YOU CAN LEAVE THEM BE. WELGOSS WILL LET YOU KNOW IF HE NEEDS ASSISTANCE.
CAPTAIN CLARK! A MESSAGE FROM CAPTAIN LEWIS!

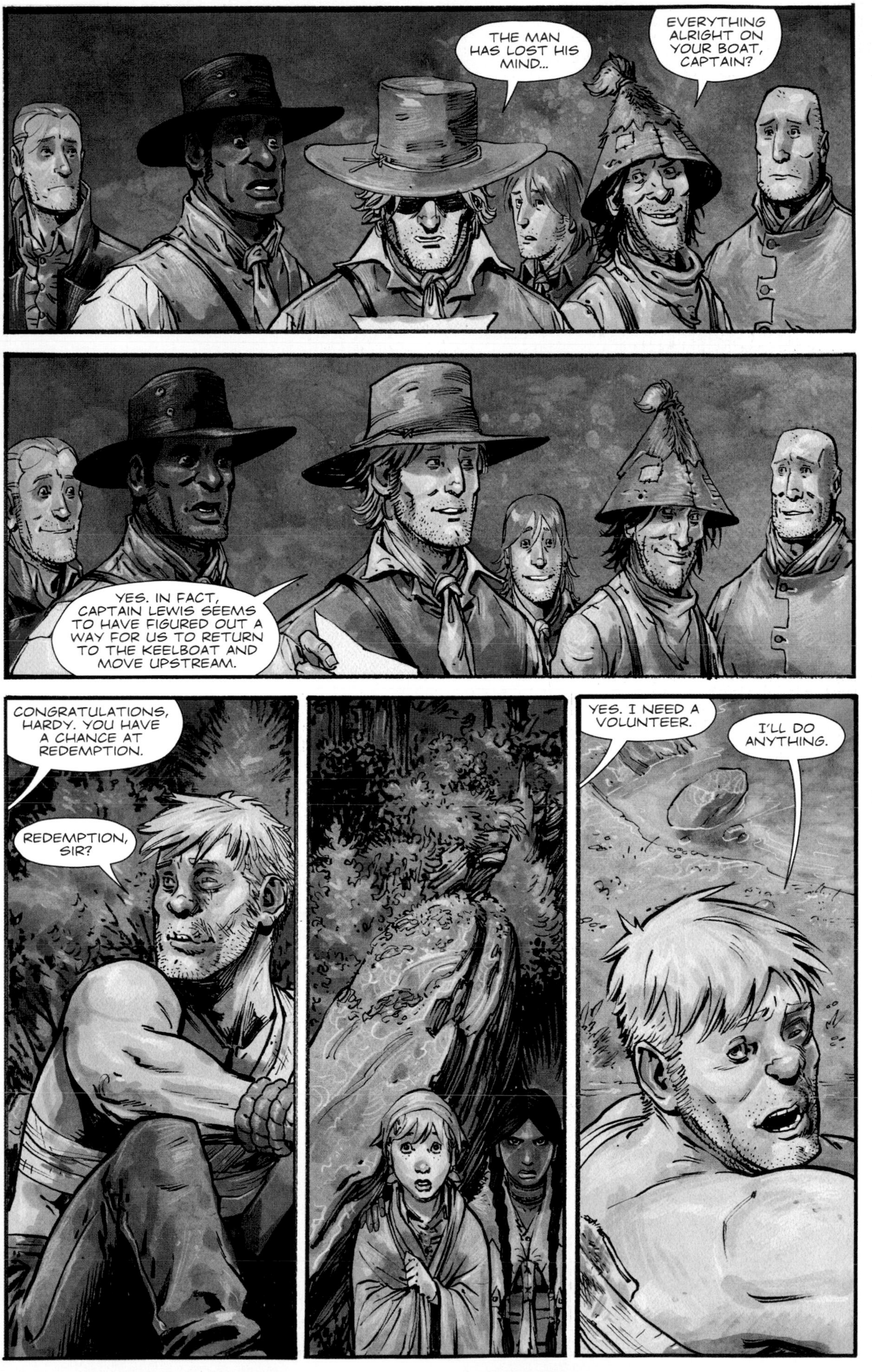
THE MAN HAS LOST HIS MIND...
EVERYTHING ALRIGHT ON YOUR BOAT, CAPTAIN?
YES. IN FACT, CAPTAIN LEWIS SEEMS TO HAVE FIGURED OUT A WAY FOR US TO RETURN TO THE KEELBOAT AND MOVE UPSTREAM.
CONGRATULATIONS, HARDY. YOU HAVE A CHANCE AT REDEMPTION.
REDEMPTION, SIR?
YES. I NEED A VOLUNTEER.
I'LL DO ANYTHING.

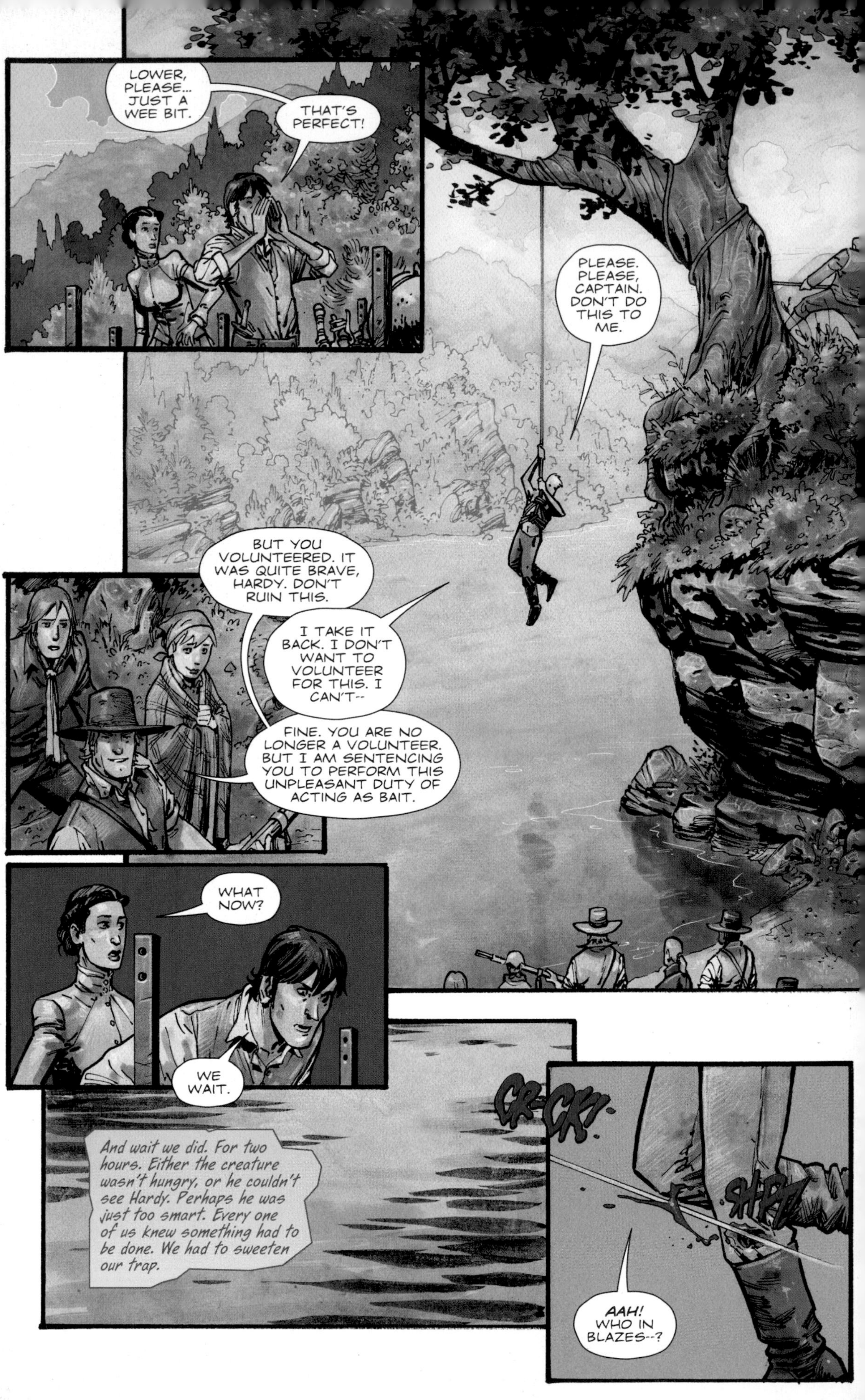

LOWER, PLEASE... JUST A WEE BIT.
THAT'S PERFECT!
PLEASE. PLEASE, CAPTAIN. DON'T DO THIS TO ME.
BUT YOU VOLUNTEERED. IT WAS QUITE BRAVE, HARDY. DON'T RUIN THIS.
I TAKE IT BACK. I DON'T WANT TO VOLUNTEER FOR THIS. I CAN'T--
FINE. YOU ARE NO LONGER A VOLUNTEER. BUT I AM SENTENCING YOU TO PERFORM THIS UNPLEASANT DUTY OF ACTING AS BAIT.
WHAT NOW?
WE WAIT.
And wait we did. For two hours. Either the creature wasn't hungry, or he couldn't see Hardy. Perhaps he was just too smart. Every one of us knew something had to be done. We had to sweeten our trap.
CR-CK!
SHPT!
AAH! WHO IN BLAZES--?

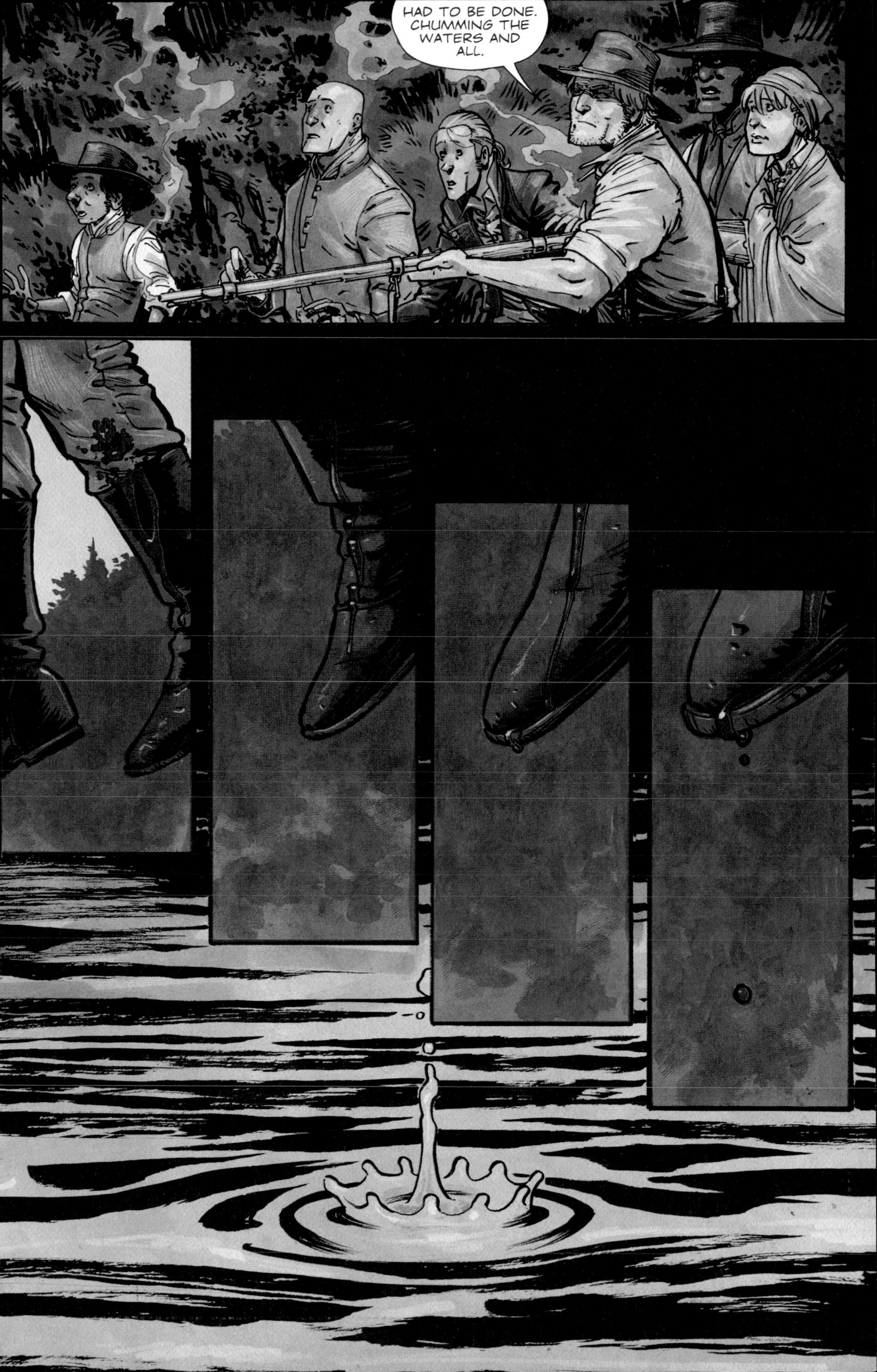
HAD TO BE DONE. CHUMMING THE WATERS AND ALL.

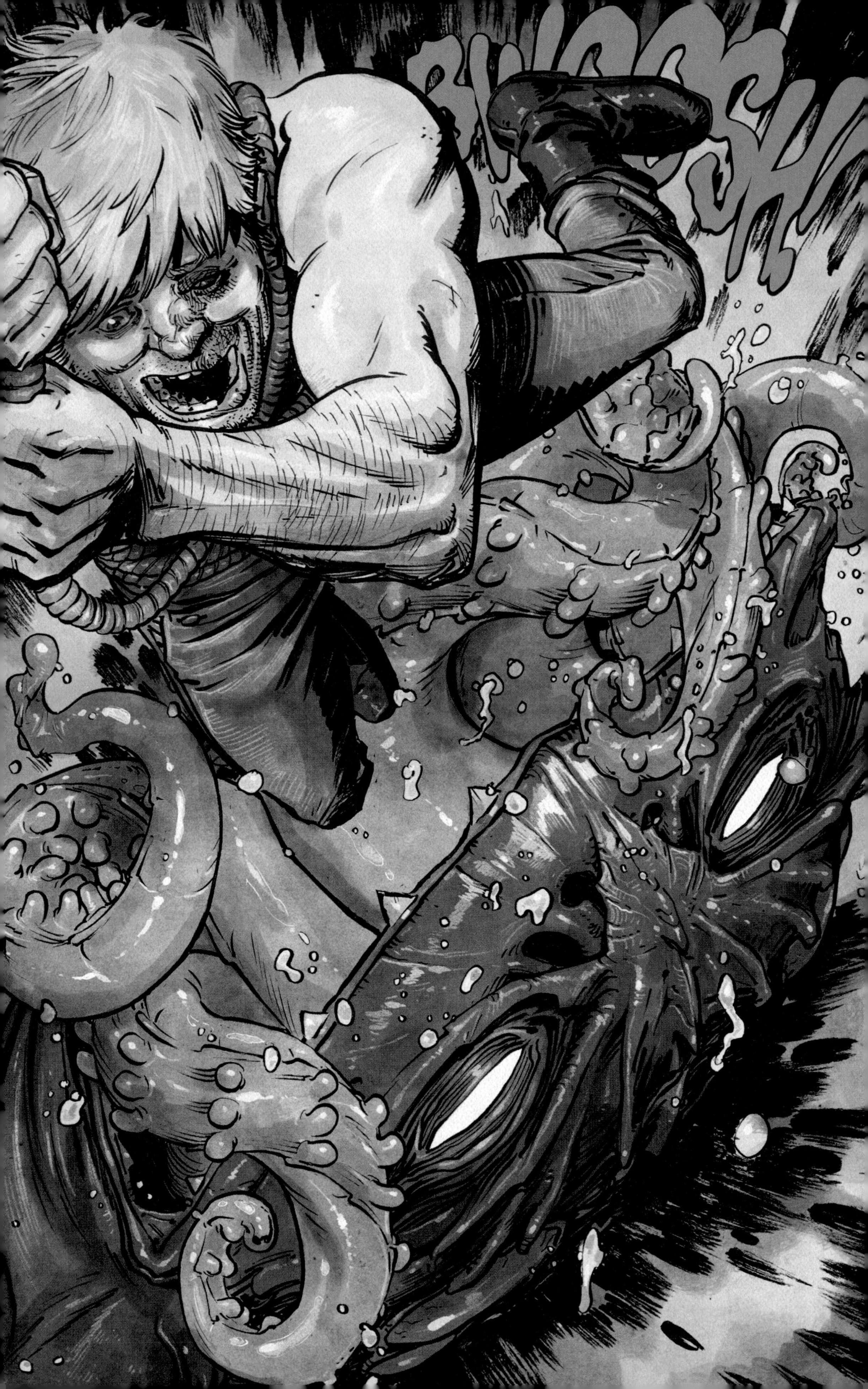
BWOOSH!

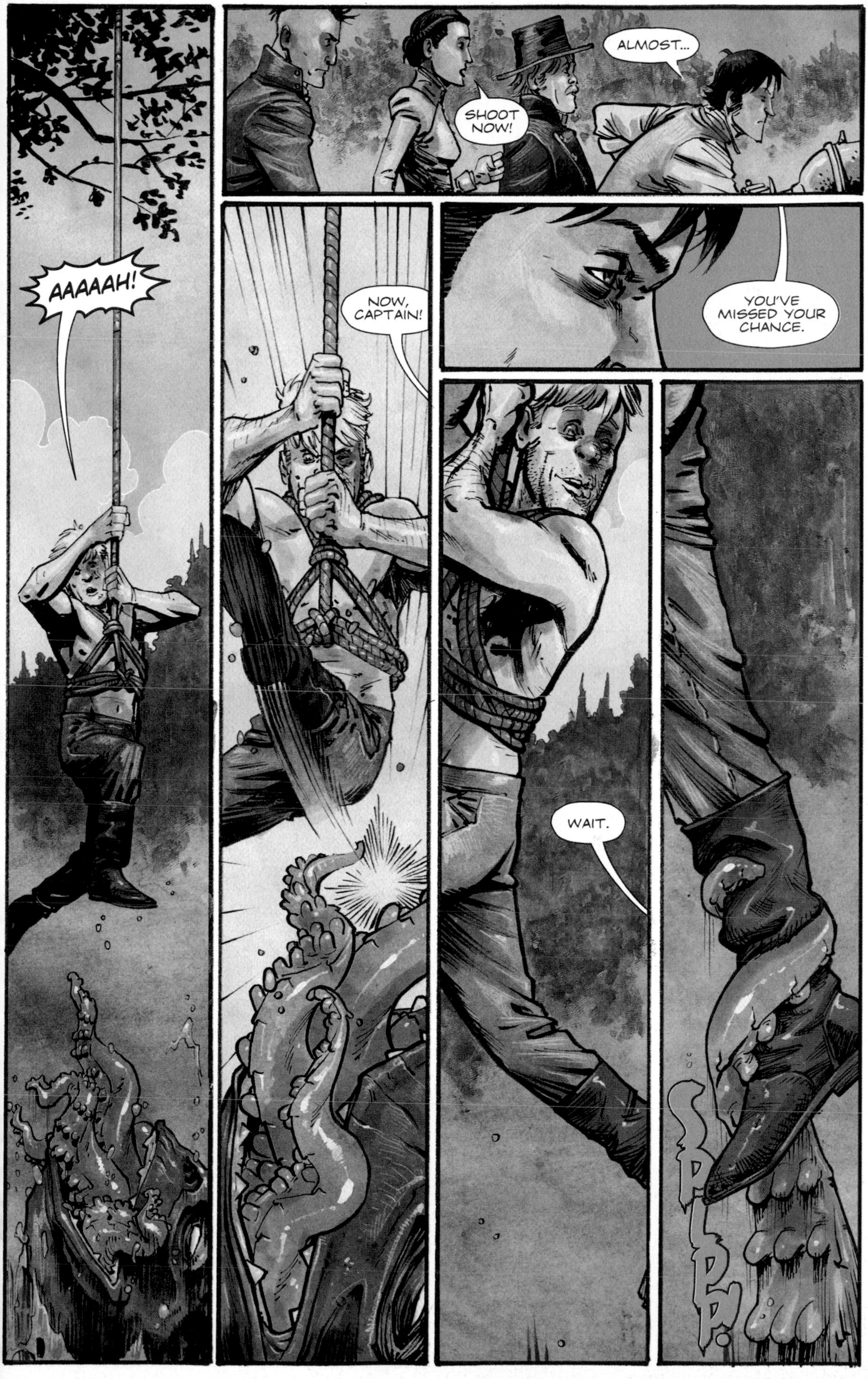
ALMOST...
SHOOT NOW!
AAAAAH!
NOW, CAPTAIN!
YOU'VE MISSED YOUR CHANCE.
WAIT.
SPLP.

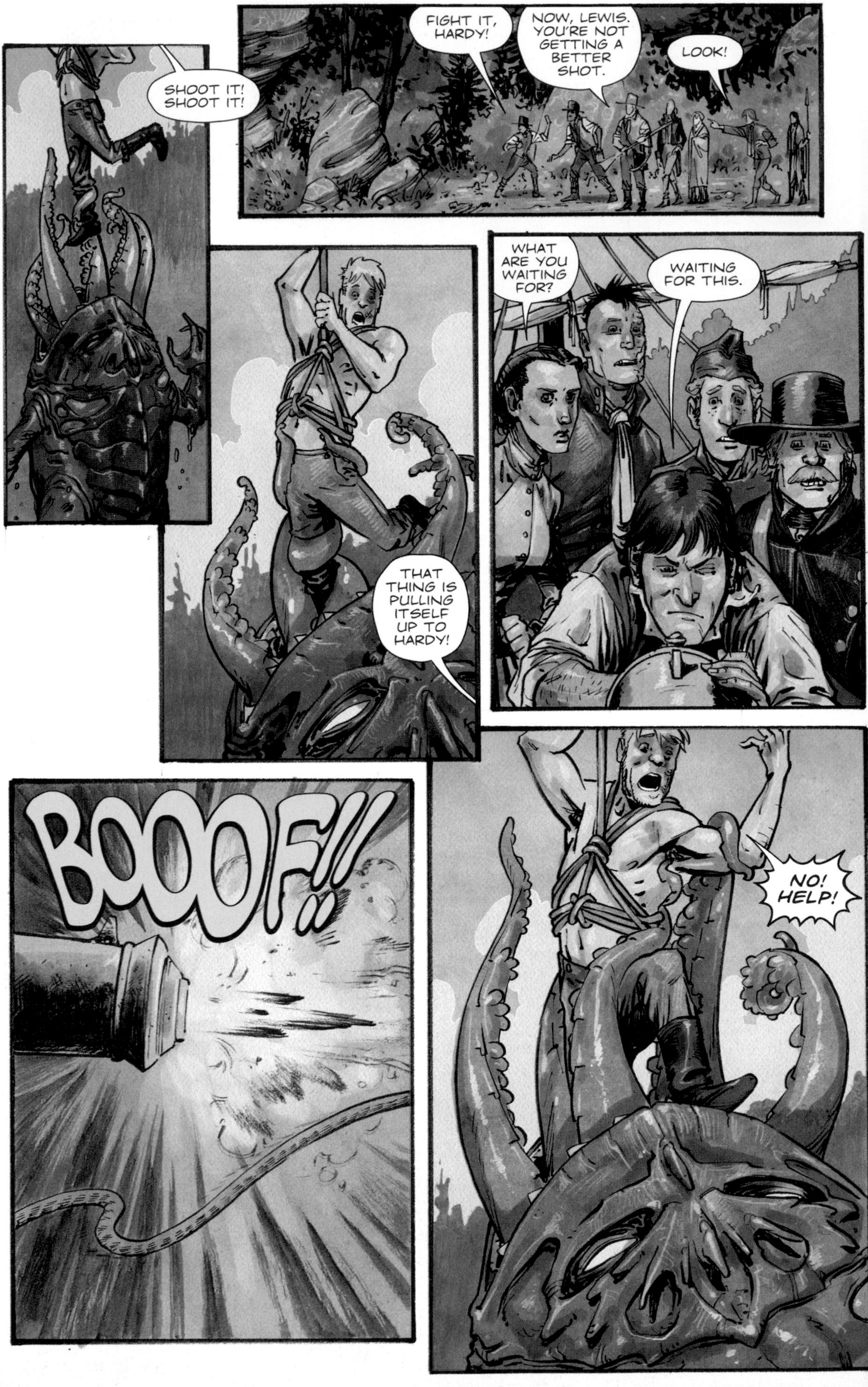
SHOOT IT! SHOOT IT!
FIGHT IT, HARDY!
NOW, LEWIS. YOU'RE NOT GETTING A BETTER SHOT.
LOOK!
THAT THING IS PULLING ITSELF UP TO HARDY!
WHAT ARE YOU WAITING FOR?
WAITING FOR THIS.
BOOOF!!
NO! HELP!

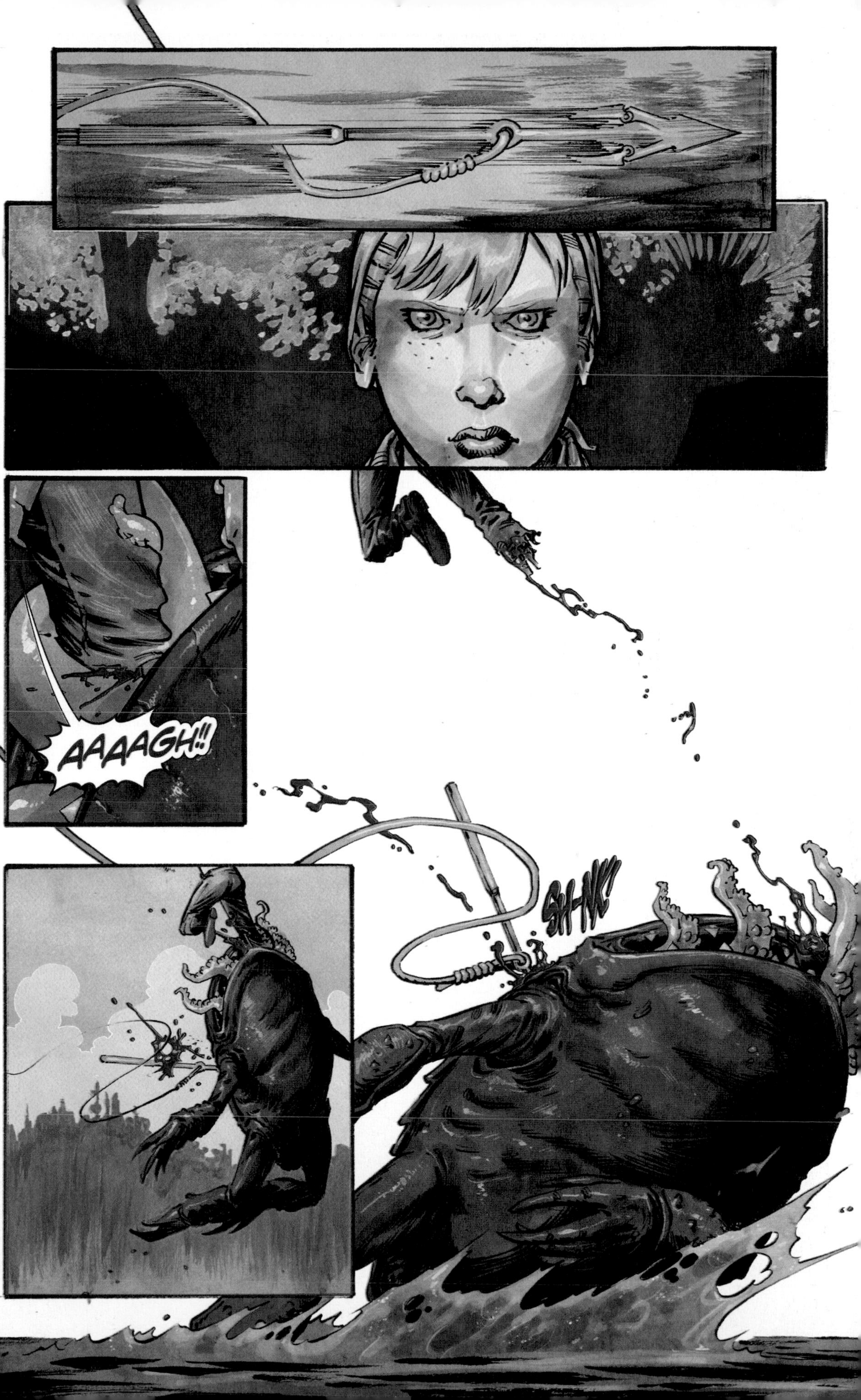
AAAAGH!!
SH-NK!

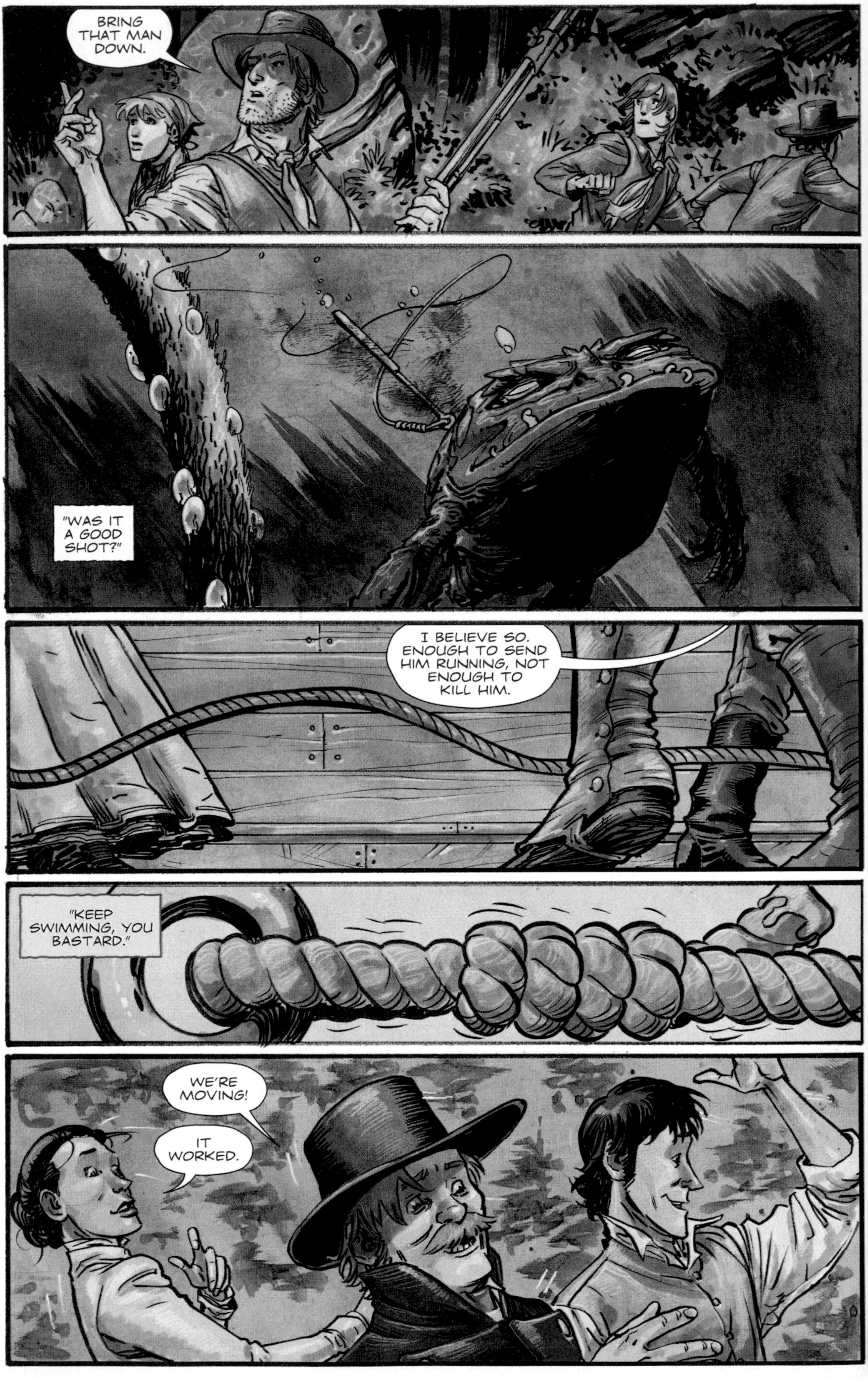
BRING THAT MAN DOWN.
"WAS IT A GOOD SHOT?"
I BELIEVE SO. ENOUGH TO SEND HIM RUNNING, NOT ENOUGH TO KILL HIM.
"KEEP SWIMMING, YOU BASTARD."
WE'RE MOVING!
IT WORKED.

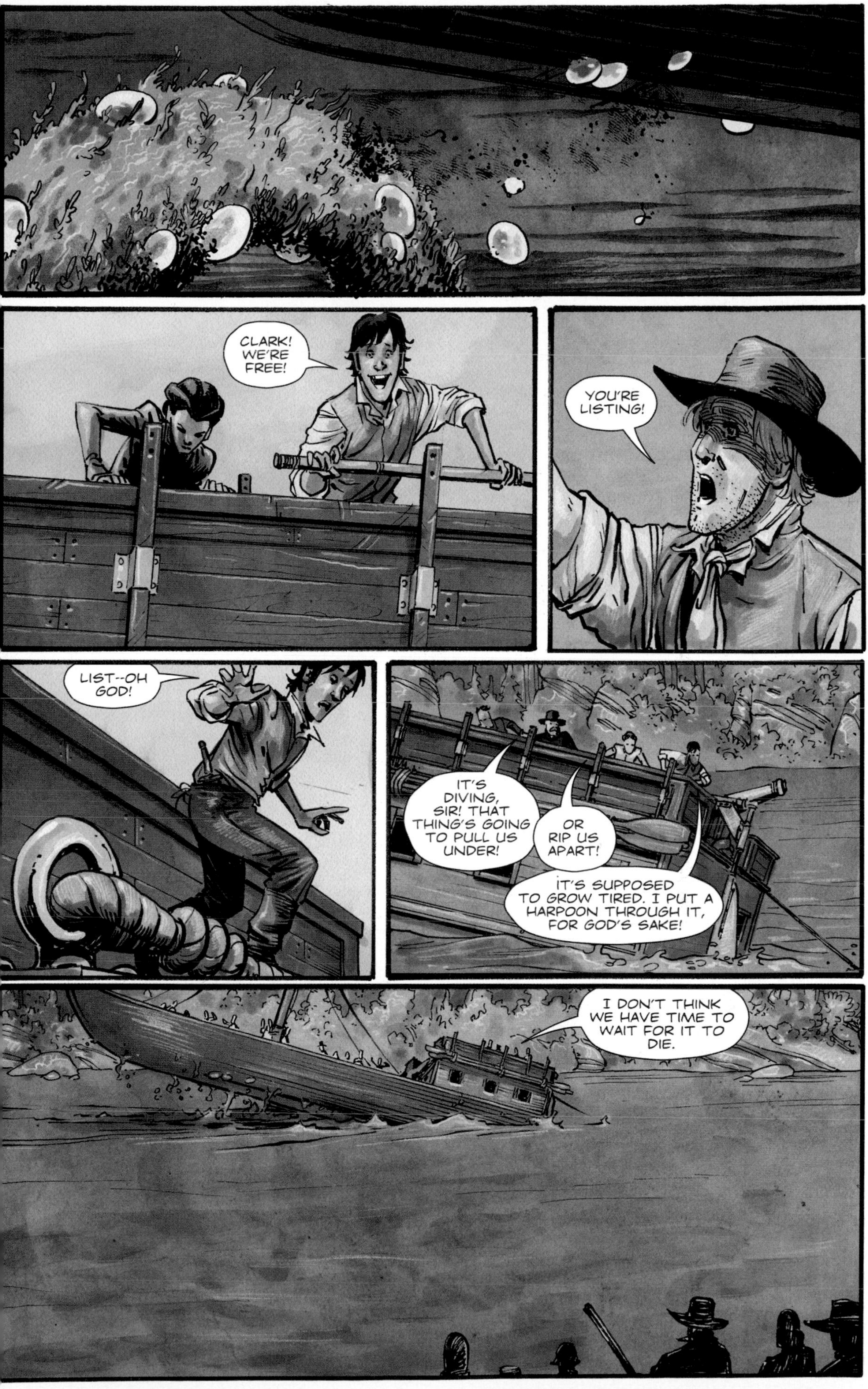
CLARK! WE'RE FREE!
YOU'RE LISTING!
LIST--OH GOD!
IT'S DIVING, SIR! THAT THING'S GOING TO PULL US UNDER!
OR RIP US APART!
IT'S SUPPOSED TO GROW TIRED. I PUT A HARPOON THROUGH IT, FOR GOD'S SAKE!
I DON'T THINK WE HAVE TIME TO WAIT FOR IT TO DIE.

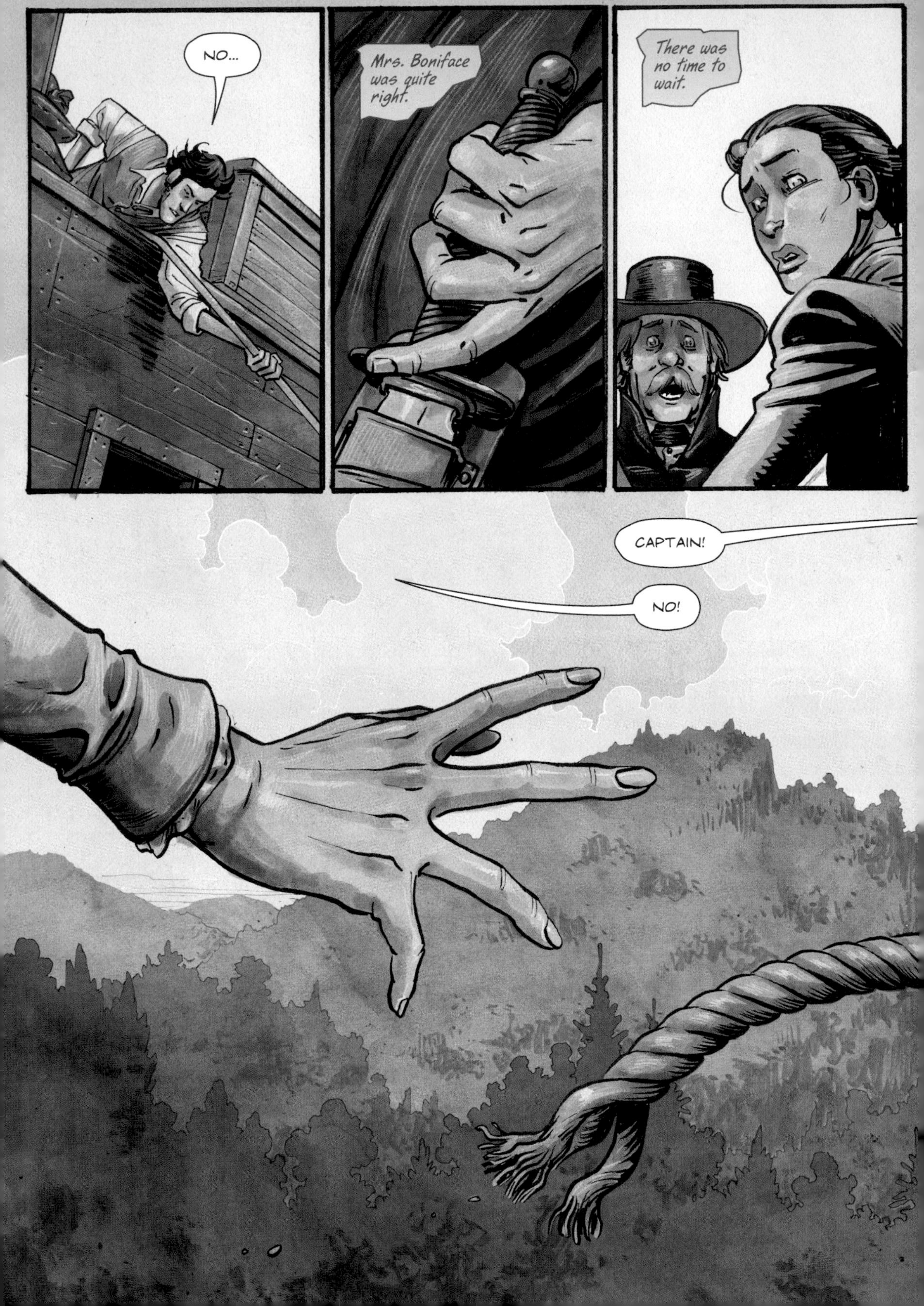
NO...
Mrs. Boniface was quite right.
There was no time to wait.
CAPTAIN!
NO!

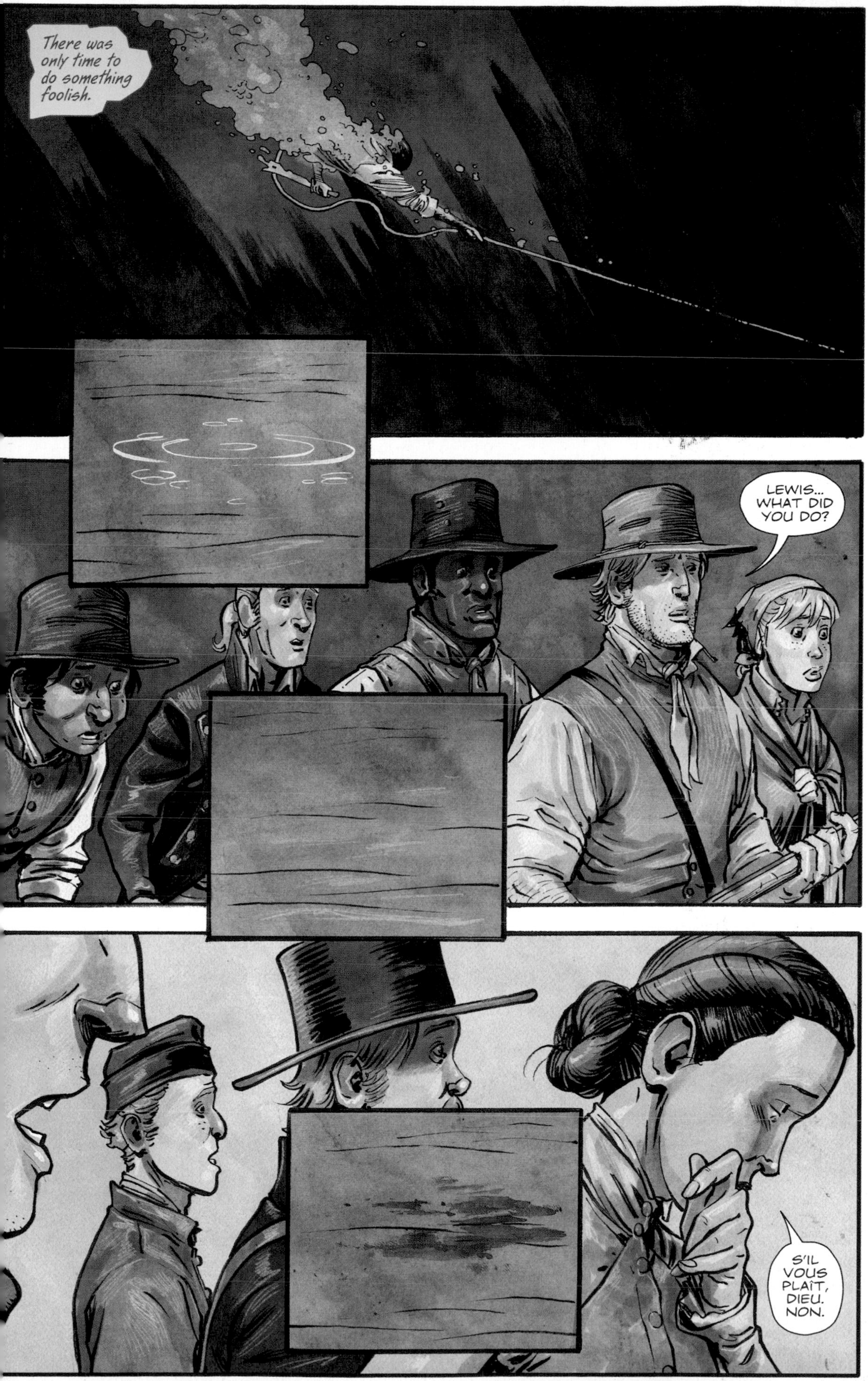
There was only time to do something foolish.
LEWIS... WHAT DID YOU DO?
S'IL VOUS PLAÎT, DIEU. NON.

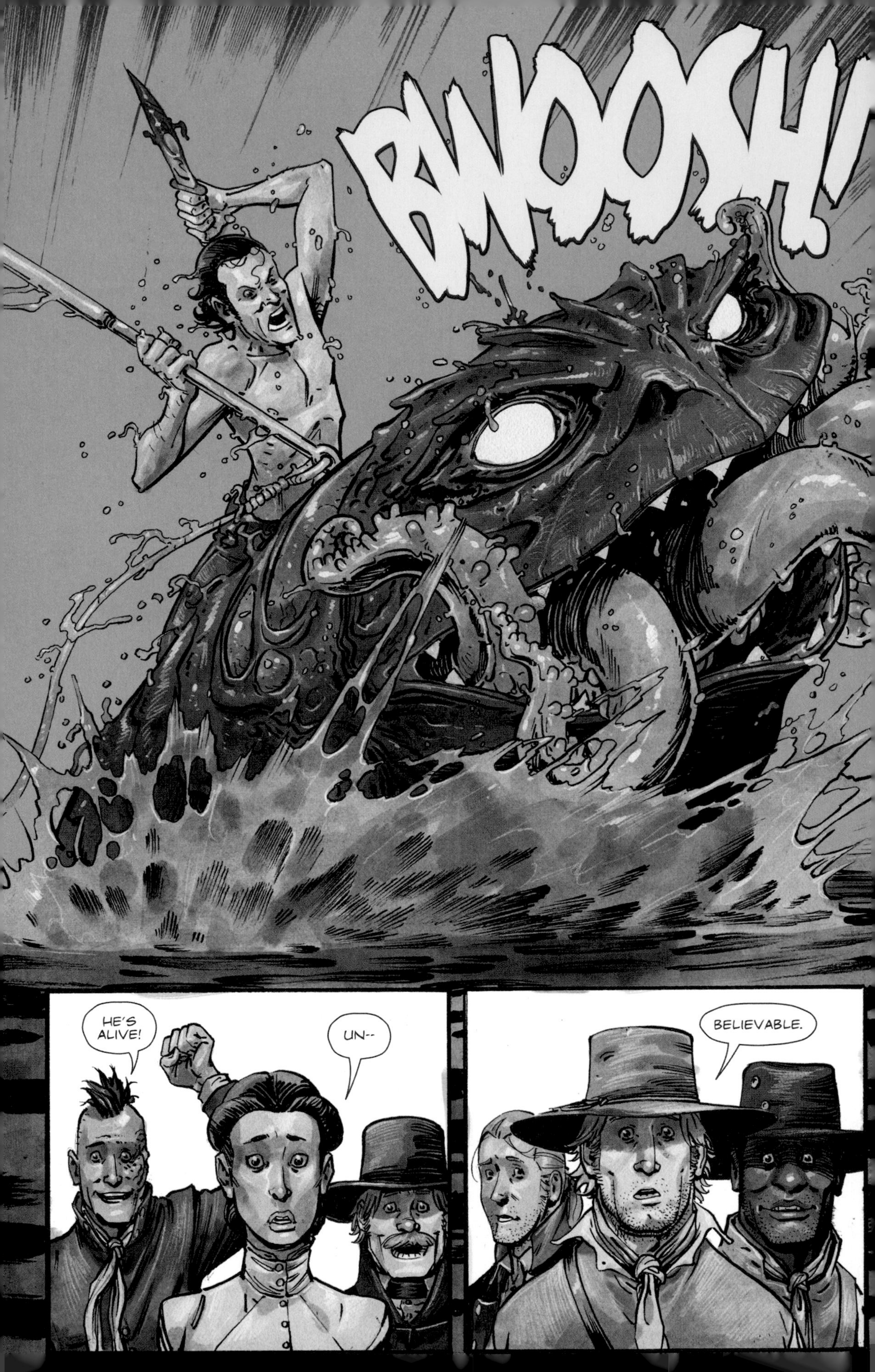
BWOOSH!
HE'S ALIVE!
UN--
BELIEVABLE.

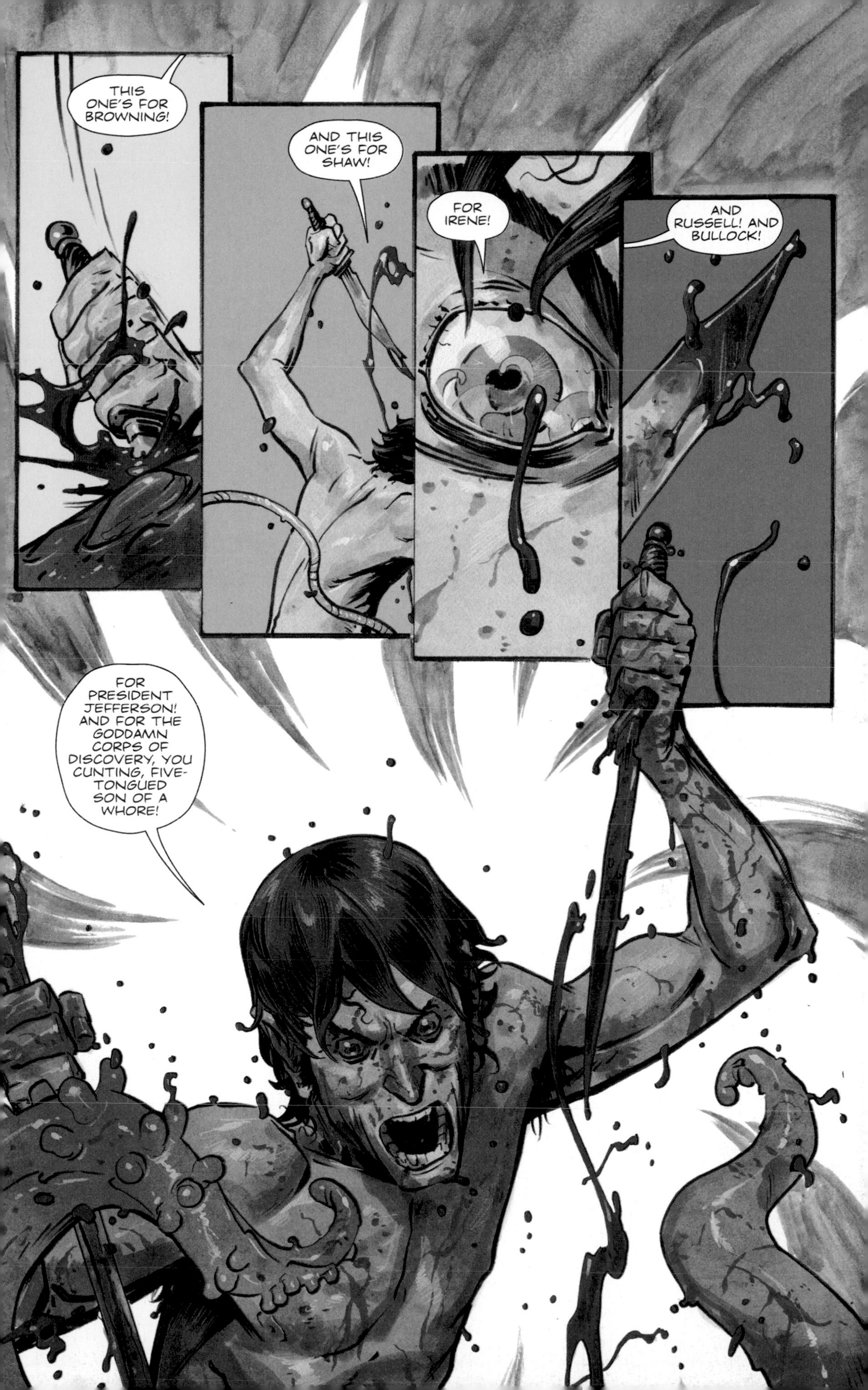
THIS ONE'S FOR BROWNING!
AND THIS ONE'S FOR SHAW!
FOR IRENE!
AND RUSSELL! AND BULLOCK!
FOR PRESIDENT JEFFERSON! AND FOR THE GODDAMN CORPS OF DISCOVERY, YOU CUNTING, FIVE-TONGUED SON OF A WHORE!

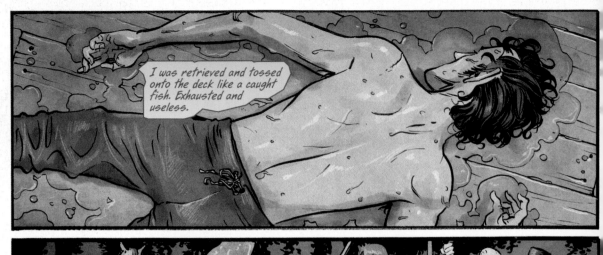

I was retrieved and tossed onto the deck like a caught fish. Exhausted and useless.

The men evacuated the shore. Hardy was clinging to life.

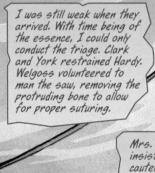

I was still weak when they arrived. With time being of the essence, I could only conduct the triage. Clark and York restrained Hardy. Welgoss volunteered to man the saw, removing the protruding bone to allow for proper suturing.

Mrs. Boniface insisted on cauterizing the wound. She claims to have done this many times in her village, for limbs lost to faulty traps.

I do not want to believe she took pleasure in Hardy's pain, but I could understand if she did.

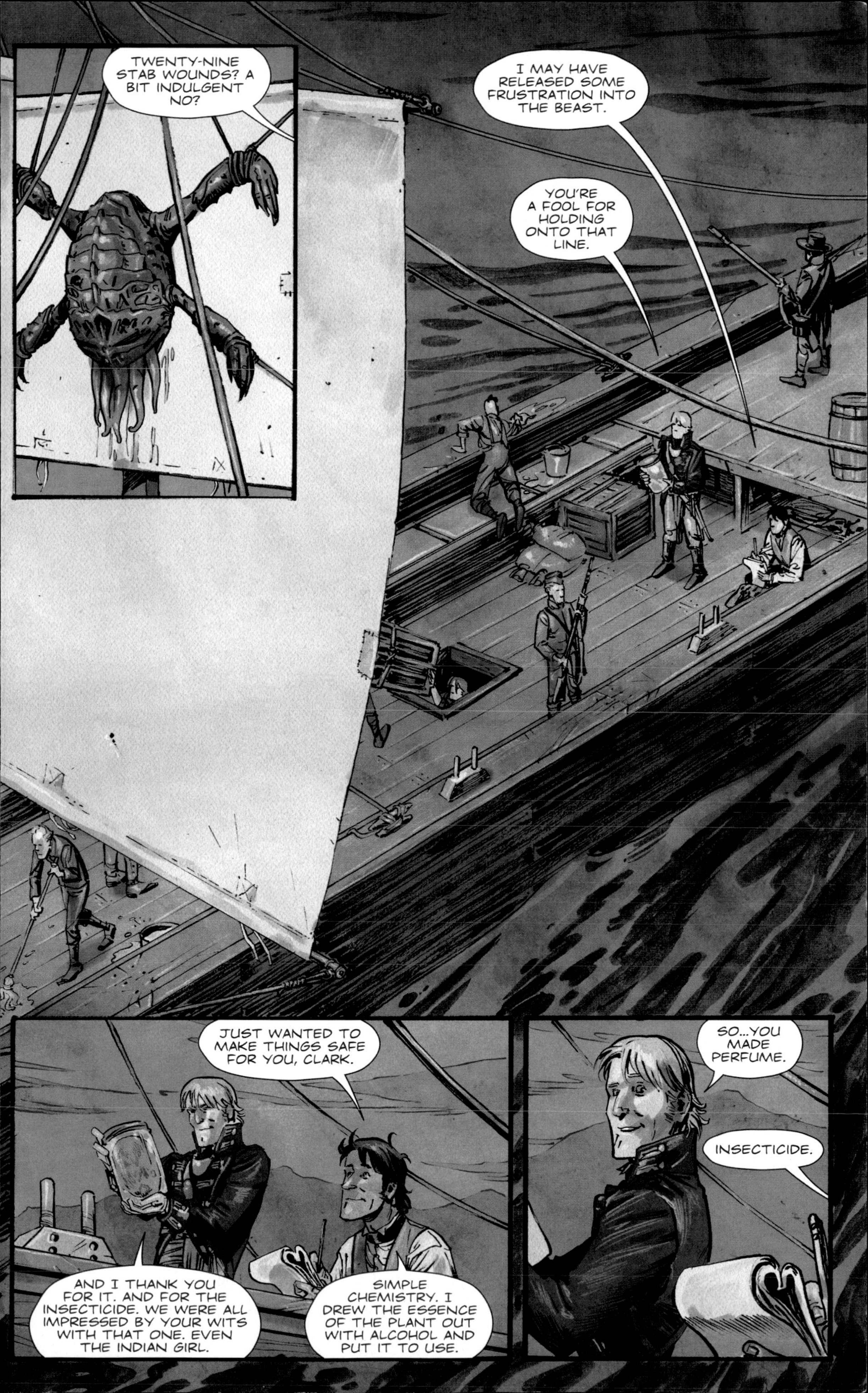
TWENTY-NINE STAB WOUNDS? A BIT INDULGENT NO?
I MAY HAVE RELEASED SOME FRUSTRATION INTO THE BEAST.
YOU'RE A FOOL FOR HOLDING ONTO THAT LINE.
JUST WANTED TO MAKE THINGS SAFE FOR YOU, CLARK.
AND I THANK YOU FOR IT. AND FOR THE INSECTICIDE. WE WERE ALL IMPRESSED BY YOUR WITS WITH THAT ONE. EVEN THE INDIAN GIRL.
SIMPLE CHEMISTRY. I DREW THE ESSENCE OF THE PLANT OUT WITH ALCOHOL AND PUT IT TO USE.
SO...YOU MADE PERFUME.
INSECTICIDE.

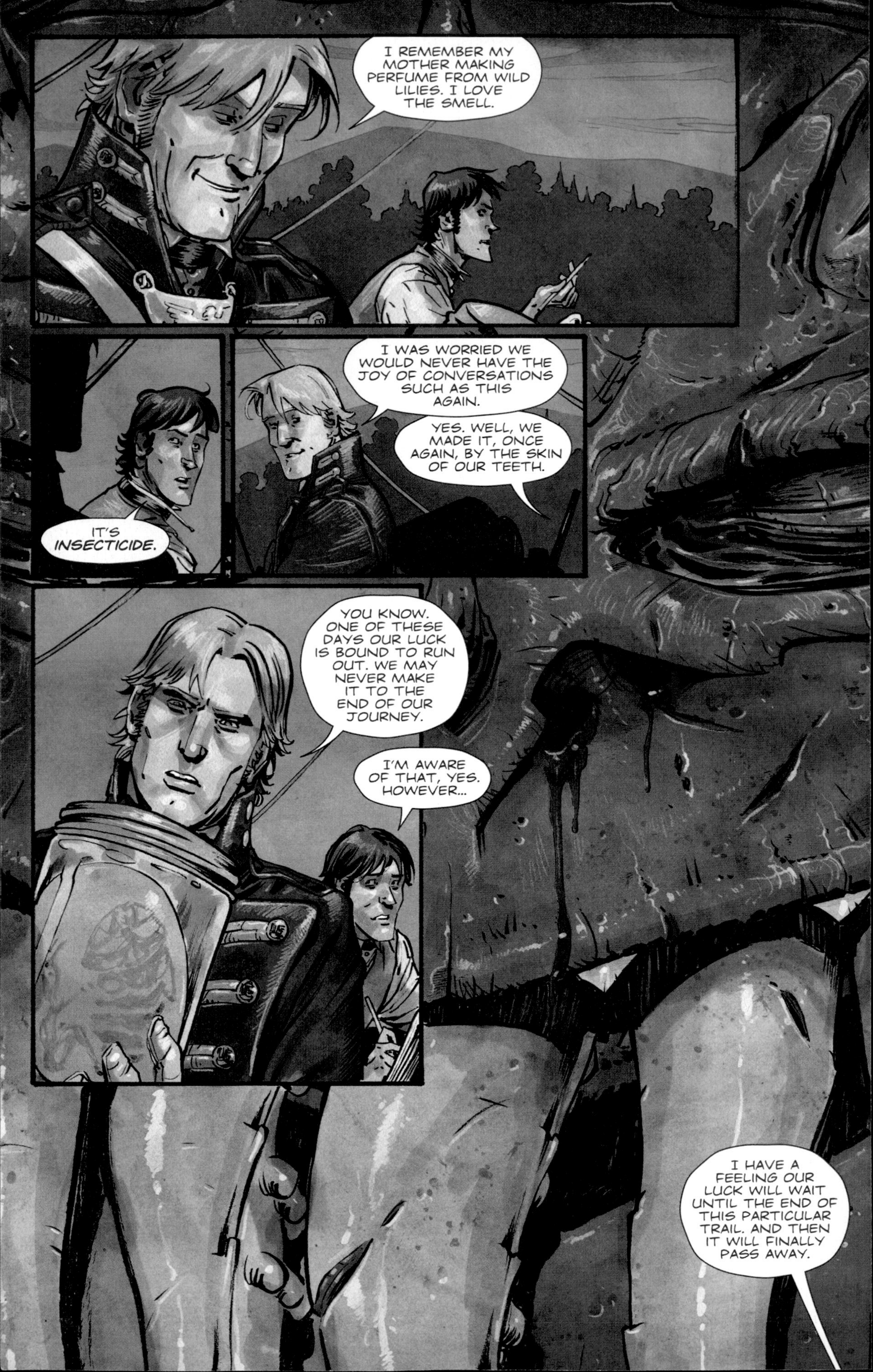
I REMEMBER MY MOTHER MAKING PERFUME FROM WILD LILIES. I LOVE THE SMELL.
IT'S INSECTICIDE.
I WAS WORRIED WE WOULD NEVER HAVE THE JOY OF CONVERSATIONS SUCH AS THIS AGAIN.
YES. WELL, WE MADE IT, ONCE AGAIN, BY THE SKIN OF OUR TEETH.
YOU KNOW. ONE OF THESE DAYS OUR LUCK IS BOUND TO RUN OUT. WE MAY NEVER MAKE IT TO THE END OF OUR JOURNEY.
I'M AWARE OF THAT, YES. HOWEVER...
I HAVE A FEELING OUR LUCK WILL WAIT UNTIL THE END OF THIS PARTICULAR TRAIL. AND THEN IT WILL FINALLY PASS AWAY.

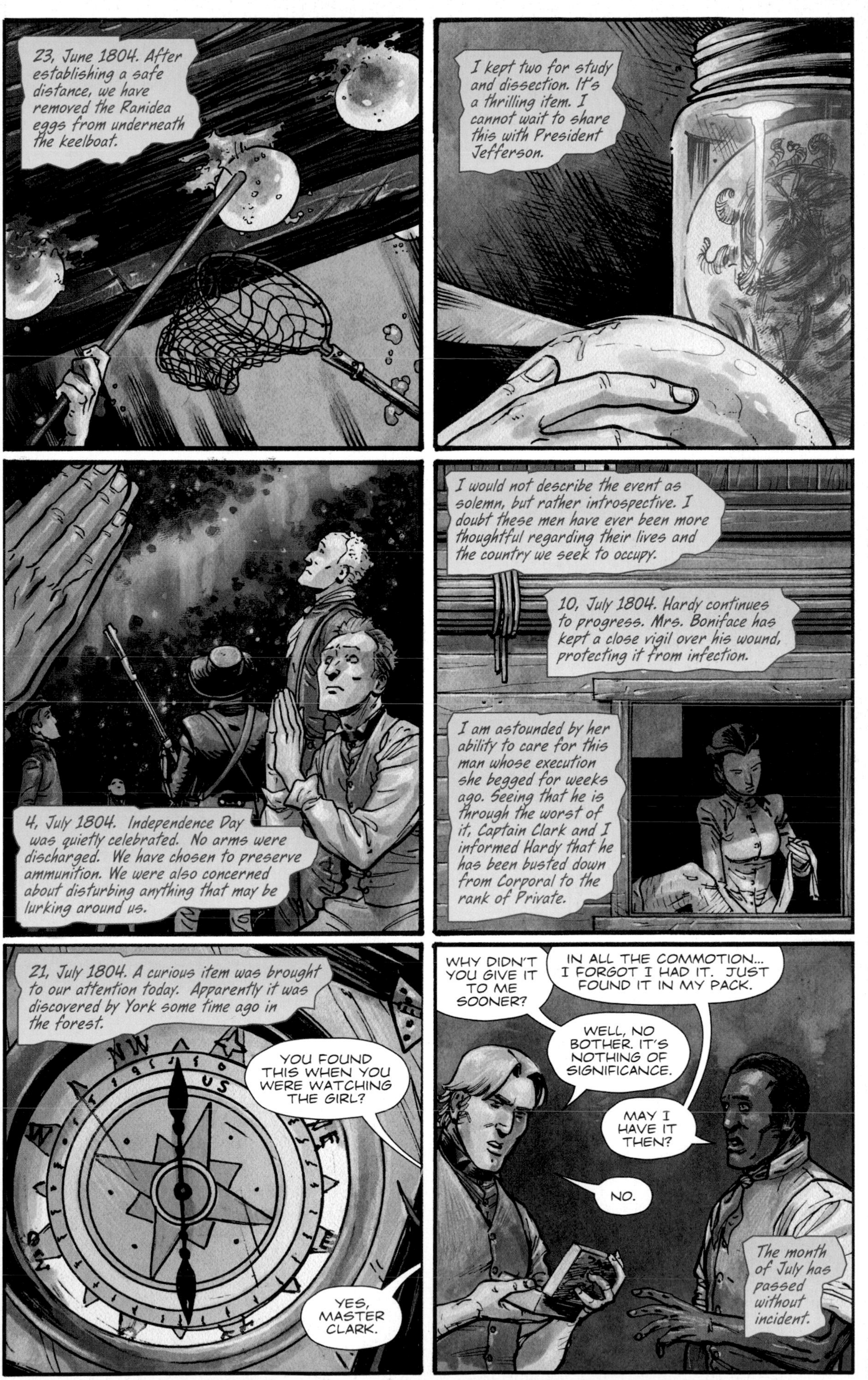
23, June 1804. After establishing a safe distance, we have removed the Ranidea eggs from underneath the keelboat.
I kept two for study and dissection. It's a thrilling item. I cannot wait to share this with President Jefferson.
4, July 1804. Independence Day was quietly celebrated. No arms were discharged. We have chosen to preserve ammunition. We were also concerned about disturbing anything that may be lurking around us.
I would not describe the event as solemn, but rather introspective. I doubt these men have ever been more thoughtful regarding their lives and the country we seek to occupy.
10, July 1804. Hardy continues to progress. Mrs. Boniface has kept a close vigil over his wound, protecting it from infection.
I am astounded by her ability to care for this man whose execution she begged for weeks ago. Seeing that he is through the worst of it, Captain Clark and I informed Hardy that he has been busted down from Corporal to the rank of Private.
21, July 1804. A curious item was brought to our attention today. Apparently it was discovered by York some time ago in the forest.
YOU FOUND THIS WHEN YOU WERE WATCHING THE GIRL?
YES, MASTER CLARK.
WHY DIDN'T YOU GIVE IT TO ME SOONER?
IN ALL THE COMMOTION... I FORGOT I HAD IT. JUST FOUND IT IN MY PACK.
WELL, NO BOTHER. IT'S NOTHING OF SIGNIFICANCE.
MAY I HAVE IT THEN?
NO.
The month of July has passed without incident.

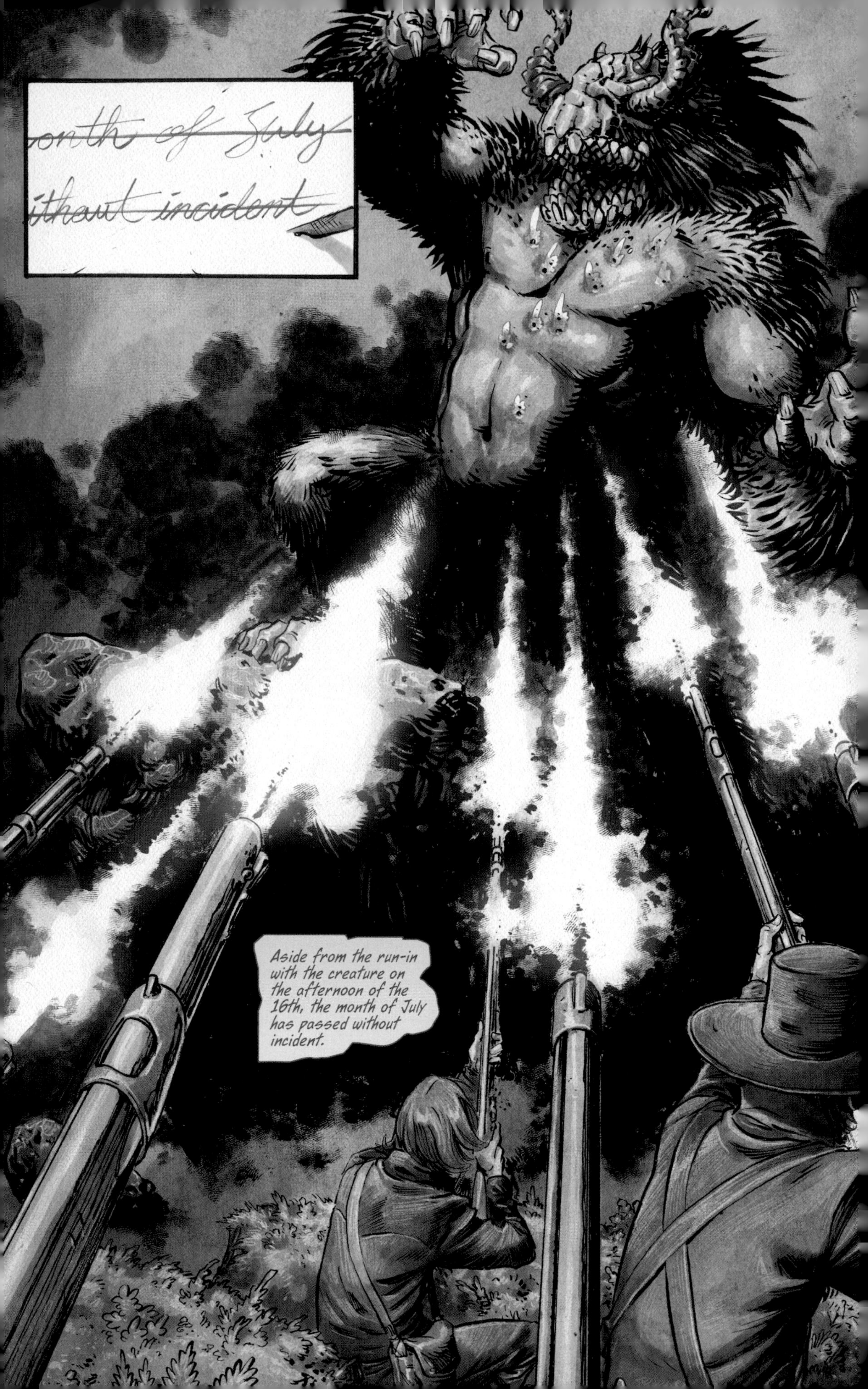
onth of July
ithout incident
Aside from the run-in with the creature on the afternoon of the 16th, the month of July has passed without incident.

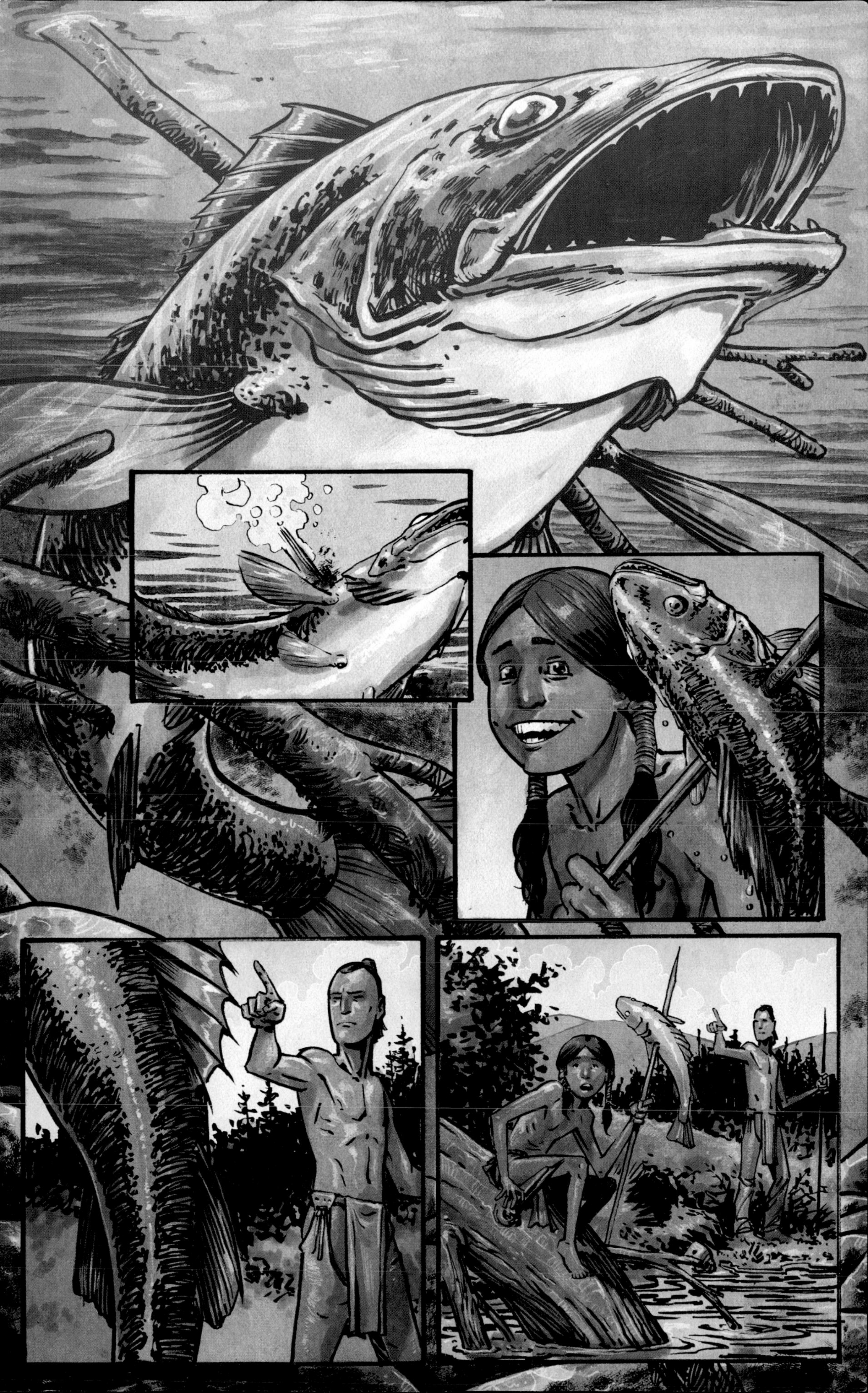

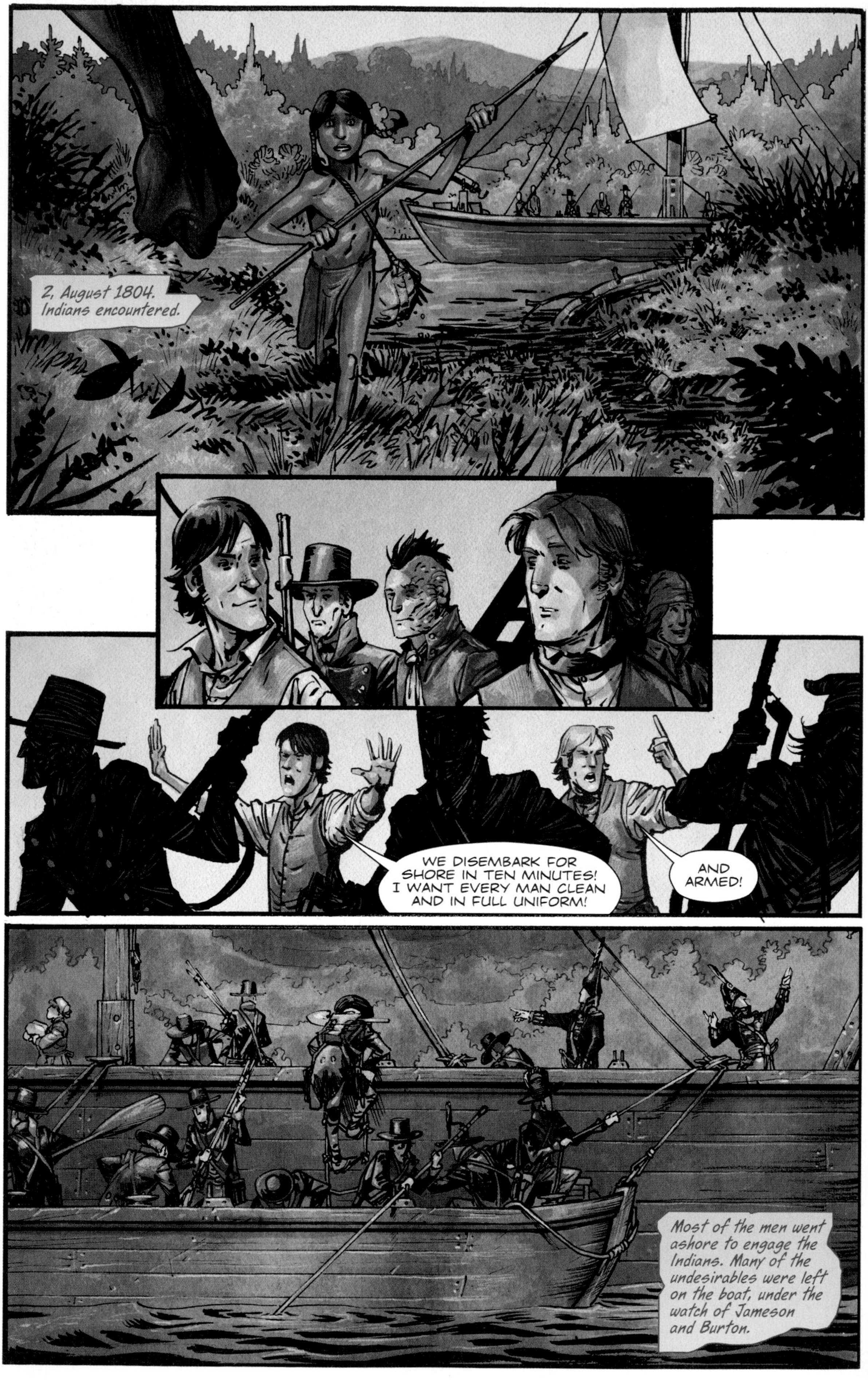
2, August 1804.
Indians encountered.
WE DISEMBARK FOR SHORE IN TEN MINUTES! I WANT EVERY MAN CLEAN AND IN FULL UNIFORM!
AND ARMED!
Most of the men went ashore to engage the Indians. Many of the undesirables were left on the boat, under the watch of Jameson and Burton.

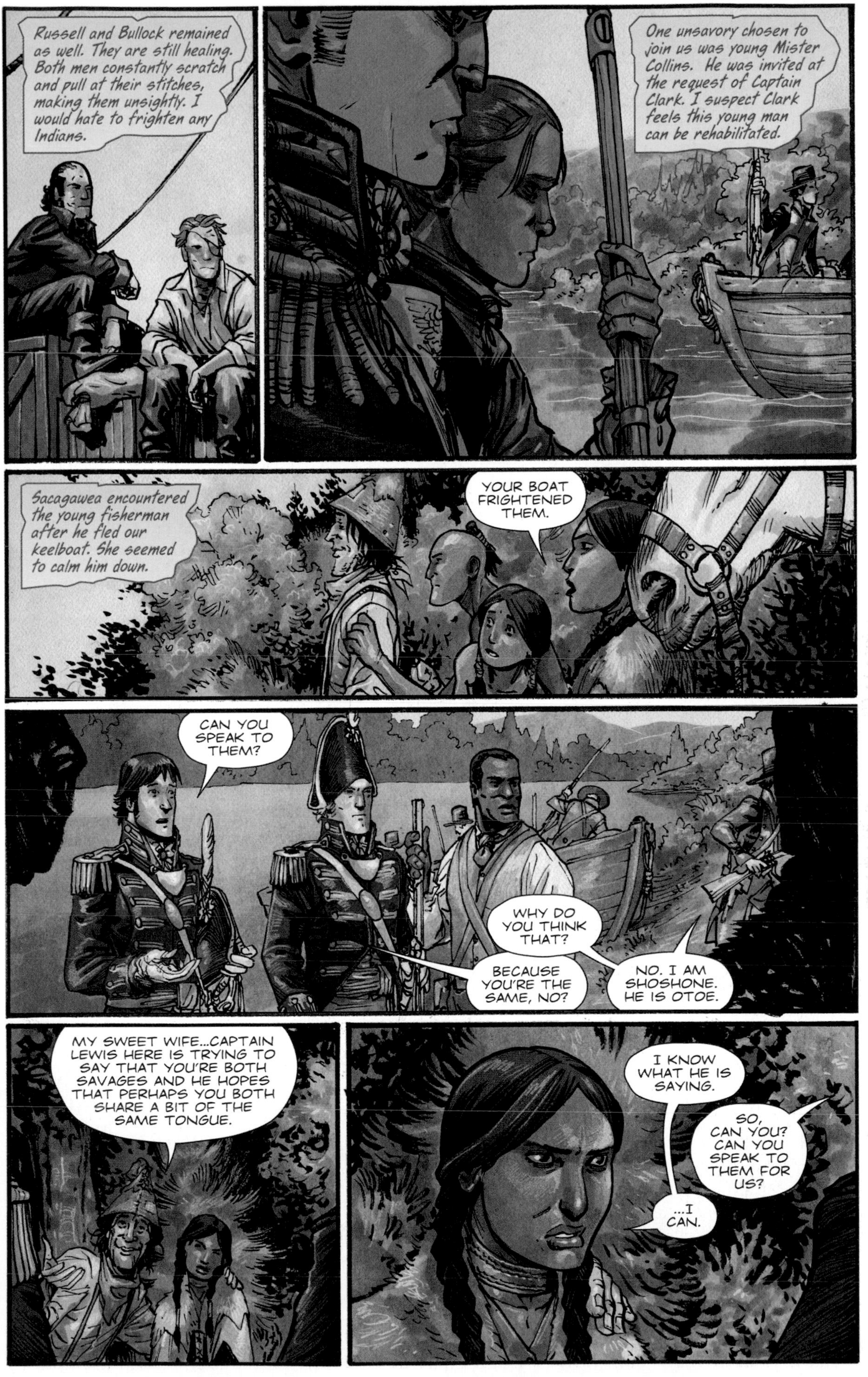
Russell and Bullock remained as well. They are still healing. Both men constantly scratch and pull at their stitches, making them unsightly. I would hate to frighten any Indians.
One unsavory chosen to join us was young Mister Collins. He was invited at the request of Captain Clark. I suspect Clark feels this young man can be rehabilitated.
Sacagawea encountered the young fisherman after he fled our keelboat. She seemed to calm him down.
YOUR BOAT FRIGHTENED THEM.
CAN YOU SPEAK TO THEM?
WHY DO YOU THINK THAT?
BECAUSE YOU'RE THE SAME, NO?
NO. I AM SHOSHONE. HE IS OTOE.
MY SWEET WIFE...CAPTAIN LEWIS HERE IS TRYING TO SAY THAT YOU'RE BOTH SAVAGES AND HE HOPES THAT PERHAPS YOU BOTH SHARE A BIT OF THE SAME TONGUE.
I KNOW WHAT HE IS SAYING.
SO, CAN YOU? CAN YOU SPEAK TO THEM FOR US?
...I CAN.

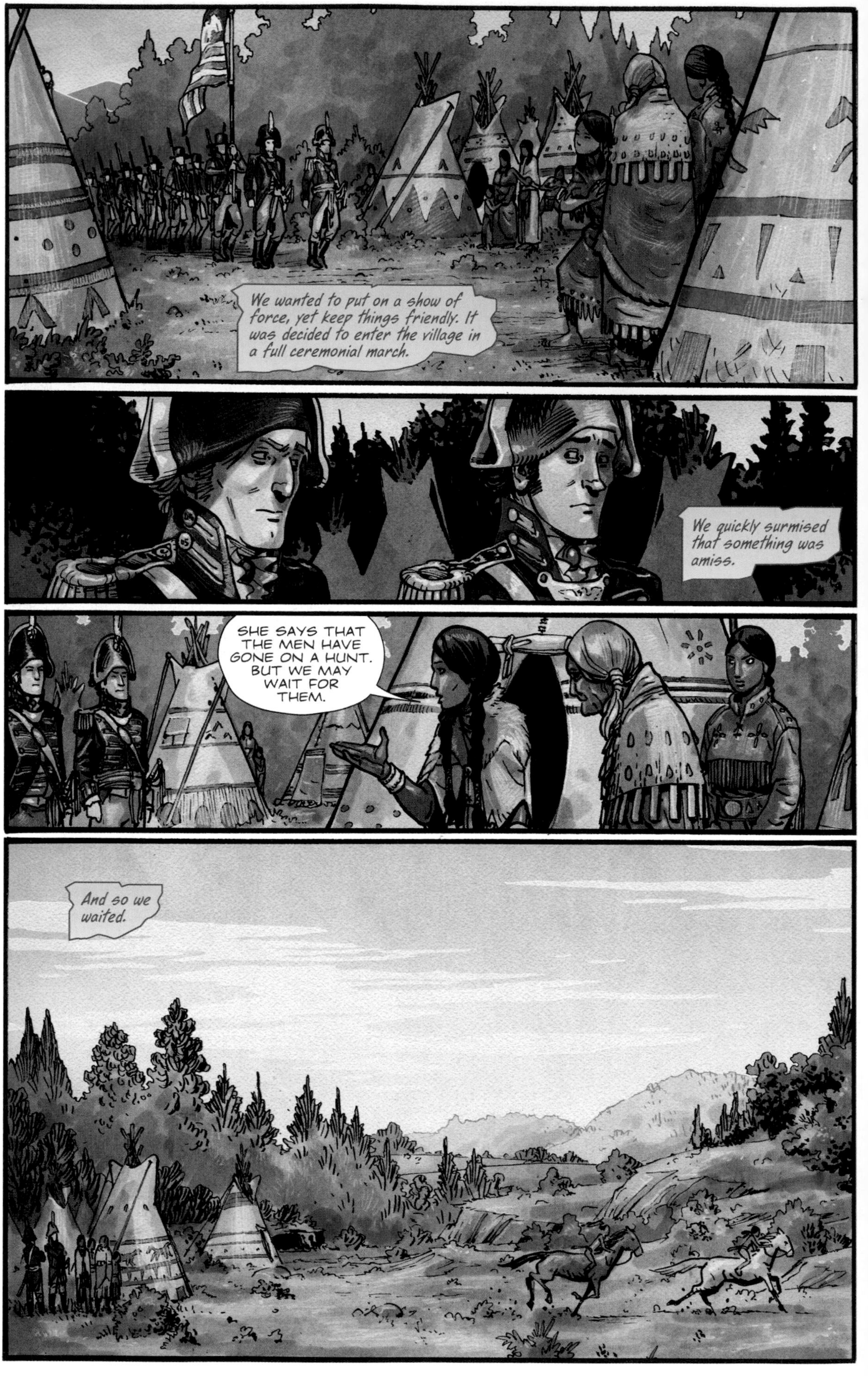
We wanted to put on a show of force, yet keep things friendly. It was decided to enter the village in a full ceremonial march.
We quickly surmised that something was amiss.
SHE SAYS THAT THE MEN HAVE GONE ON A HUNT. BUT WE MAY WAIT FOR THEM.
And so we waited.

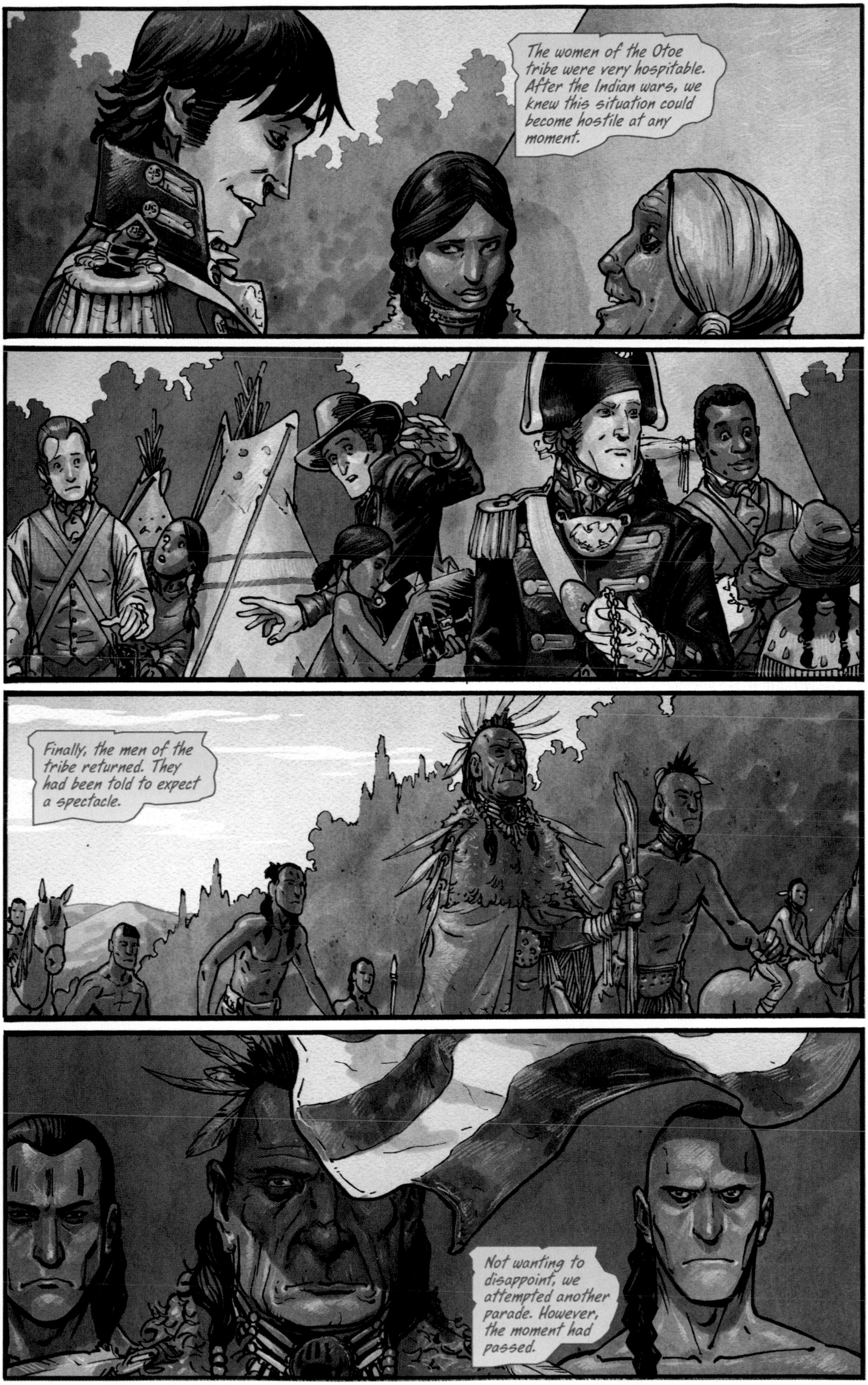
The women of the Otoe tribe were very hospitable. After the Indian wars, we knew this situation could become hostile at any moment.
Finally, the men of the tribe returned. They had been told to expect a spectacle.
Not wanting to disappoint, we attempted another parade. However, the moment had passed.

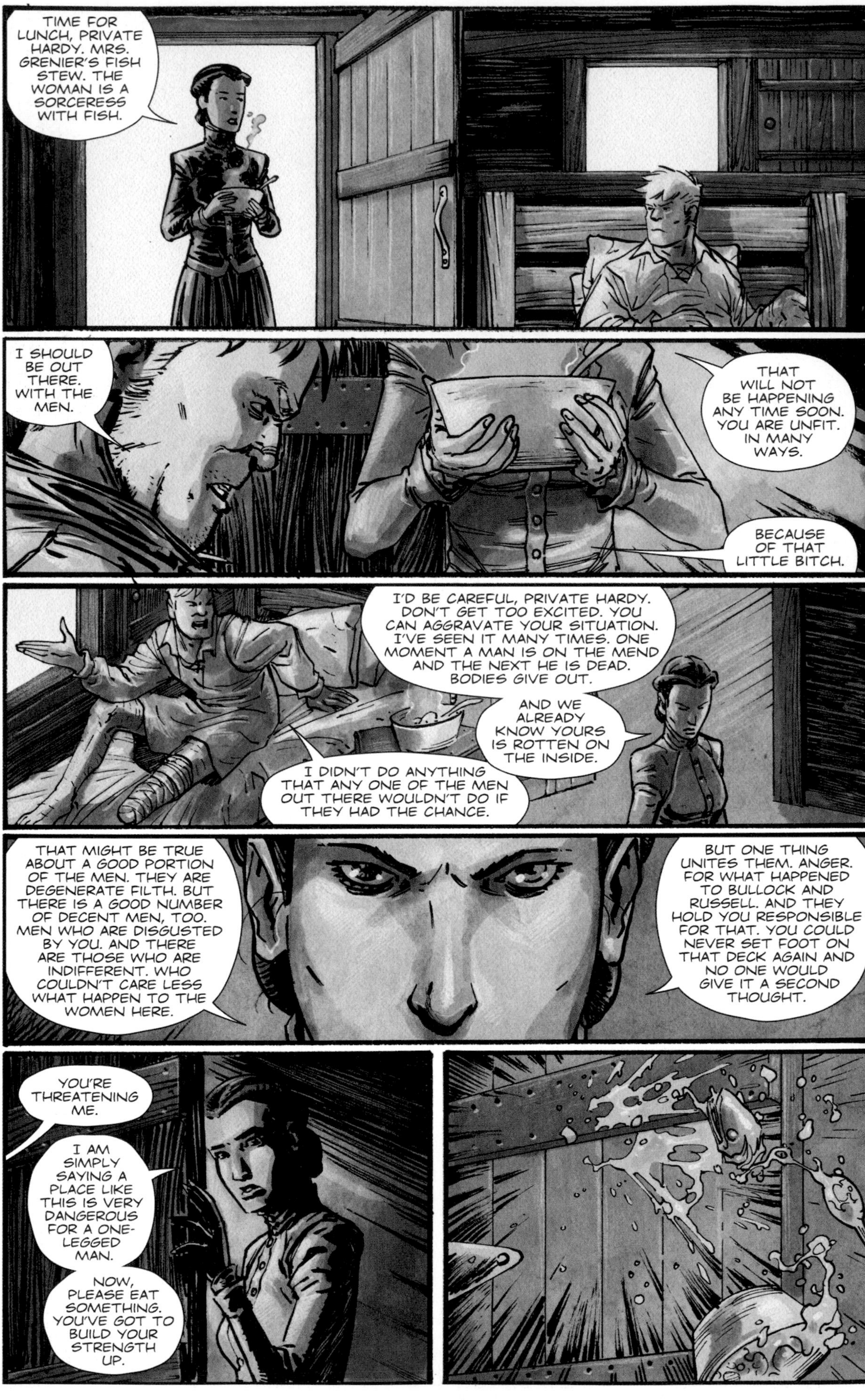
TIME FOR LUNCH, PRIVATE HARDY. MRS. GRENIER'S FISH STEW. THE WOMAN IS A SORCERESS WITH FISH.
I SHOULD BE OUT THERE. WITH THE MEN.
THAT WILL NOT BE HAPPENING ANY TIME SOON. YOU ARE UNFIT. IN MANY WAYS.
BECAUSE OF THAT LITTLE BITCH.
I'D BE CAREFUL, PRIVATE HARDY. DON'T GET TOO EXCITED. YOU CAN AGGRAVATE YOUR SITUATION. I'VE SEEN IT MANY TIMES. ONE MOMENT A MAN IS ON THE MEND AND THE NEXT HE IS DEAD. BODIES GIVE OUT.
AND WE ALREADY KNOW YOURS IS ROTTEN ON THE INSIDE.
I DIDN'T DO ANYTHING THAT ANY ONE OF THE MEN OUT THERE WOULDN'T DO IF THEY HAD THE CHANCE.
THAT MIGHT BE TRUE ABOUT A GOOD PORTION OF THE MEN. THEY ARE DEGENERATE FILTH. BUT THERE IS A GOOD NUMBER OF DECENT MEN, TOO. MEN WHO ARE DISGUSTED BY YOU. AND THERE ARE THOSE WHO ARE INDIFFERENT. WHO COULDN'T CARE LESS WHAT HAPPEN TO THE WOMEN HERE.
BUT ONE THING UNITES THEM. ANGER. FOR WHAT HAPPENED TO BULLOCK AND RUSSELL. AND THEY HOLD YOU RESPONSIBLE FOR THAT. YOU COULD NEVER SET FOOT ON THAT DECK AGAIN AND NO ONE WOULD GIVE IT A SECOND THOUGHT.
YOU'RE THREATENING ME.
I AM SIMPLY SAYING A PLACE LIKE THIS IS VERY DANGEROUS FOR A ONE-LEGGED MAN.
NOW, PLEASE EAT SOMETHING. YOU'VE GOT TO BUILD YOUR STRENGTH UP.

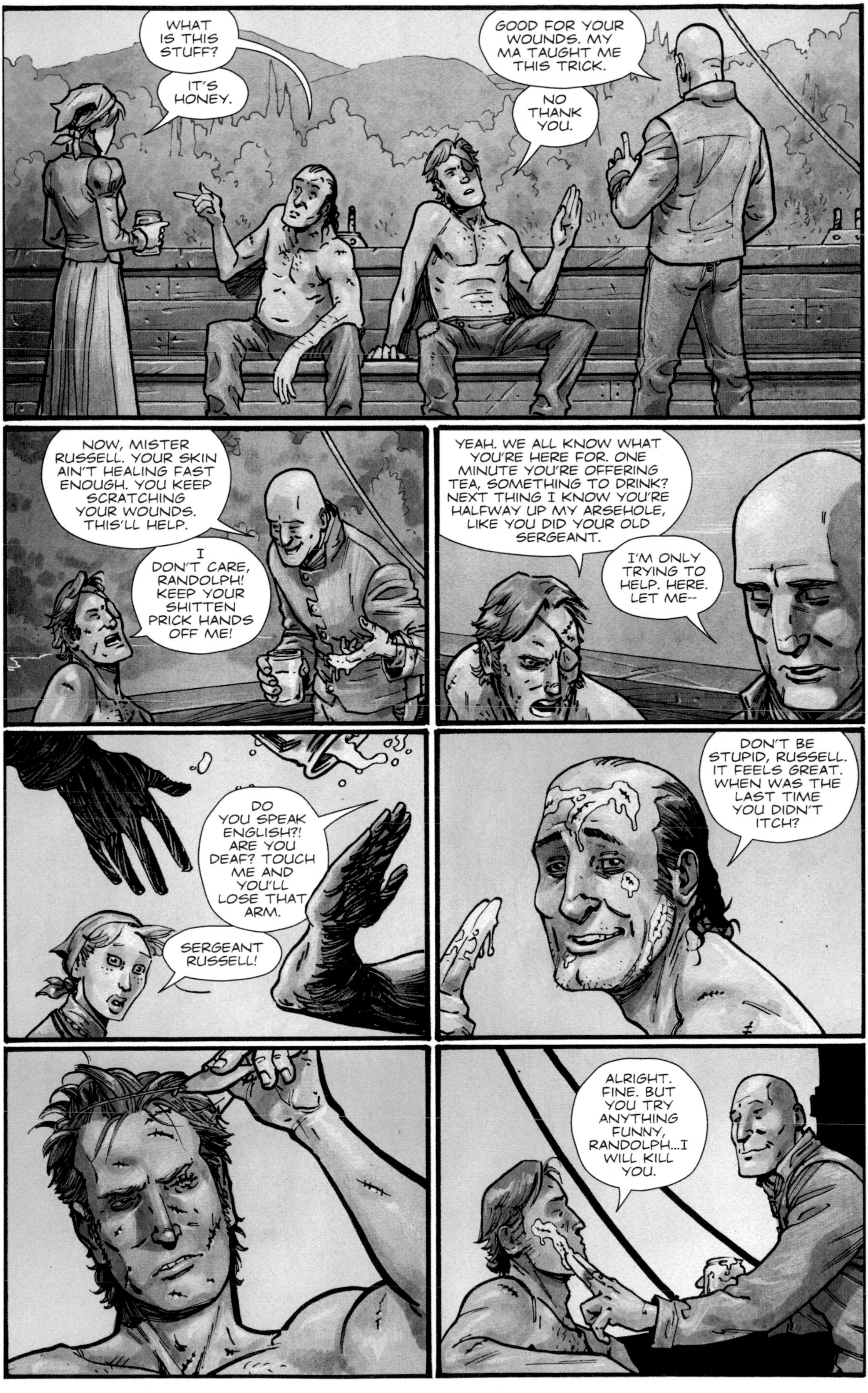
WHAT IS THIS STUFF?
IT'S HONEY.
GOOD FOR YOUR WOUNDS. MY MA TAUGHT ME THIS TRICK.
NO THANK YOU.
NOW, MISTER RUSSELL. YOUR SKIN AIN'T HEALING FAST ENOUGH. YOU KEEP SCRATCHING YOUR WOUNDS. THIS'LL HELP.
I DON'T CARE, RANDOLPH! KEEP YOUR SHITTEN PRICK HANDS OFF ME!
YEAH. WE ALL KNOW WHAT YOU'RE HERE FOR. ONE MINUTE YOU'RE OFFERING TEA, SOMETHING TO DRINK? NEXT THING I KNOW YOU'RE HALFWAY UP MY ARSEHOLE, LIKE YOU DID YOUR OLD SERGEANT.
I'M ONLY TRYING TO HELP. HERE. LET ME--
DO YOU SPEAK ENGLISH?! ARE YOU DEAF? TOUCH ME AND YOU'LL LOSE THAT ARM.
SERGEANT RUSSELL!
DON'T BE STUPID, RUSSELL. IT FEELS GREAT. WHEN WAS THE LAST TIME YOU DIDN'T ITCH?
ALRIGHT. FINE. BUT YOU TRY ANYTHING FUNNY, RANDOLPH...I WILL KILL YOU.

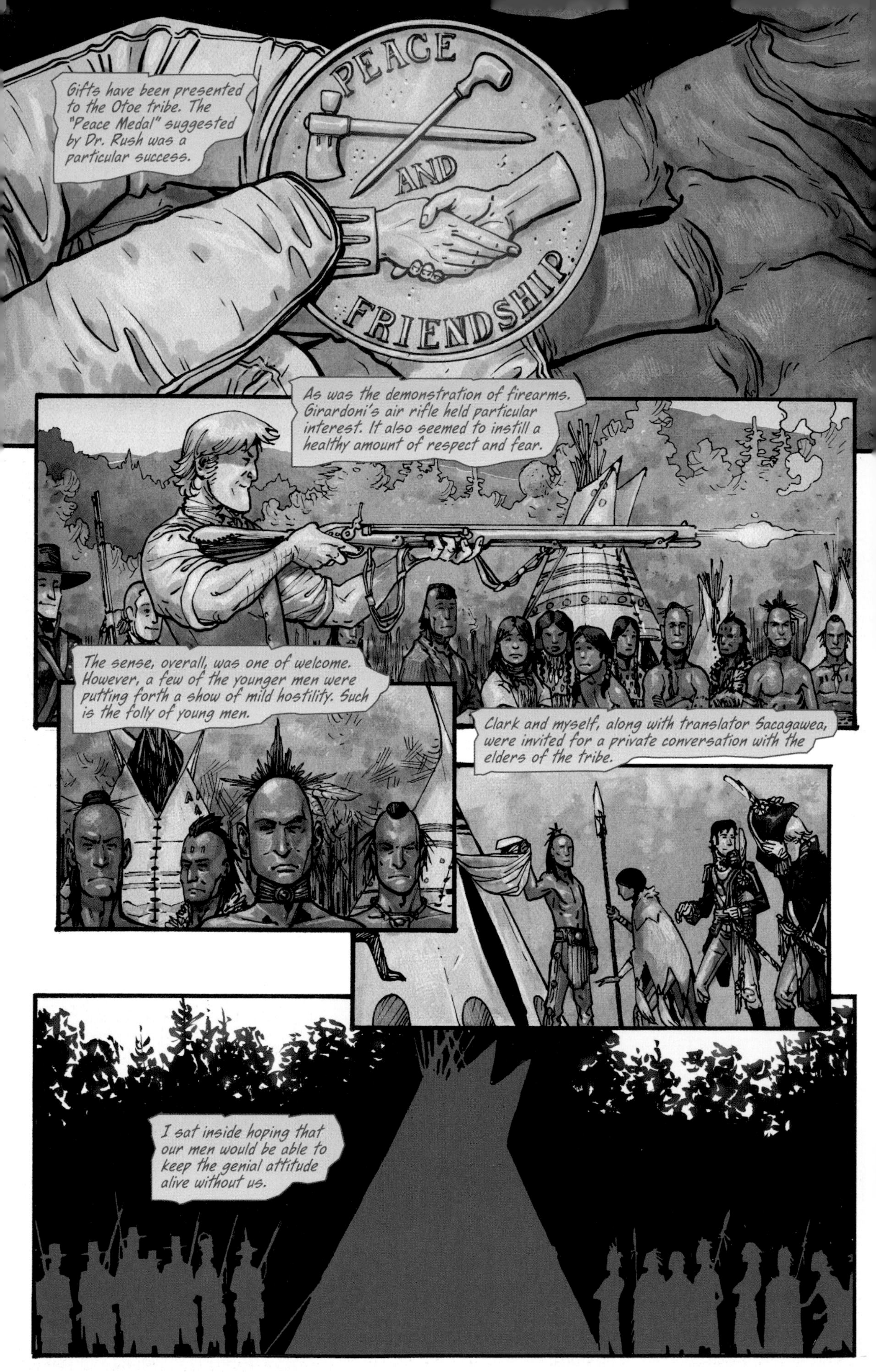

Gifts have been presented to the Otoe tribe. The "Peace Medal" suggested by Dr. Rush was a particular success.
PEACE
AND
FRIENDSHIP
As was the demonstration of firearms. Girardoni's air rifle held particular interest. It also seemed to instill a healthy amount of respect and fear.
The sense, overall, was one of welcome. However, a few of the younger men were putting forth a show of mild hostility. Such is the folly of young men.
Clark and myself, along with translator Sacagawea, were invited for a private conversation with the elders of the tribe.
I sat inside hoping that our men would be able to keep the genial attitude alive without us.

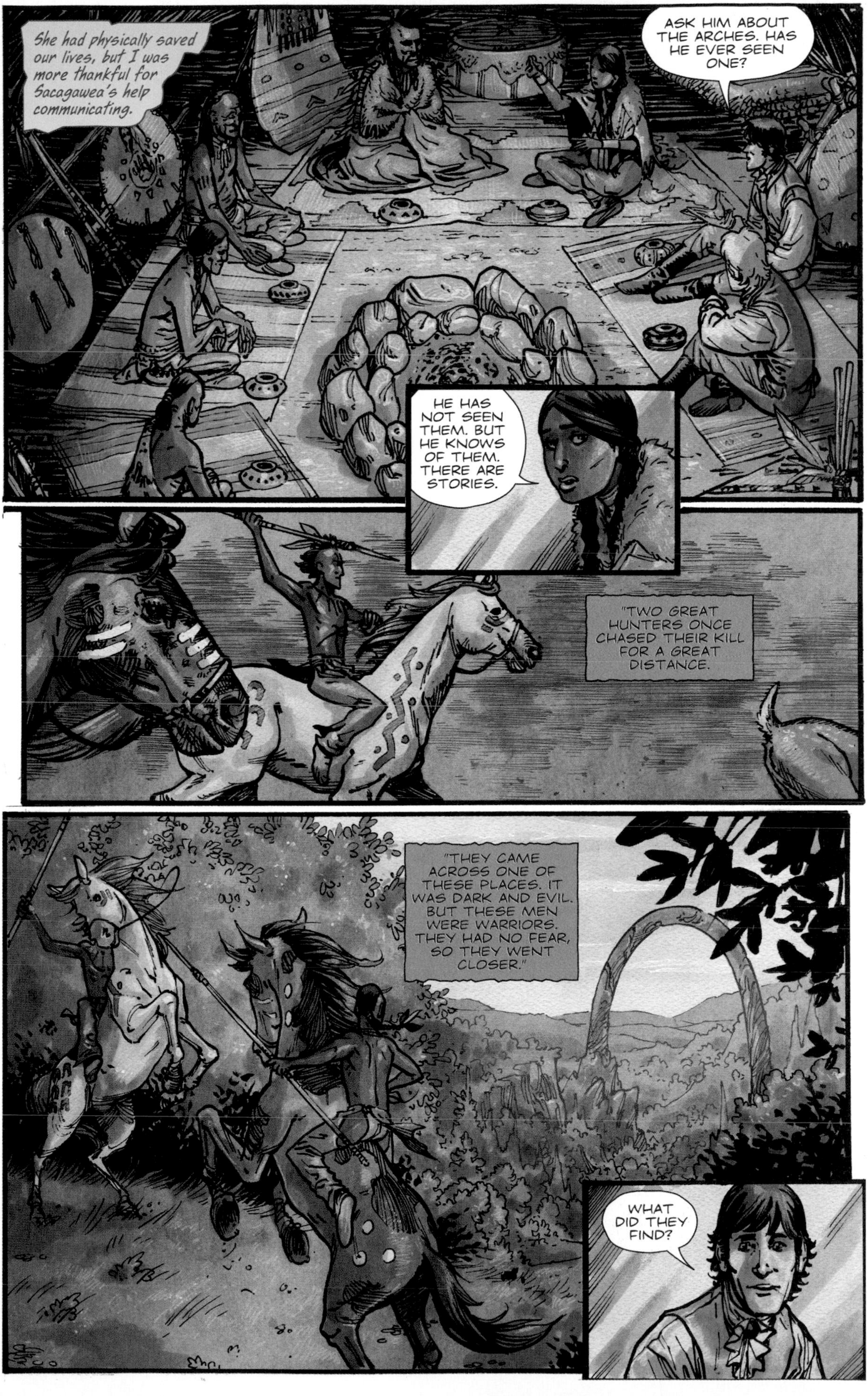
She had physically saved our lives, but I was more thankful for Sacagawea's help communicating.
ASK HIM ABOUT THE ARCHES. HAS HE EVER SEEN ONE?
HE HAS NOT SEEN THEM. BUT HE KNOWS OF THEM. THERE ARE STORIES.
"TWO GREAT HUNTERS ONCE CHASED THEIR KILL FOR A GREAT DISTANCE.
"THEY CAME ACROSS ONE OF THESE PLACES. IT WAS DARK AND EVIL. BUT THESE MEN WERE WARRIORS. THEY HAD NO FEAR, SO THEY WENT CLOSER."
WHAT DID THEY FIND?

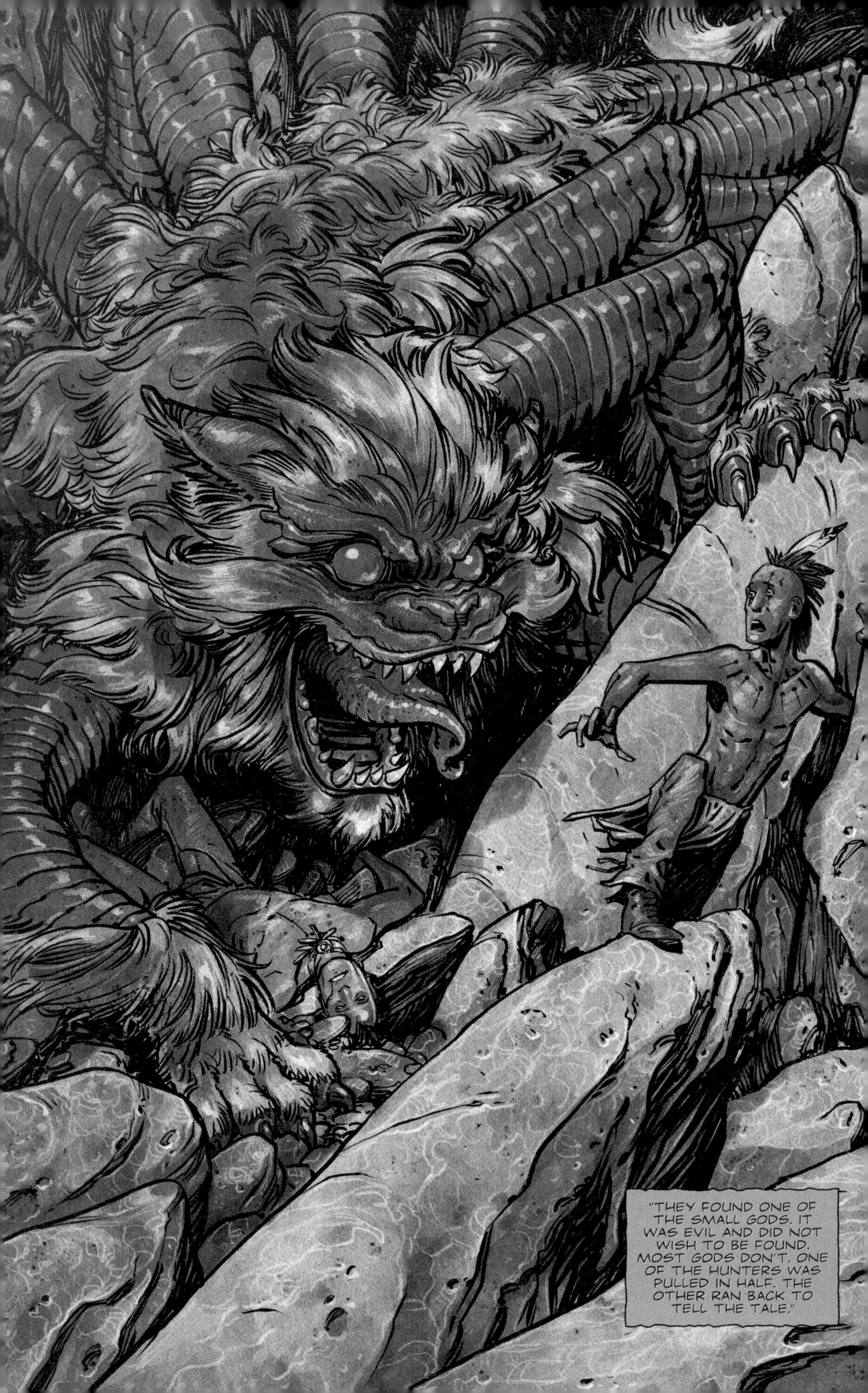
"THEY FOUND ONE OF THE SMALL GODS. IT WAS EVIL AND DID NOT WISH TO BE FOUND. MOST GODS DON'T. ONE OF THE HUNTERS WAS PULLED IN HALF. THE OTHER RAN BACK TO TELL THE TALE."

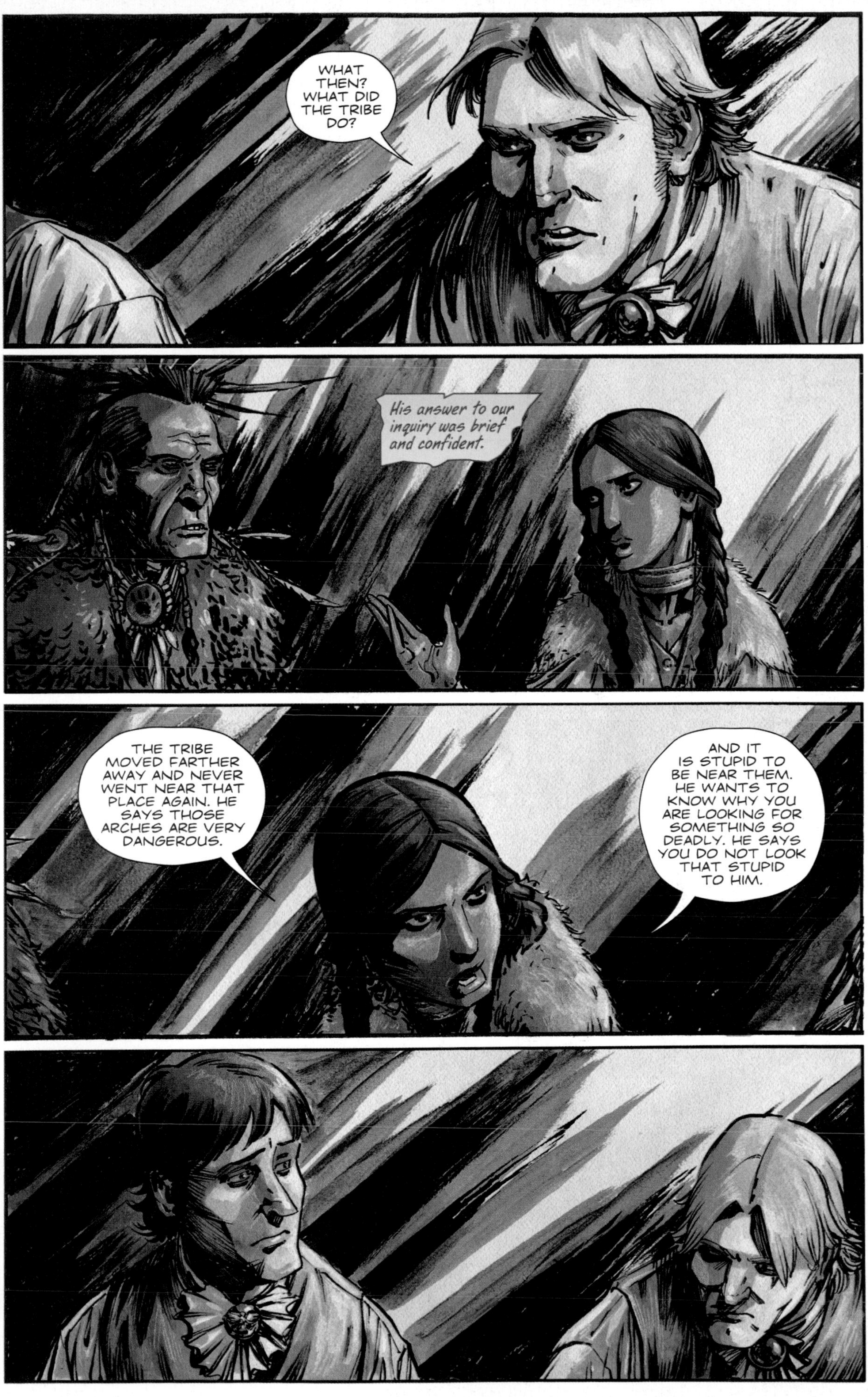
WHAT THEN? WHAT DID THE TRIBE DO?
His answer to our inquiry was brief and confident.
THE TRIBE MOVED FARTHER AWAY AND NEVER WENT NEAR THAT PLACE AGAIN. HE SAYS THOSE ARCHES ARE VERY DANGEROUS.
AND IT IS STUPID TO BE NEAR THEM. HE WANTS TO KNOW WHY YOU ARE LOOKING FOR SOMETHING SO DEADLY. HE SAYS YOU DO NOT LOOK THAT STUPID TO HIM.

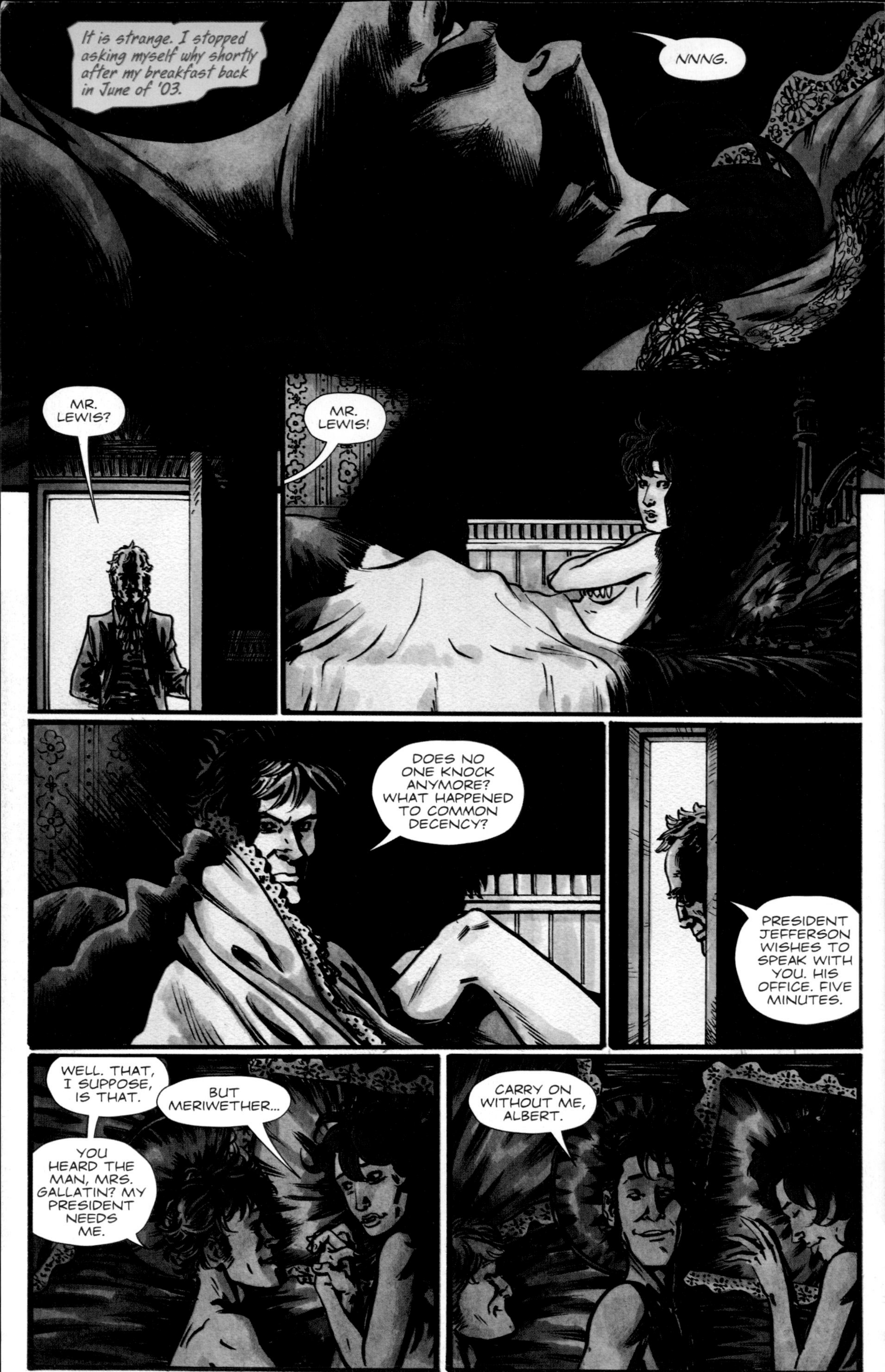
It is strange. I stopped asking myself why shortly after my breakfast back in June of '03.
NNNG.
MR. LEWIS?
MR. LEWIS!
DOES NO ONE KNOCK ANYMORE? WHAT HAPPENED TO COMMON DECENCY?
PRESIDENT JEFFERSON WISHES TO SPEAK WITH YOU. HIS OFFICE. FIVE MINUTES.
WELL. THAT, I SUPPOSE, IS THAT.
YOU HEARD THE MAN, MRS. GALLATIN? MY PRESIDENT NEEDS ME.
BUT MERIWETHER...
CARRY ON WITHOUT ME, ALBERT.

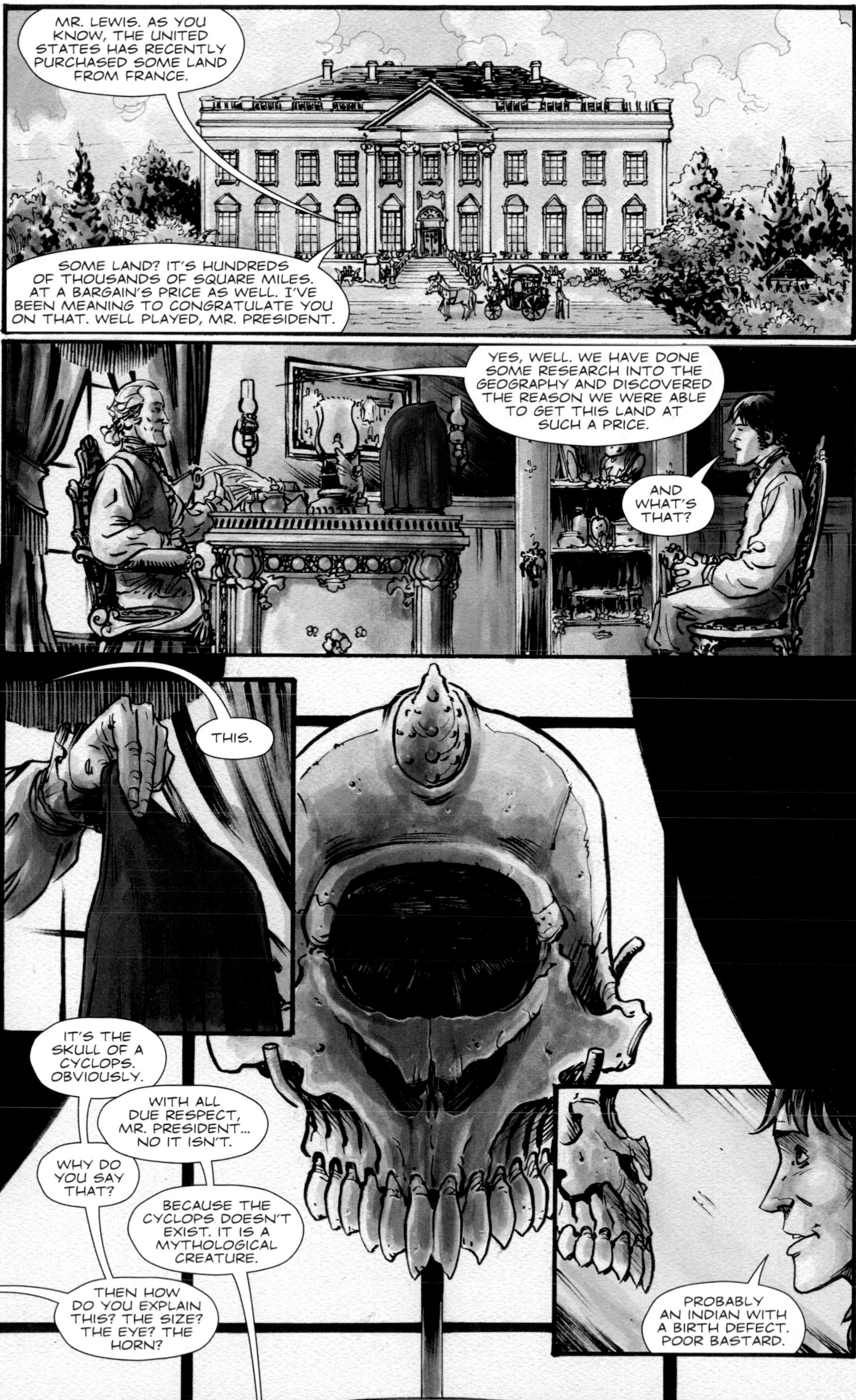
MR. LEWIS. AS YOU KNOW, THE UNITED STATES HAS RECENTLY PURCHASED SOME LAND FROM FRANCE.
SOME LAND? IT'S HUNDREDS OF THOUSANDS OF SQUARE MILES. AT A BARGAIN'S PRICE AS WELL. I'VE BEEN MEANING TO CONGRATULATE YOU ON THAT. WELL PLAYED, MR. PRESIDENT.
YES, WELL. WE HAVE DONE SOME RESEARCH INTO THE GEOGRAPHY AND DISCOVERED THE REASON WE WERE ABLE TO GET THIS LAND AT SUCH A PRICE.
AND WHAT'S THAT?
THIS.
IT'S THE SKULL OF A CYCLOPS. OBVIOUSLY.
WITH ALL DUE RESPECT, MR. PRESIDENT... NO IT ISN'T.
WHY DO YOU SAY THAT?
BECAUSE THE CYCLOPS DOESN'T EXIST. IT IS A MYTHOLOGICAL CREATURE.
THEN HOW DO YOU EXPLAIN THIS? THE SIZE? THE EYE? THE HORN?
PROBABLY AN INDIAN WITH A BIRTH DEFECT. POOR BASTARD.

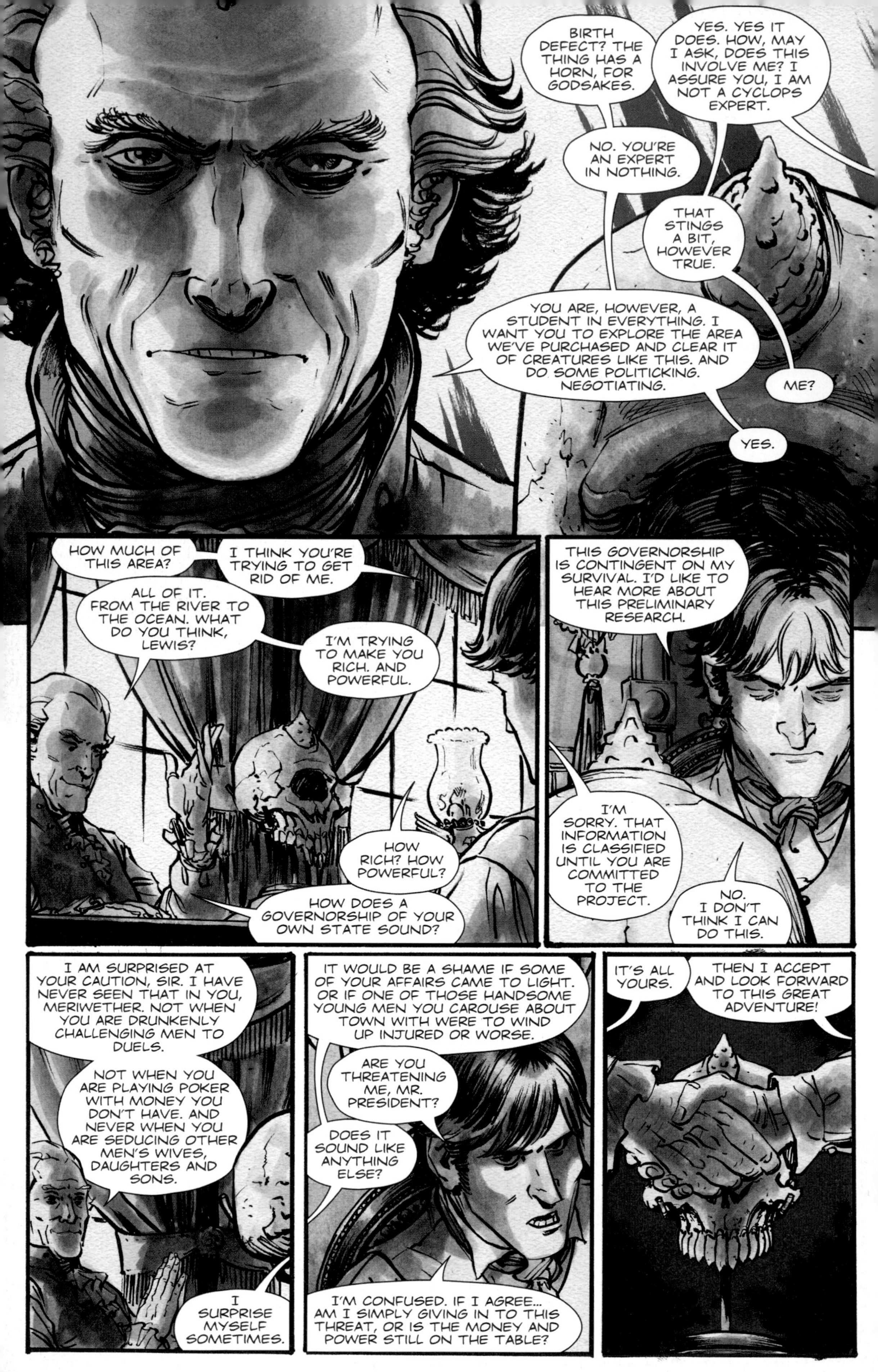
BIRTH DEFECT? THE THING HAS A HORN, FOR GODSAKES.
YES. YES IT DOES. HOW, MAY I ASK, DOES THIS INVOLVE ME? I ASSURE YOU, I AM NOT A CYCLOPS EXPERT.
NO. YOU'RE AN EXPERT IN NOTHING.
THAT STINGS A BIT, HOWEVER TRUE.
YOU ARE, HOWEVER, A STUDENT IN EVERYTHING. I WANT YOU TO EXPLORE THE AREA WE'VE PURCHASED AND CLEAR IT OF CREATURES LIKE THIS. AND DO SOME POLITICKING. NEGOTIATING.
ME?
YES.
HOW MUCH OF THIS AREA?
I THINK YOU'RE TRYING TO GET RID OF ME.
ALL OF IT. FROM THE RIVER TO THE OCEAN. WHAT DO YOU THINK, LEWIS?
I'M TRYING TO MAKE YOU RICH. AND POWERFUL.
HOW RICH? HOW POWERFUL?
HOW DOES A GOVERNORSHIP OF YOUR OWN STATE SOUND?
THIS GOVERNORSHIP IS CONTINGENT ON MY SURVIVAL. I'D LIKE TO HEAR MORE ABOUT THIS PRELIMINARY RESEARCH.
I'M SORRY. THAT INFORMATION IS CLASSIFIED UNTIL YOU ARE COMMITTED TO THE PROJECT.
NO. I DON'T THINK I CAN DO THIS.
I AM SURPRISED AT YOUR CAUTION, SIR. I HAVE NEVER SEEN THAT IN YOU, MERIWETHER. NOT WHEN YOU ARE DRUNKENLY CHALLENGING MEN TO DUELS.
NOT WHEN YOU ARE PLAYING POKER WITH MONEY YOU DON'T HAVE. AND NEVER WHEN YOU ARE SEDUCING OTHER MEN'S WIVES, DAUGHTERS AND SONS.
I SURPRISE MYSELF SOMETIMES.
IT WOULD BE A SHAME IF SOME OF YOUR AFFAIRS CAME TO LIGHT. OR IF ONE OF THOSE HANDSOME YOUNG MEN YOU CAROUSE ABOUT TOWN WITH WERE TO WIND UP INJURED OR WORSE.
ARE YOU THREATENING ME, MR. PRESIDENT?
DOES IT SOUND LIKE ANYTHING ELSE?
I'M CONFUSED. IF I AGREE... AM I SIMPLY GIVING IN TO THIS THREAT, OR IS THE MONEY AND POWER STILL ON THE TABLE?
IT'S ALL YOURS.
THEN I ACCEPT AND LOOK FORWARD TO THIS GREAT ADVENTURE!

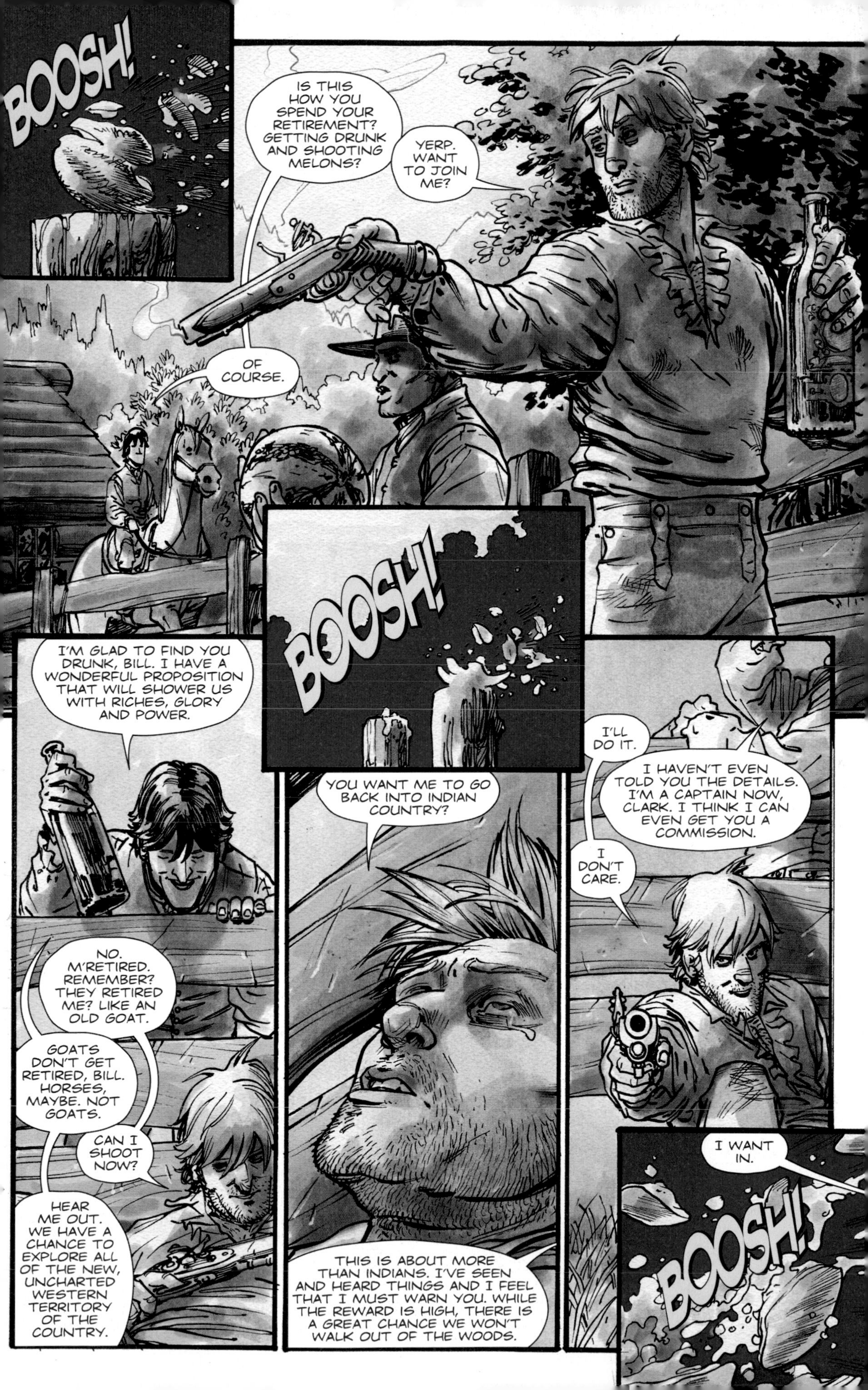

BOOSH!
IS THIS HOW YOU SPEND YOUR RETIREMENT? GETTING DRUNK AND SHOOTING MELONS?
YERP. WANT TO JOIN ME?
OF COURSE.
BOOSH!
I'M GLAD TO FIND YOU DRUNK, BILL. I HAVE A WONDERFUL PROPOSITION THAT WILL SHOWER US WITH RICHES, GLORY AND POWER.
NO. M'RETIRED. REMEMBER? THEY RETIRED ME? LIKE AN OLD GOAT.
GOATS DON'T GET RETIRED, BILL. HORSES, MAYBE. NOT GOATS.
CAN I SHOOT NOW?
HEAR ME OUT. WE HAVE A CHANCE TO EXPLORE ALL OF THE NEW, UNCHARTED WESTERN TERRITORY OF THE COUNTRY.
YOU WANT ME TO GO BACK INTO INDIAN COUNTRY?
THIS IS ABOUT MORE THAN INDIANS. I'VE SEEN AND HEARD THINGS AND I FEEL THAT I MUST WARN YOU. WHILE THE REWARD IS HIGH, THERE IS A GREAT CHANCE WE WON'T WALK OUT OF THE WOODS.
I'LL DO IT.
I HAVEN'T EVEN TOLD YOU THE DETAILS. I'M A CAPTAIN NOW, CLARK. I THINK I CAN EVEN GET YOU A COMMISSION.
I DON'T CARE.
I WANT IN.
BOOSH!

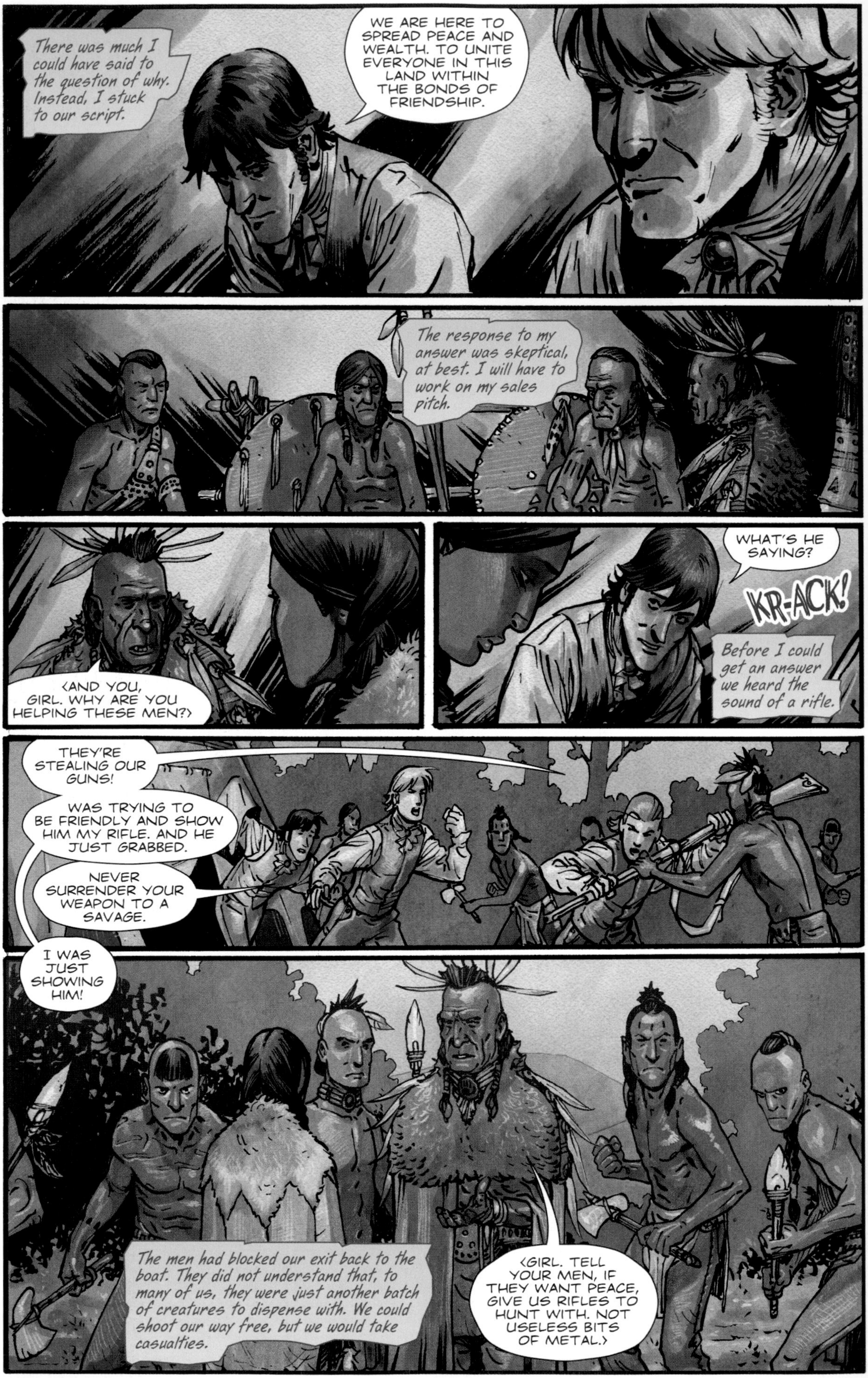
There was much I could have said to the question of why. Instead, I stuck to our script.
WE ARE HERE TO SPREAD PEACE AND WEALTH. TO UNITE EVERYONE IN THIS LAND WITHIN THE BONDS OF FRIENDSHIP.
The response to my answer was skeptical, at best. I will have to work on my sales pitch.
<AND YOU, GIRL. WHY ARE YOU HELPING THESE MEN?>
WHAT'S HE SAYING?
KR-ACK!
Before I could get an answer we heard the sound of a rifle.
THEY'RE STEALING OUR GUNS!
WAS TRYING TO BE FRIENDLY AND SHOW HIM MY RIFLE. AND HE JUST GRABBED.
NEVER SURRENDER YOUR WEAPON TO A SAVAGE.
I WAS JUST SHOWING HIM!
The men had blocked our exit back to the boat. They did not understand that, to many of us, they were just another batch of creatures to dispense with. We could shoot our way free, but we would take casualties.
<GIRL. TELL YOUR MEN, IF THEY WANT PEACE, GIVE US RIFLES TO HUNT WITH. NOT USELESS BITS OF METAL.>

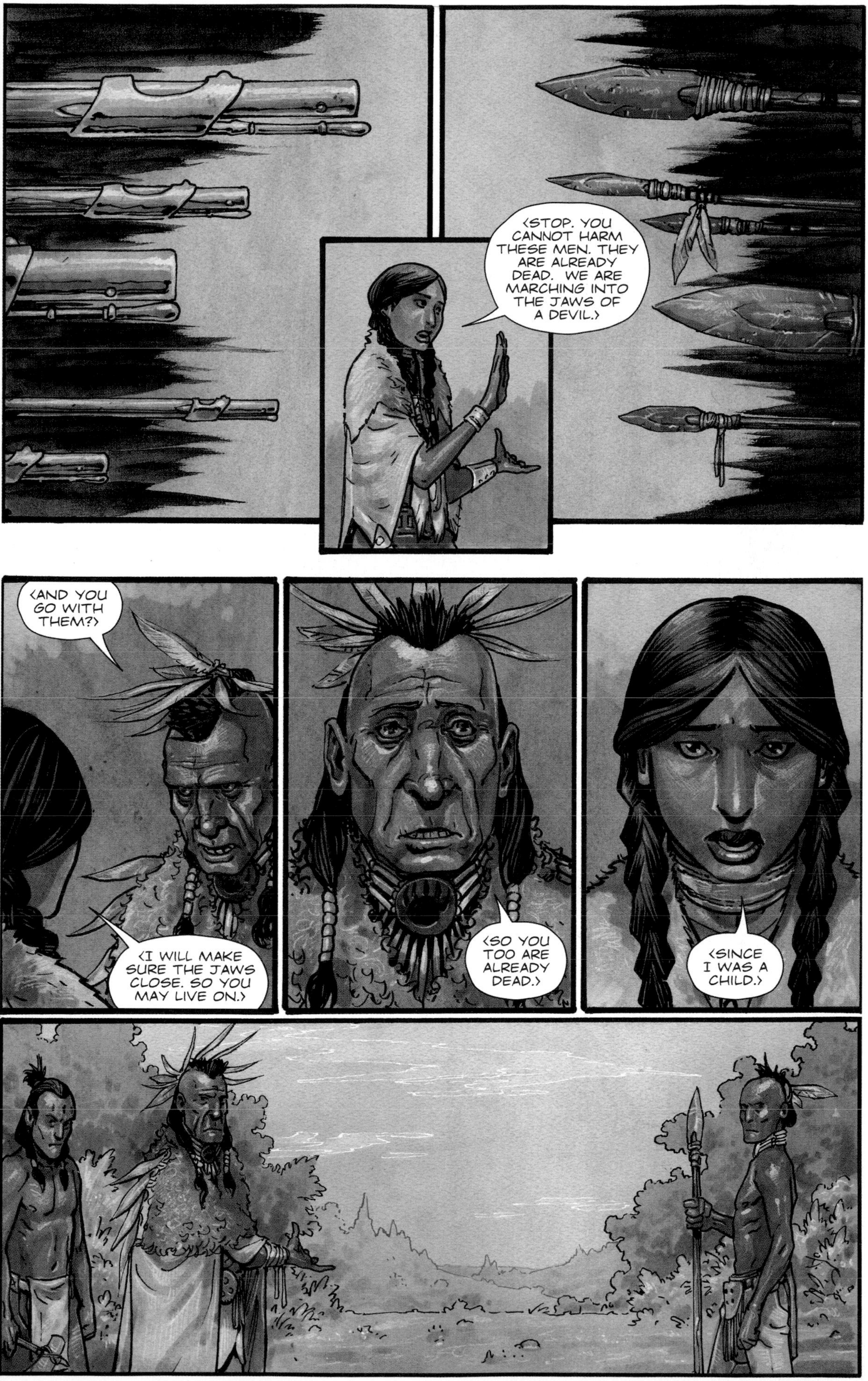
<STOP. YOU CANNOT HARM THESE MEN. THEY ARE ALREADY DEAD. WE ARE MARCHING INTO THE JAWS OF A DEVIL.>
<AND YOU GO WITH THEM?>
<I WILL MAKE SURE THE JAWS CLOSE. SO YOU MAY LIVE ON.>
<SO YOU TOO ARE ALREADY DEAD.>
<SINCE I WAS A CHILD.>

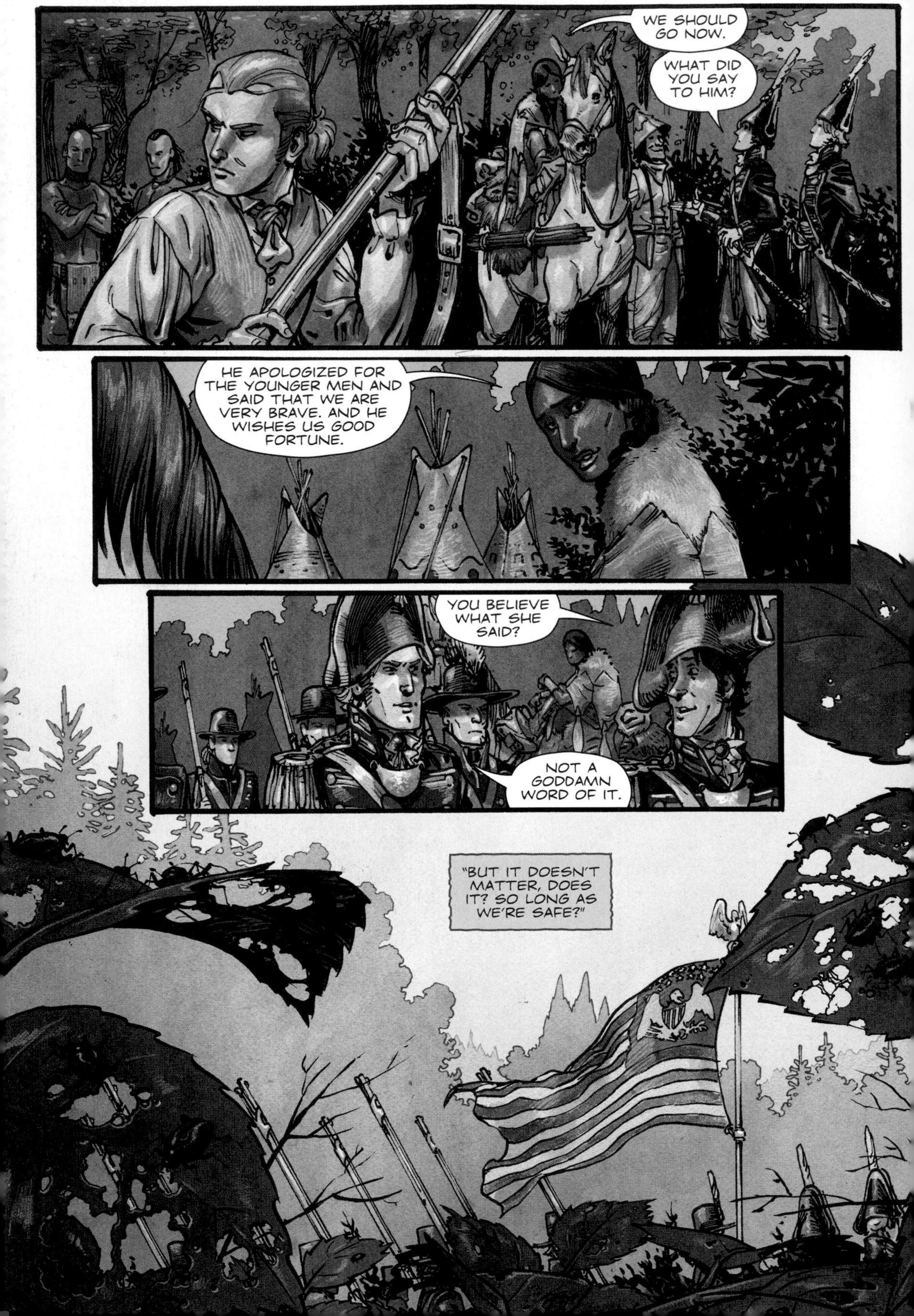
WE SHOULD GO NOW.
WHAT DID YOU SAY TO HIM?
HE APOLOGIZED FOR THE YOUNGER MEN AND SAID THAT WE ARE VERY BRAVE. AND HE WISHES US GOOD FORTUNE.
YOU BELIEVE WHAT SHE SAID?
NOT A GODDAMN WORD OF IT.
"BUT IT DOESN'T MATTER, DOES IT? SO LONG AS WE'RE SAFE?"

To be continued...

SKYBOUND INSIDER

Join the **Skybound Insider** program and get updates on all of Skybound's great content including **The Walking Dead**.

- Get a **monthly** newsletter
- **Invites** to members-only events
- **Sneak peeks** of new comics
- **Discounts** on merchandise at the Skybound and Walking Dead online stores.

Membership is **free** and it only takes a minute to sign up.

BECOME A SKYBOUND INSIDER TODAY!
insider.skybound.com

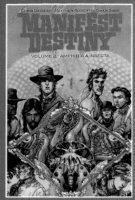

FOR MORE OF INVINCIBLE

TRADEPAPERBACKS

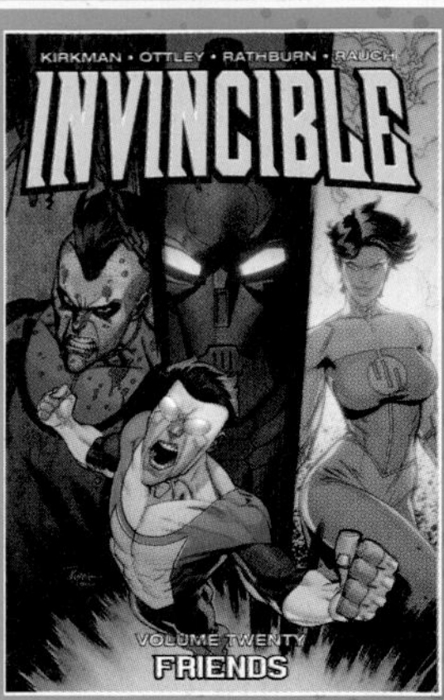
KIRKMAN • OTTLEY • RATHBURN • RAUCH
INVINCIBLE
VOLUME TWENTY
FRIENDS

VOL. 1: FAMILY MATTERS TP
ISBN: 978-1-58240-711-1
$12.99
VOL. 2: EIGHT IS ENOUGH TP
ISBN: 978-1-58240-347-2
$12.99
VOL. 3: PERFECT STRANGERS TP
ISBN: 978-1-58240-793-7
$12.99
VOL. 4: HEAD OF THE CLASS TP
ISBN: 978-1-58240-440-2
$14.95
VOL. 5: THE FACTS OF LIFE TP
ISBN: 978-1-58240-554-4
$14.99
VOL. 6: A DIFFERENT WORLD TP
ISBN: 978-1-58240-579-7
$14.99
VOL. 7: THREE'S COMPANY TP
ISBN: 978-1-58240-656-5
$14.99
VOL. 8: MY FAVORITE MARTIAN TP
ISBN: 978-1-58240-683-1
$14.99
VOL. 9: OUT OF THIS WORLD TP
ISBN: 978-1-58240-827-9
$14.99
VOL. 10: WHO'S THE BOSS TP
ISBN: 978-1-60706-013-0
$16.99
VOL. 11: HAPPY DAYS TP
ISBN: 978-1-60706-062-8
$16.99
VOL. 12: STILL STANDING TP
ISBN: 978-1-60706-166-3
$16.99
VOL. 13: GROWING PAINS TP
ISBN: 978-1-60706-251-6
$16.99
VOL. 14: THE VILTRUMITE WAR TP
ISBN: 978-1-60706-367-4
$19.99
VOL. 15: GET SMART TP
ISBN: 978-1-60706-498-5
$16.99
VOL. 16: FAMILY TIES TP
ISBN: 978-1-60706-579-1
$16.99
VOL. 17: WHAT'S HAPPENING TP
ISBN: 978-1-60706-662-0
$16.99
VOL. 18: DEATH OF EVERYONE TP
ISBN: 978-1-60706-762-7
$16.99
VOL. 19: THE WAR AT HOME TP
ISBN: 978-1-60706-856-3
$16.99
VOL. 20: FRIENDS TP
ISBN: 978-1-63215-043-1
$16.99
THE OFFICIAL HANDBOOK OF
THE INVINCIBLE UNIVERSE TP
ISBN: 978-1-58240-831-6
$12.99
INVINCIBLE PRESENTS,
VOL. 1: ATOM EVE & REX SPLODE TP
ISBN: 978-1-60706-255-4
$14.99

COMPLETE LIBRARY

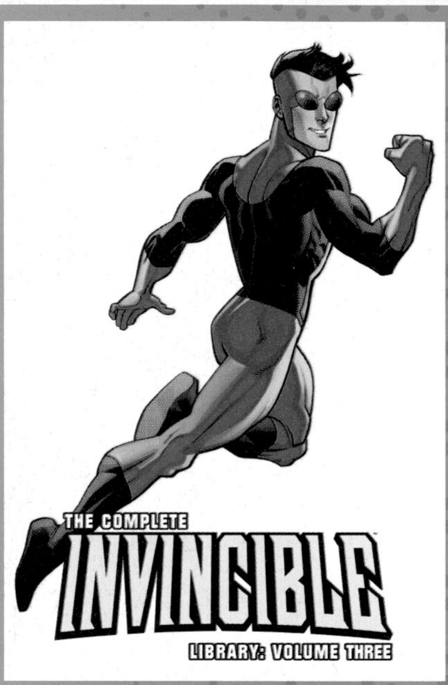
THE COMPLETE
INVINCIBLE
LIBRARY: VOLUME THREE

THE COMPLETE INVINCIBLE LIBRARY, VOL. 2 HC
ISBN: 978-1-60706-112-0
$125.00
THE COMPLETE INVINCIBLE LIBRARY, VOL. 3 HC
ISBN: 978-1-60706-421-3
$125.00

COMPENDIUMS

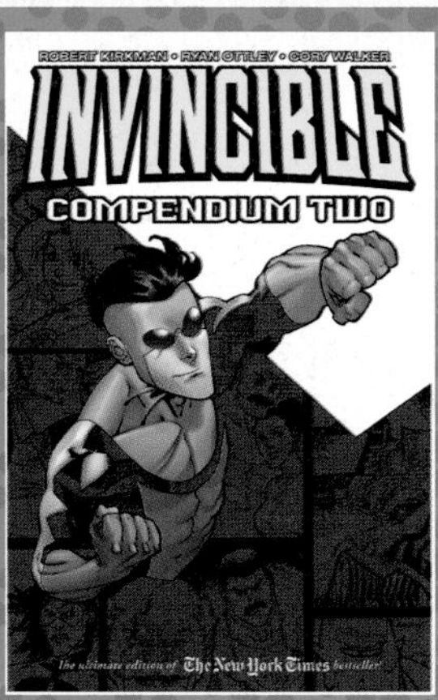
ROBERT KIRKMAN • RYAN OTTLEY • CORY WALKER
INVINCIBLE
COMPENDIUM TWO
The ultimate edition of The New York Times bestseller!

COMPENDIUM VOL. 1
ISBN: 978-1-60706-411-4
$64.99
COMPENDIUM VOL. 2
ISBN: 978-1-60706-772-6
$64.99

ULTIMATE COLLECTIONS

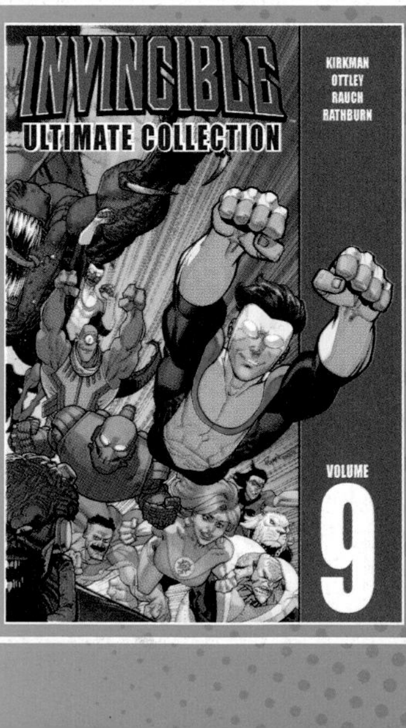
INVINCIBLE
ULTIMATE COLLECTION
KIRKMAN
OTTLEY
RAUCH
RATHBURN
VOLUME
9

ULTIMATE COLLECTION, VOL. 1 HC
ISBN 978-1-58240-500-1
$34.95
ULTIMATE COLLECTION, VOL. 2 HC
ISBN: 978-1-58240-594-0
$34.99
ULTIMATE COLLECTION, VOL. 3 HC
ISBN: 978-1-58240-763-0
$34.99
ULTIMATE COLLECTION, VOL. 4 HC
ISBN: 978-1-58240-989-4
$34.99
ULTIMATE COLLECTION, VOL. 5 HC
ISBN: 978-1-60706-116-8
$34.99
ULTIMATE COLLECTION, VOL. 6 HC
ISBN: 978-1-60706-360-5
$34.99
ULTIMATE COLLECTION, VOL. 7 HC
ISBN: 978-1-60706-509-8
$39.99
ULTIMATE COLLECTION, VOL. 8 HC
ISBN: 978-1-60706-680-4
$39.99
ULTIMATE COLLECTION, VOL. 9 HC
ISBN: 978-1-63215-032-5
$39.99

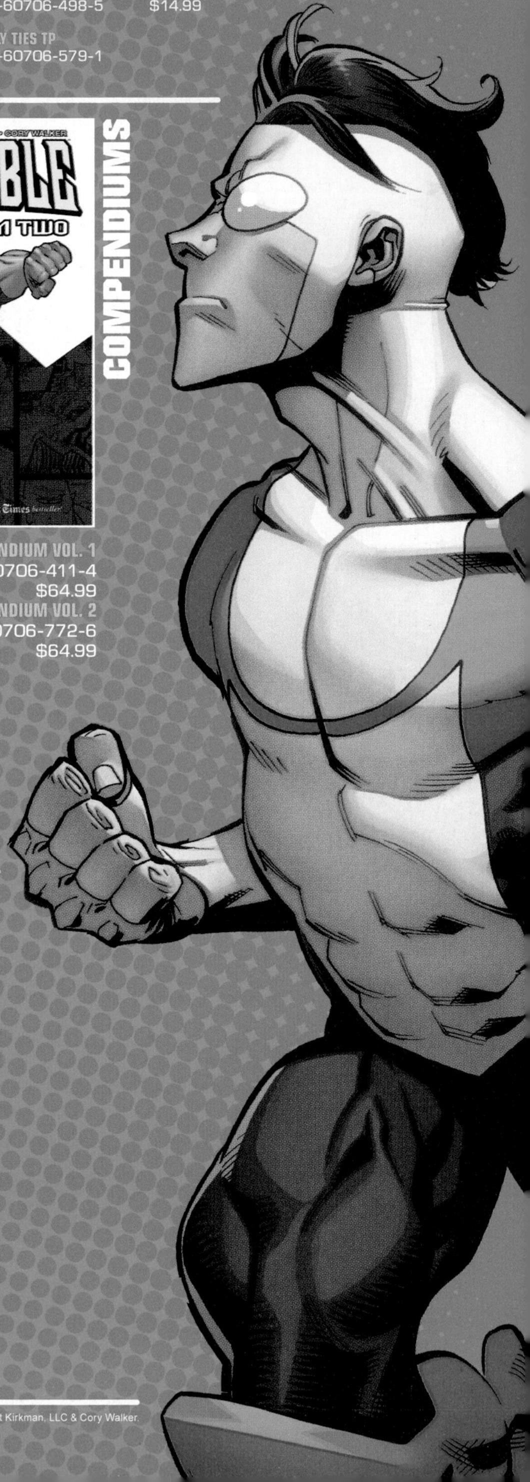

FOR MORE OF THE WALKING DEAD

TRADEPAPERBACKS

ROBERT KIRKMAN TONY MOORE
THE WALKING DEAD
VOLUME 1
DAYS GONE BYE

VOL. 1: DAYS GONE BYE TP
ISBN: 978-1-58240-672-5
$14.99
VOL. 2: MILES BEHIND US TP
ISBN: 978-1-58240-775-3
$14.99
VOL. 3: SAFETY BEHIND BARS TP
ISBN: 978-1-58240-805-7
$14.99
VOL. 4: THE HEART'S DESIRE TP
ISBN: 978-1-58240-530-8
$14.99
VOL. 5: THE BEST DEFENSE TP
ISBN: 978-1-58240-612-1
$14.99
VOL. 6: THIS SORROWFUL LIFE TP
ISBN: 978-1-58240-684-8
$14.99
VOL. 7: THE CALM BEFORE TP
ISBN: 978-1-58240-828-6
$14.99

VOL. 8: MADE TO SUFFER TP
ISBN: 978-1-58240-883-5
$14.99
VOL. 9: HERE WE REMAIN TP
ISBN: 978-1-60706-022-2
$14.99
VOL. 10: WHAT WE BECOME TP
ISBN: 978-1-60706-075-8
$14.99
VOL. 11: FEAR THE HUNTERS TP
ISBN: 978-1-60706-181-6
$14.99
VOL. 12: LIFE AMONG THEM TP
ISBN: 978-1-60706-254-7
$14.99
VOL. 13: TOO FAR GONE TP
ISBN: 978-1-60706-329-2
$14.99
VOL. 14: NO WAY OUT TP
ISBN: 978-1-60706-392-6
$14.99

VOL. 15: WE FIND OURSELVES TP
ISBN: 978-1-60706-440-4
$14.99
VOL. 16: A LARGER WORLD TP
ISBN: 978-1-60706-559-3
$14.99
VOL. 17: SOMETHING TO FEAR TP
ISBN: 978-1-60706-615-6
$14.99
VOL. 18: WHAT COMES AFTER TP
ISBN: 978-1-60706-687-3
$14.99
VOL. 19: MARCH TO WAR TP
ISBN: 978-1-60706-818-1
$14.99
VOL. 20: ALL OUT WAR PART ONE TP
ISBN: 978-1-60706-882-2
$14.99
VOL. 21: ALL OUT WAR PART TWO TP
ISBN: 978-1-63215-030-1
$14.99

VOL. 1: SPANISH EDITION TP
ISBN: 978-1-60706-797-9
$14.99
VOL. 2: SPANISH EDITION TP
ISBN: 978-1-60706-845-7
$14.99
VOL. 3: SPANISH EDITION TP
ISBN: 978-1-60706-883-9
$14.99
VOL. 4: SPANISH EDITION TP
ISBN: 978-1-63215-035-6
$14.99

HARDCOVERS

THE WALKING DEAD
BOOK ONE
a continuing story of survival horror.

BOOK ONE HC
ISBN: 978-1-58240-619-0
$34.99
BOOK TWO HC
ISBN: 978-1-58240-698-5
$34.99
BOOK THREE HC
ISBN: 978-1-58240-825-5
$34.99
BOOK FOUR HC
ISBN: 978-1-60706-000-0
$34.99
BOOK FIVE HC
ISBN: 978-1-60706-171-7
$34.99
BOOK SIX HC
ISBN: 978-1-60706-327-8
$34.99
BOOK SEVEN HC
ISBN: 978-1-60706-439-8
$34.99
BOOK EIGHT HC
ISBN: 978-1-60706-593-7
$34.99
BOOK NINE HC
ISBN: 978-1-60706-798-6
$34.99
BOOK TEN HC
ISBN: 978-1-63215-034-9
$34.99

COMPENDIUMS

The ultimate edition of The New York Times bestseller!
THE WALKING DEAD
COMPENDIUM ONE
Robert Kirkman • Charlie Adlard • Tony Moore • Cliff Rathburn

COMPENDIUM TP, VOL. 1
ISBN: 978-1-60706-076-5
$59.99
COMPENDIUM TP, VOL. 2
ISBN: 978-1-60706-596-8
$59.99

SPECIALTY BOOKS

THE WALKING DEAD
THE COVERS

THE WALKING DEAD: THE COVERS, VOL. 1 HC
ISBN: 978-1-60706-002-4
$24.99
THE WALKING DEAD SURVIVORS' GUIDE
ISBN: 978-1-60706-458-9
$12.99
THE WALKING DEAD: ALL OUT WAR HC
ISBN: 978-1-60706-002-4
$24.99

OMNIBUS

THE WALKING DEAD

OMNIBUS, VOL. 1
ISBN: 978-1-60706-503-6
$100.00
OMNIBUS, VOL. 2
ISBN: 978-1-60706-515-9
$100.00
OMNIBUS, VOL. 3
ISBN: 978-1-60706-330-8
$100.00
OMNIBUS, VOL. 4
ISBN: 978-1-60706-616-3
$100.00
OMNIBUS, VOL. 5
ISBN: 978-1-63215-042-4
$100.00

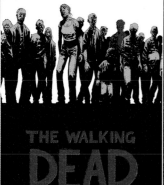

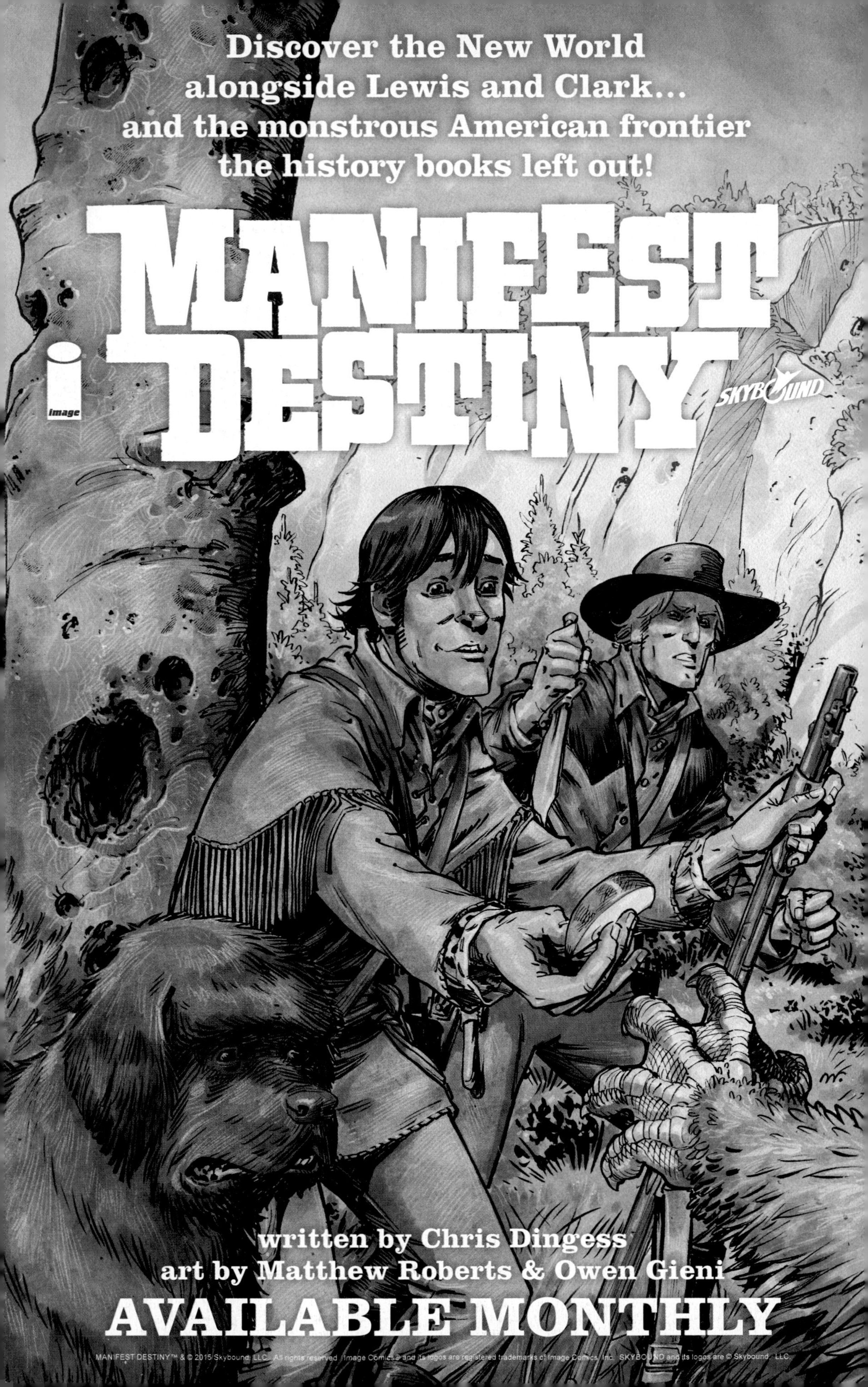

Discover the New World
alongside Lewis and Clark...
and the monstrous American frontier
the history books left out!
MANIFEST DESTINY
image
SKYBOUND
written by Chris Dingess
art by Matthew Roberts & Owen Gieni
AVAILABLE MONTHLY
MANIFEST DESTINY™ & © 2015 Skybound, LLC. All rights reserved. Image Comics® and its logos are registered trademarks of Image Comics, Inc. SKYBOUND and its logos are © Skybound, LLC.